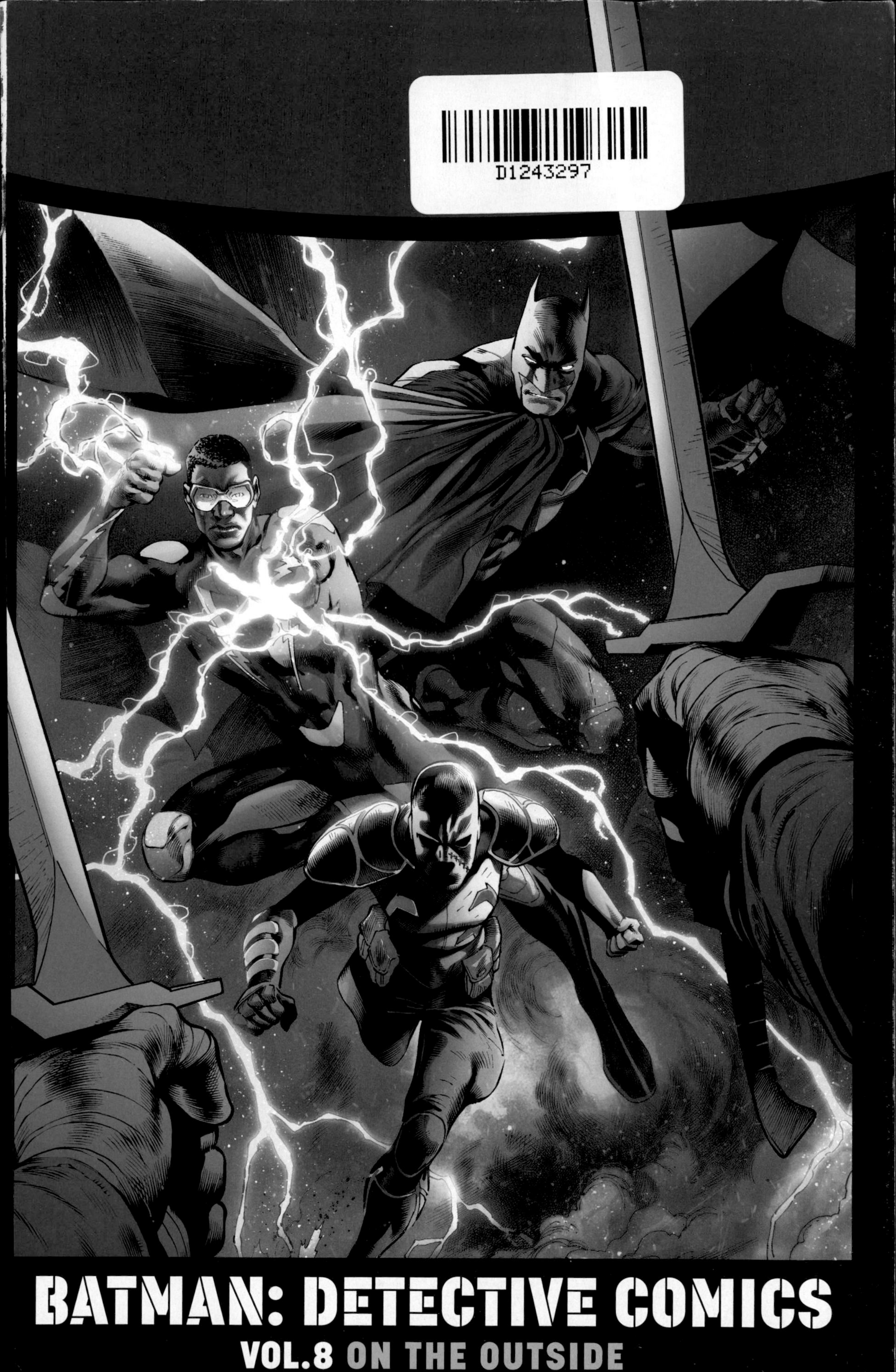

BATMAN: DETECTIVE COMICS

VOL.8 ON THE OUTSIDE

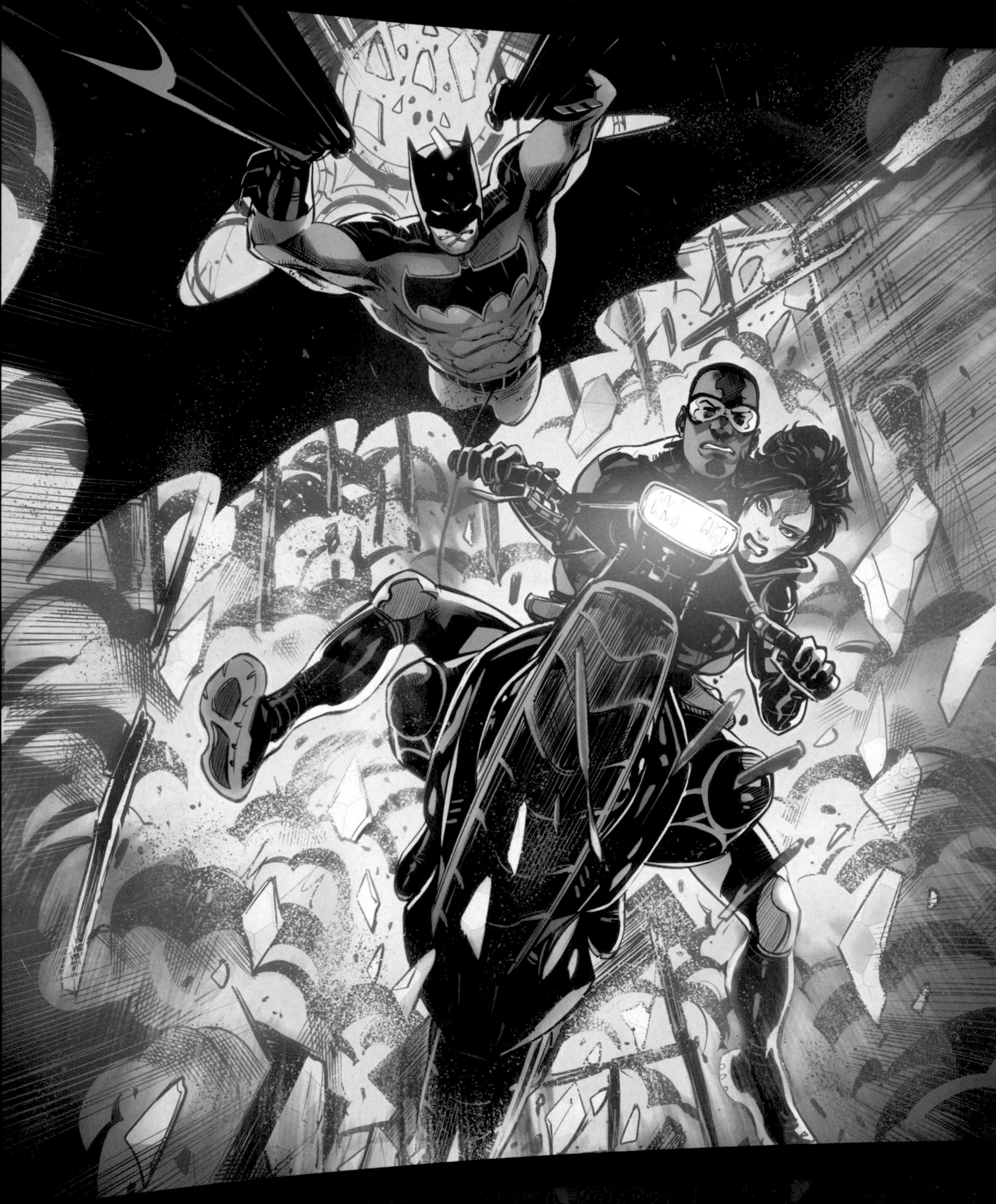

BATMAN: DETECTIVE COMICS
VOL.8 ON THE OUTSIDE

BRYAN HILL ∗ **MICHAEL MORECI**
writers

MIGUEL MENDONÇA ∗ **PHILIPPE BRIONES**
DIANA EGEA ∗ **SEBASTIAN FIUMARA**
artists

ADRIANO LUCAS ∗ **DAVE STEWART**
colorists

SAL CIPRIANO ∗ **CLEM ROBINS**
letterers

EDUARDO PANSICA, JULIO FERREIRA and **ADRIANO LUCAS**
collection cover artists

BATMAN created by BOB KANE with BILL FINGER
SUPERMAN created by JERRY SIEGEL and JOE SHUSTER
By special arrangement with the Jerry Siegel family

CHRIS CONROY Editor - Original Series ✳ DAVE WIELGOSZ Assistant Editor - Original Series
JEB WOODARD Group Editor - Collected Editions ✳ ROBIN WILDMAN Editor - Collected Edition
STEVE COOK Design Director - Books ✳ DAMIAN RYLAND Publication Design

BOB HARRAS Senior VP - Editor-in-Chief, DC Comics ✳ PAT McCALLUM Executive Editor, DC Comics

DAN DiDIO Publisher ✳ JIM LEE Publisher & Chief Creative Officer
AMIT DESAI Executive VP - Business & Marketing Strategy, Direct to Consumer & Global Franchise Management
BOBBIE CHASE VP & Executive Editor, Young Reader & Talent Development ✳ MARK CHIARELLO Senior VP - Art, Design & Collected Editions
JOHN CUNNINGHAM Senior VP - Sales & Trade Marketing ✳ BRIAR DARDEN VP - Business Affairs
ANNE DePIES Senior VP - Business Strategy, Finance & Administration ✳ DON FALLETTI VP - Manufacturing Operations
LAWRENCE GANEM VP - Editorial Administration & Talent Relations ✳ ALISON GILL Senior VP - Manufacturing & Operations
JASON GREENBERG VP - Business Strategy & Finance ✳ HANK KANALZ Senior VP - Editorial Strategy & Administration
JAY KOGAN Senior VP - Legal Affairs ✳ NICK J. NAPOLITANO VP - Manufacturing Administration ✳ LISETTE OSTERLOH VP - Digital Marketing & Events
EDDIE SCANNELL VP - Consumer Marketing ✳ COURTNEY SIMMONS Senior VP - Publicity & Communications
JIM (SKI) SOKOLOWSKI VP - Comic Book Specialty Sales & Trade Marketing
NANCY SPEARS VP - Mass, Book, Digital Sales & Trade Marketing ✳ MICHELE R. WELLS VP - Content Strategy

BATMAN: DETECTIVE COMICS VOL. 8—ON THE OUTSIDE

DC Comics, 2900 West Alameda Ave., Burbank, CA 91505
Printed by LSC Communications, Kendallville, IN, USA. 11/2/18. First Printing.
ISBN: 978-1-4012-8528-9

Library of Congress Cataloging-in-Publication Data is available.

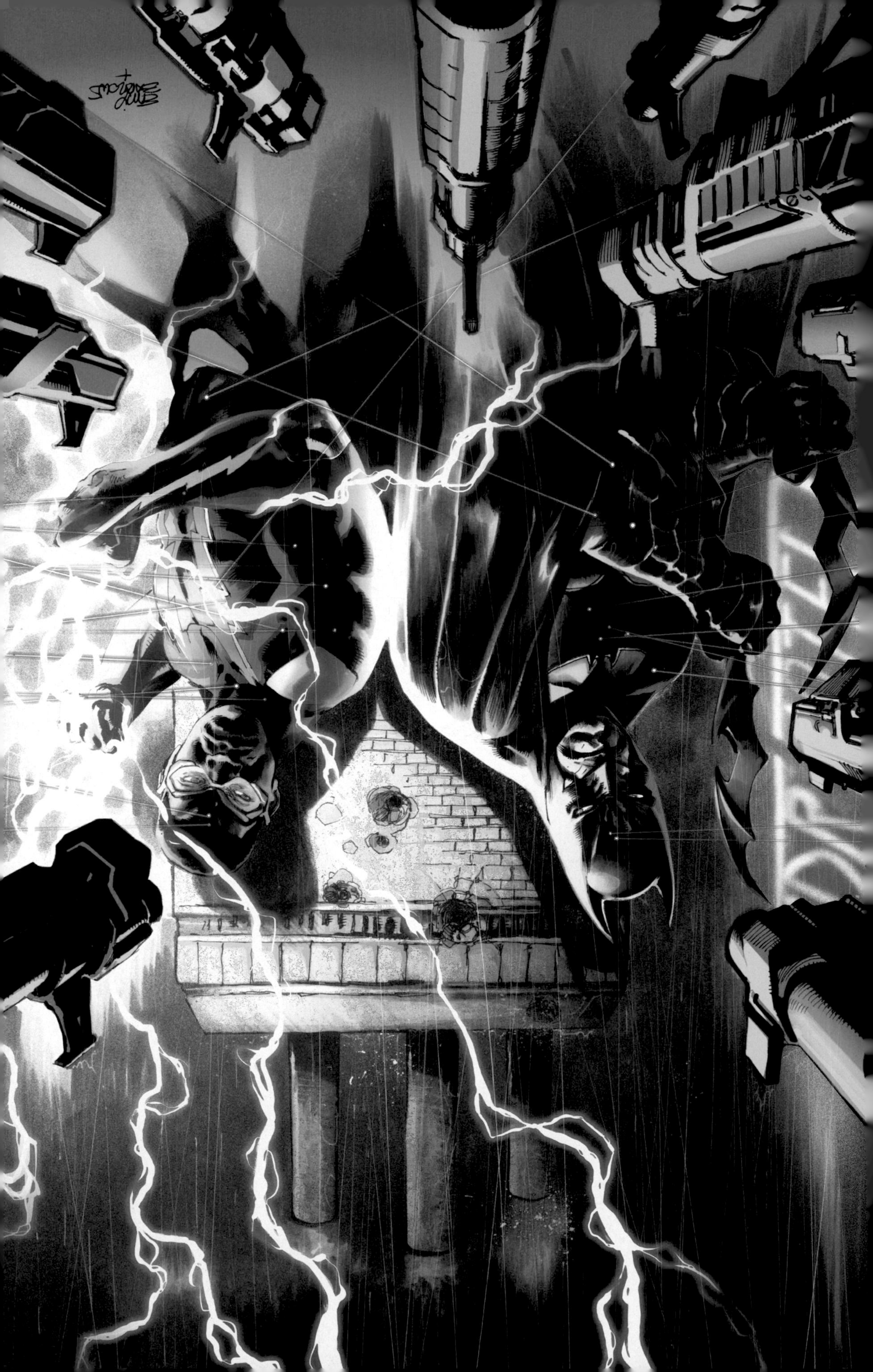

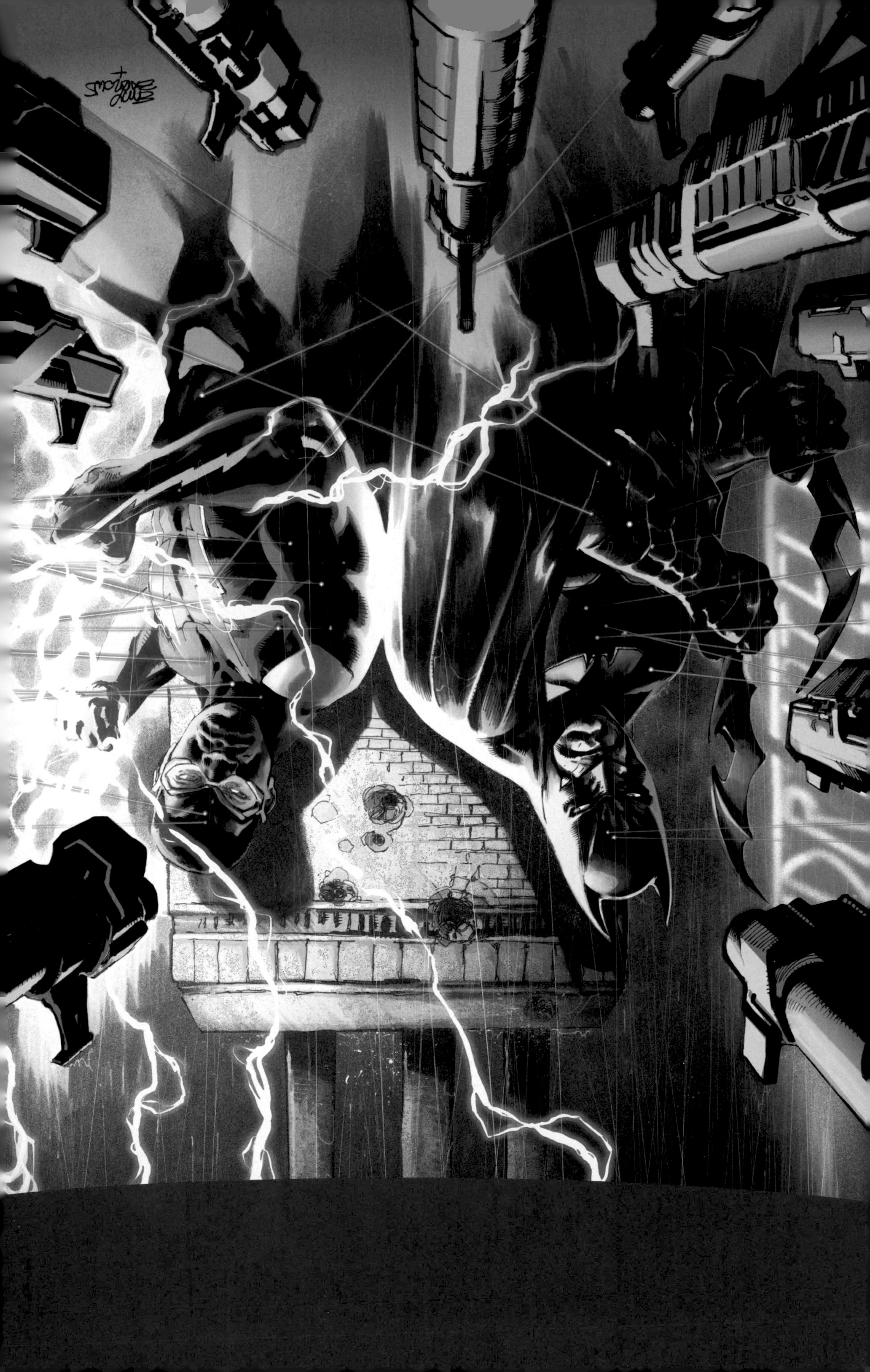

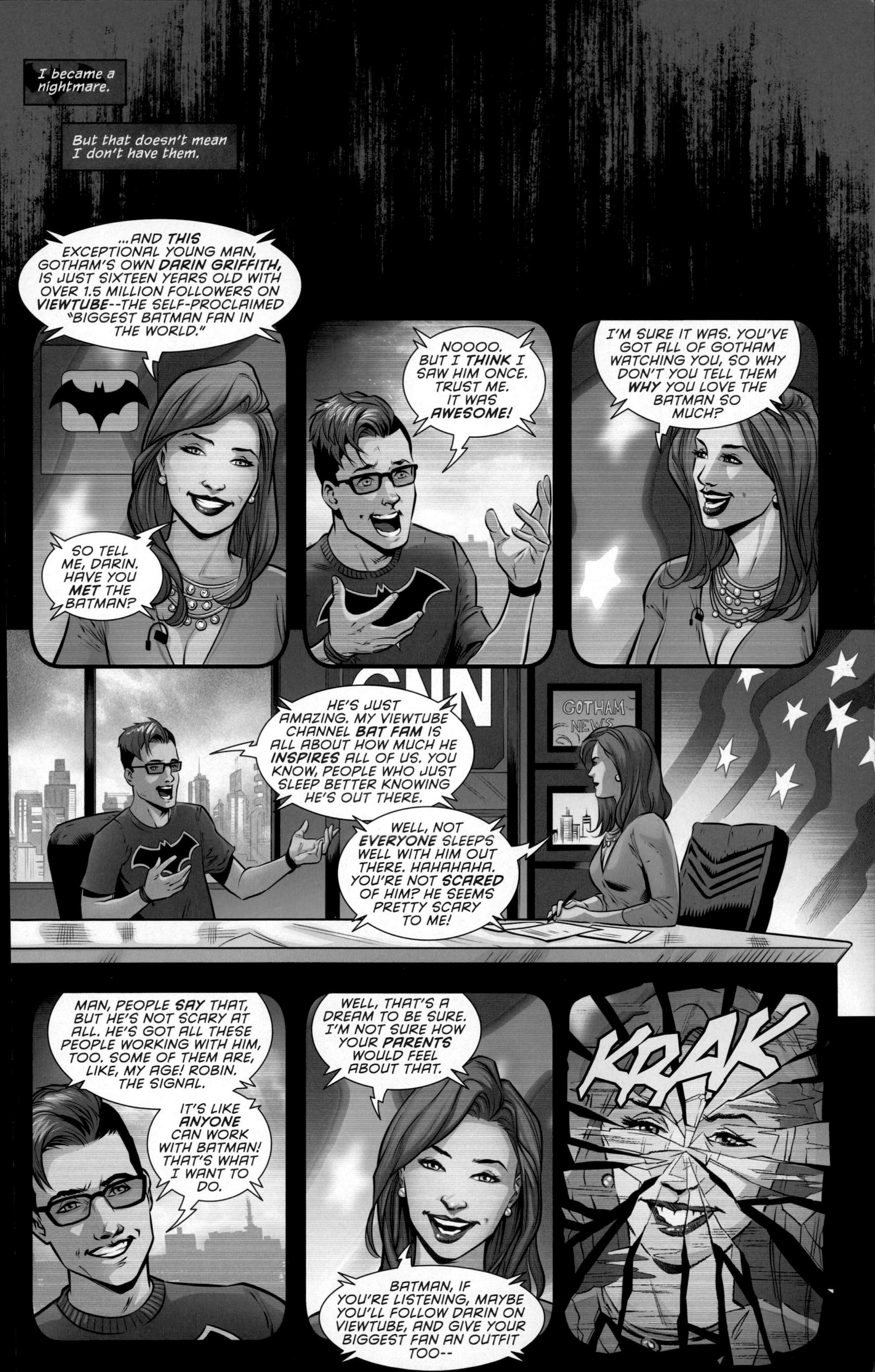

I became a nightmare.
But that doesn't mean I don't have them.
...AND THIS EXCEPTIONAL YOUNG MAN, GOTHAM'S OWN DARIN GRIFFITH, IS JUST SIXTEEN YEARS OLD WITH OVER 1.5 MILLION FOLLOWERS ON VIEWTUBE--THE SELF-PROCLAIMED "BIGGEST BATMAN FAN IN THE WORLD."
SO TELL ME, DARIN. HAVE YOU MET THE BATMAN?
NOOOO. BUT I THINK I SAW HIM ONCE. TRUST ME. IT WAS AWESOME!
I'M SURE IT WAS. YOU'VE GOT ALL OF GOTHAM WATCHING YOU, SO WHY DON'T YOU TELL THEM WHY YOU LOVE THE BATMAN SO MUCH?
GNN
GOTHAM NEWS
HE'S JUST AMAZING. MY VIEWTUBE CHANNEL BAT FAM IS ALL ABOUT HOW MUCH HE INSPIRES ALL OF US. YOU KNOW, PEOPLE WHO JUST SLEEP BETTER KNOWING HE'S OUT THERE.
WELL, NOT EVERYONE SLEEPS WELL WITH HIM OUT THERE. HAHAHAHA. YOU'RE NOT SCARED OF HIM? HE SEEMS PRETTY SCARY TO ME!
MAN, PEOPLE SAY THAT, BUT HE'S NOT SCARY AT ALL. HE'S GOT ALL THESE PEOPLE WORKING WITH HIM, TOO. SOME OF THEM ARE, LIKE, MY AGE! ROBIN. THE SIGNAL.
IT'S LIKE ANYONE CAN WORK WITH BATMAN! THAT'S WHAT I WANT TO DO.
WELL, THAT'S A DREAM TO BE SURE. I'M NOT SURE HOW YOUR PARENTS WOULD FEEL ABOUT THAT.
BATMAN, IF YOU'RE LISTENING, MAYBE YOU'LL FOLLOW DARIN ON VIEWTUBE, AND GIVE YOUR BIGGEST FAN AN OUTFIT TOO--
KRAK

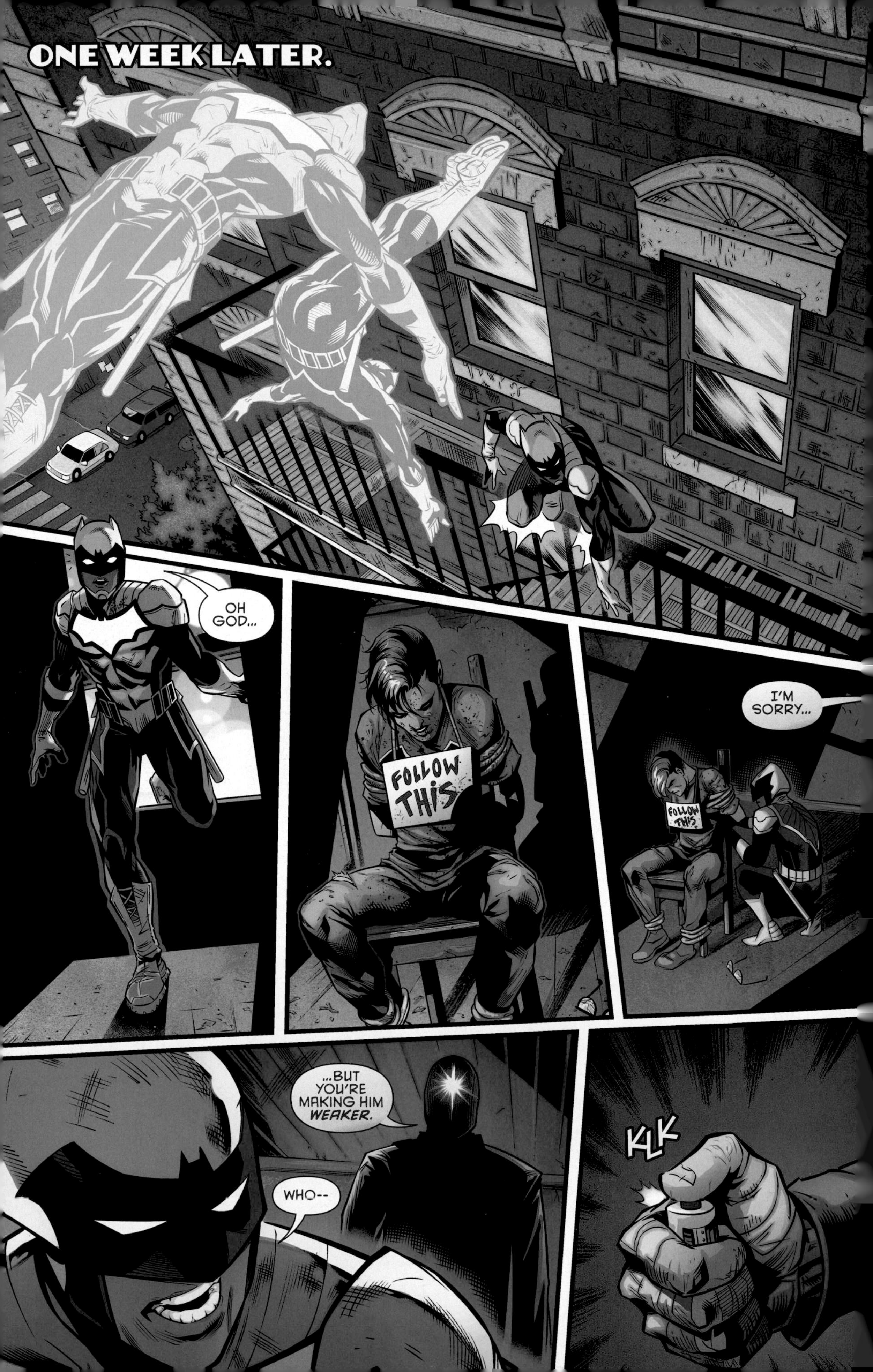
ONE WEEK LATER.
OH GOD...
FOLLOW THIS
I'M SORRY...
FOLLOW THIS
...BUT YOU'RE MAKING HIM *WEAKER*.
WHO--
KLK

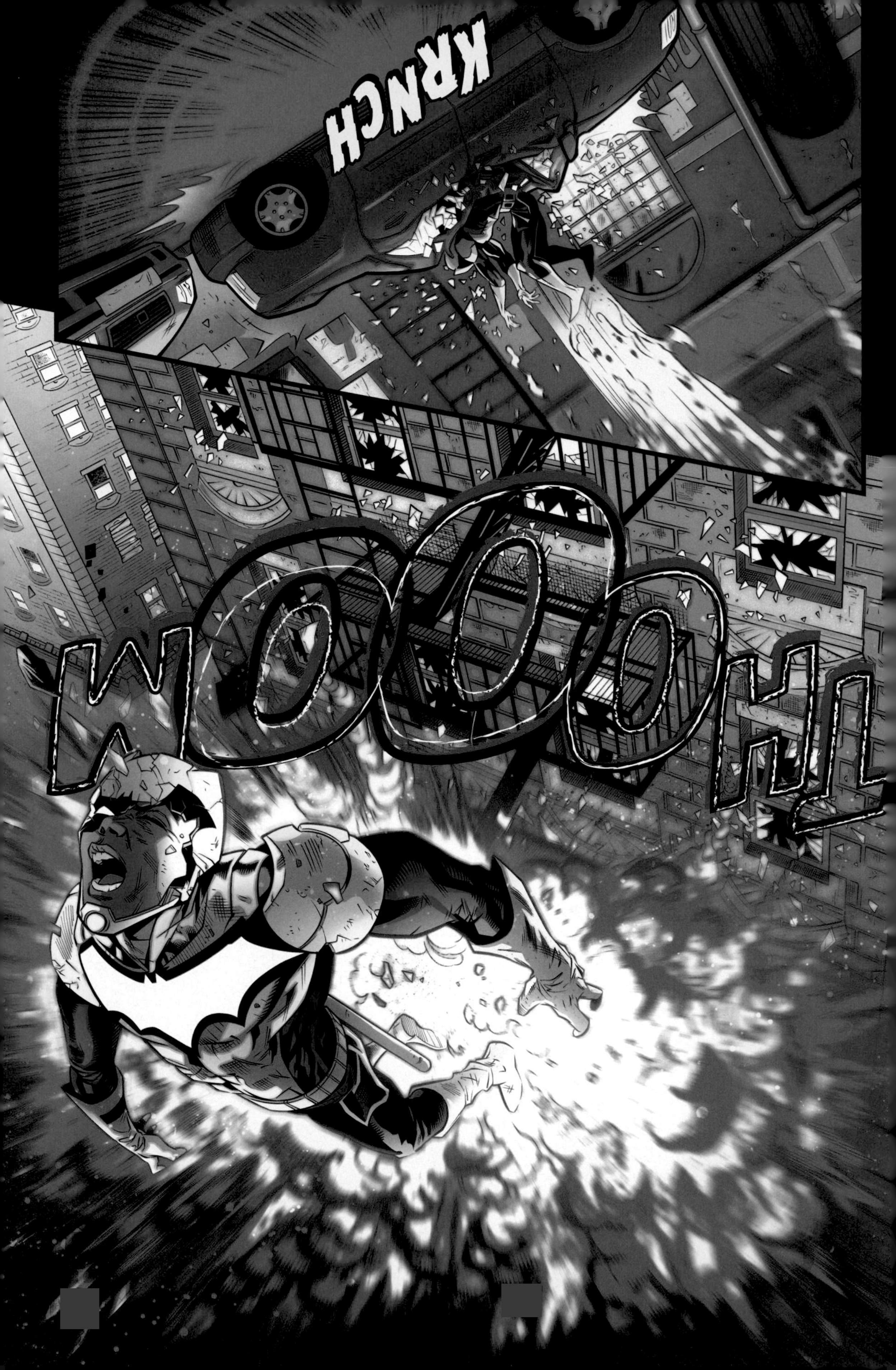
KRNCH

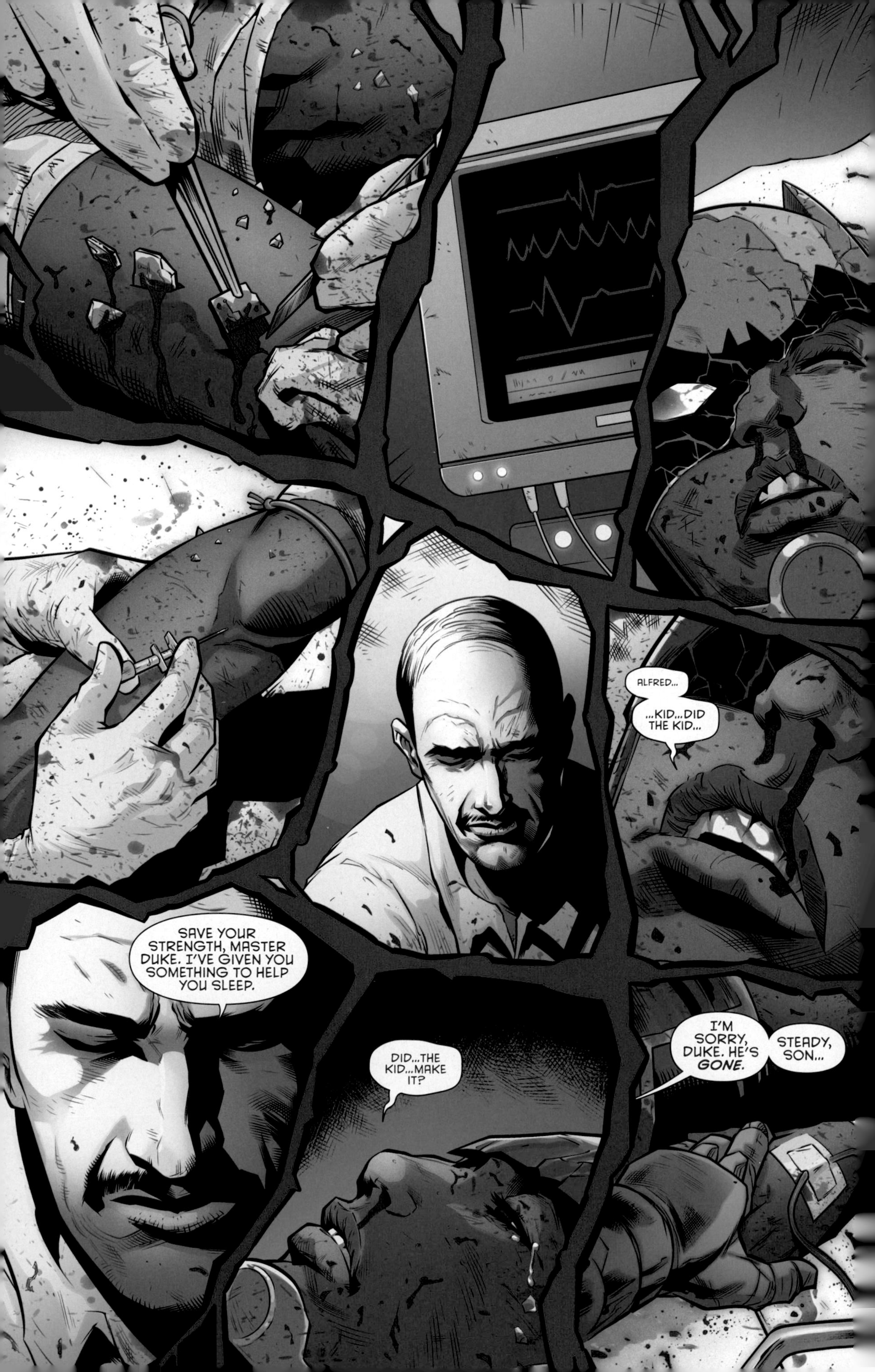
ALFRED...
...KID...DID THE KID...
SAVE YOUR STRENGTH, MASTER DUKE. I'VE GIVEN YOU SOMETHING TO HELP YOU SLEEP.
DID...THE KID...MAKE IT?
I'M SORRY, DUKE. HE'S *GONE*.
STEADY, SON...

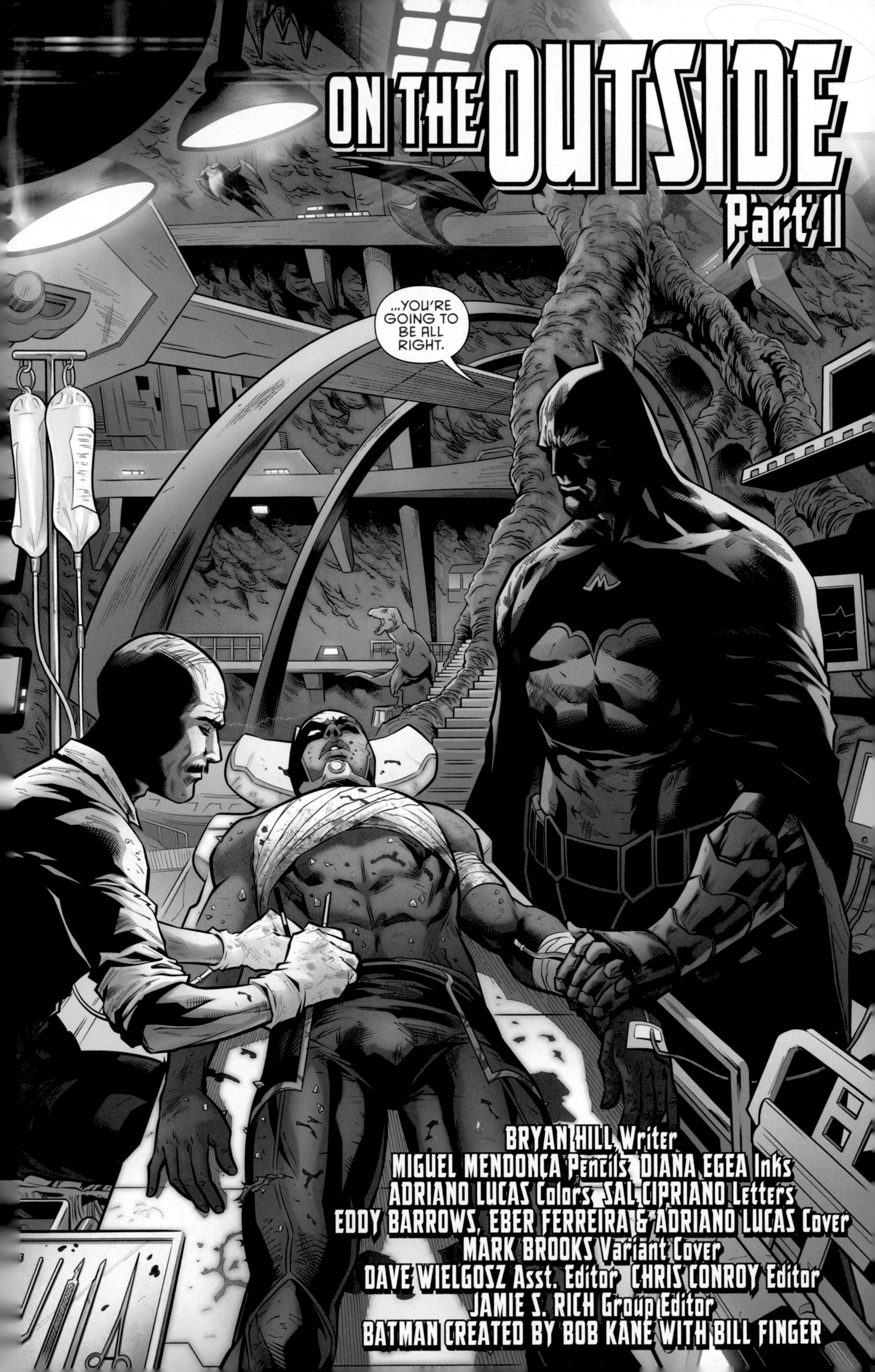
ON THE OUTSIDE
Part 1
...YOU'RE GOING TO BE ALL RIGHT.

BRYAN HILL Writer
MIGUEL MENDONÇA Pencils DIANA EGEA Inks
ADRIANO LUCAS Colors SAL CIPRIANO Letters
EDDY BARROWS, EBER FERREIRA & ADRIANO LUCAS Cover
MARK BROOKS Variant Cover
DAVE WIELGOSZ Asst. Editor CHRIS CONROY Editor
JAMIE S. RICH Group Editor
BATMAN CREATED BY BOB KANE WITH BILL FINGER

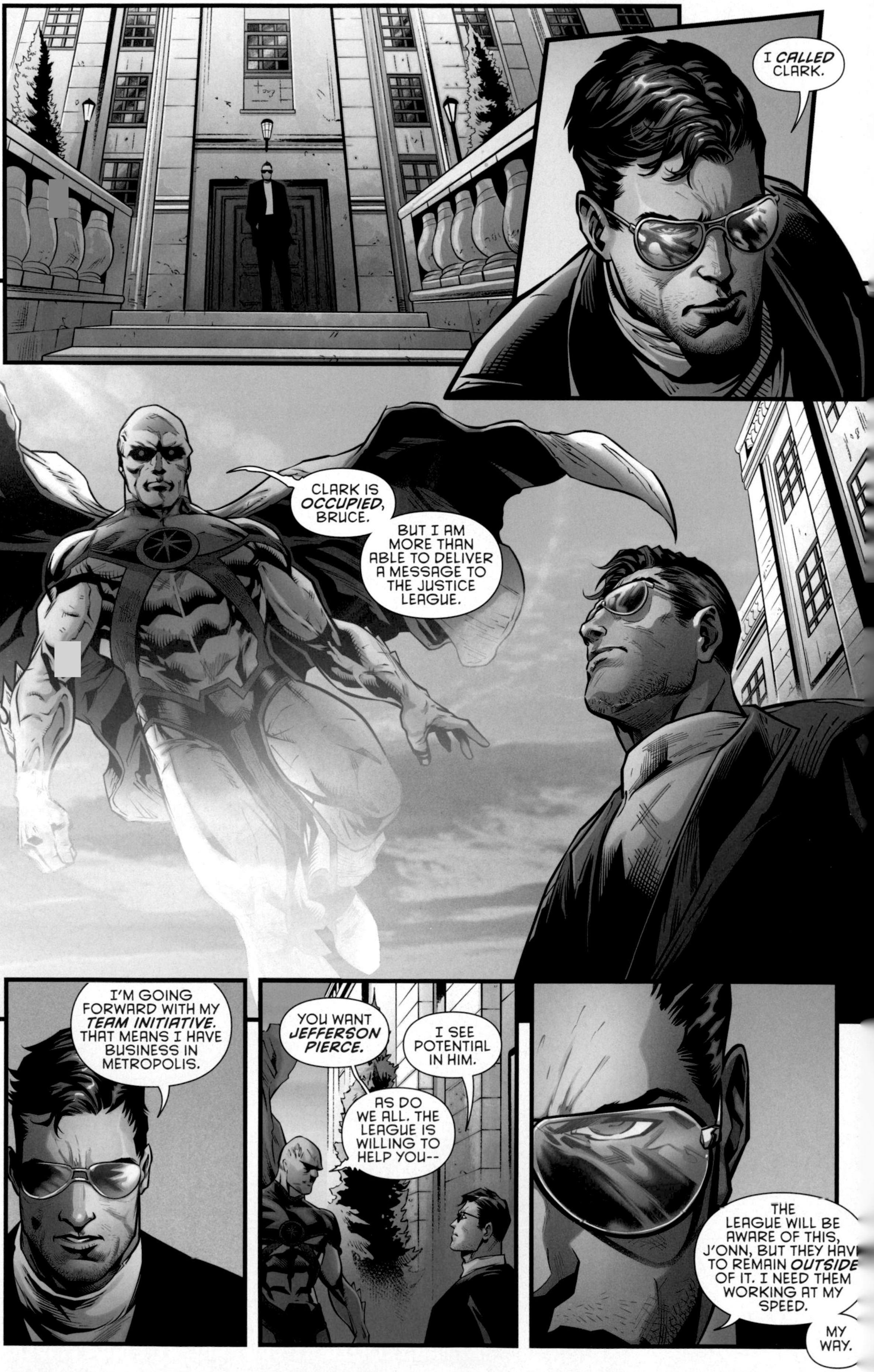
I *CALLED* CLARK.
CLARK IS *OCCUPIED*, BRUCE.
BUT I AM MORE THAN ABLE TO DELIVER A MESSAGE TO THE JUSTICE LEAGUE.
I'M GOING FORWARD WITH MY *TEAM INITIATIVE*. THAT MEANS I HAVE BUSINESS IN METROPOLIS.
YOU WANT *JEFFERSON PIERCE*.
I SEE POTENTIAL IN HIM.
AS DO WE ALL. THE LEAGUE IS WILLING TO HELP YOU--
THE LEAGUE WILL BE AWARE OF THIS, J'ONN, BUT THEY HAVE TO REMAIN *OUTSIDE* OF IT. I NEED THEM WORKING AT MY SPEED.
MY WAY.

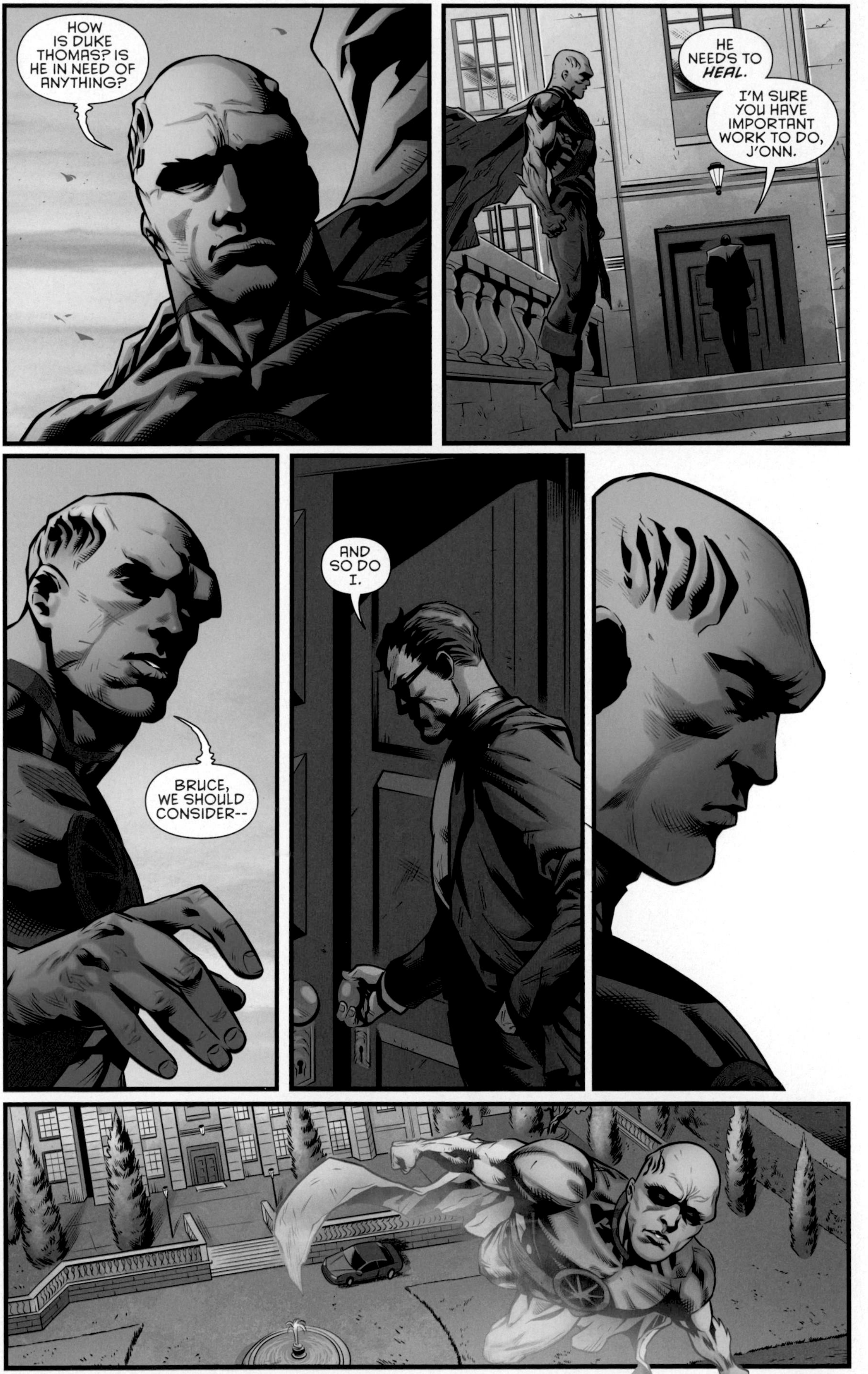
HOW IS DUKE THOMAS? IS HE IN NEED OF ANYTHING?
HE NEEDS TO *HEAL.*
I'M SURE YOU HAVE IMPORTANT WORK TO DO, J'ONN.
BRUCE, WE SHOULD CONSIDER--
AND SO DO I.

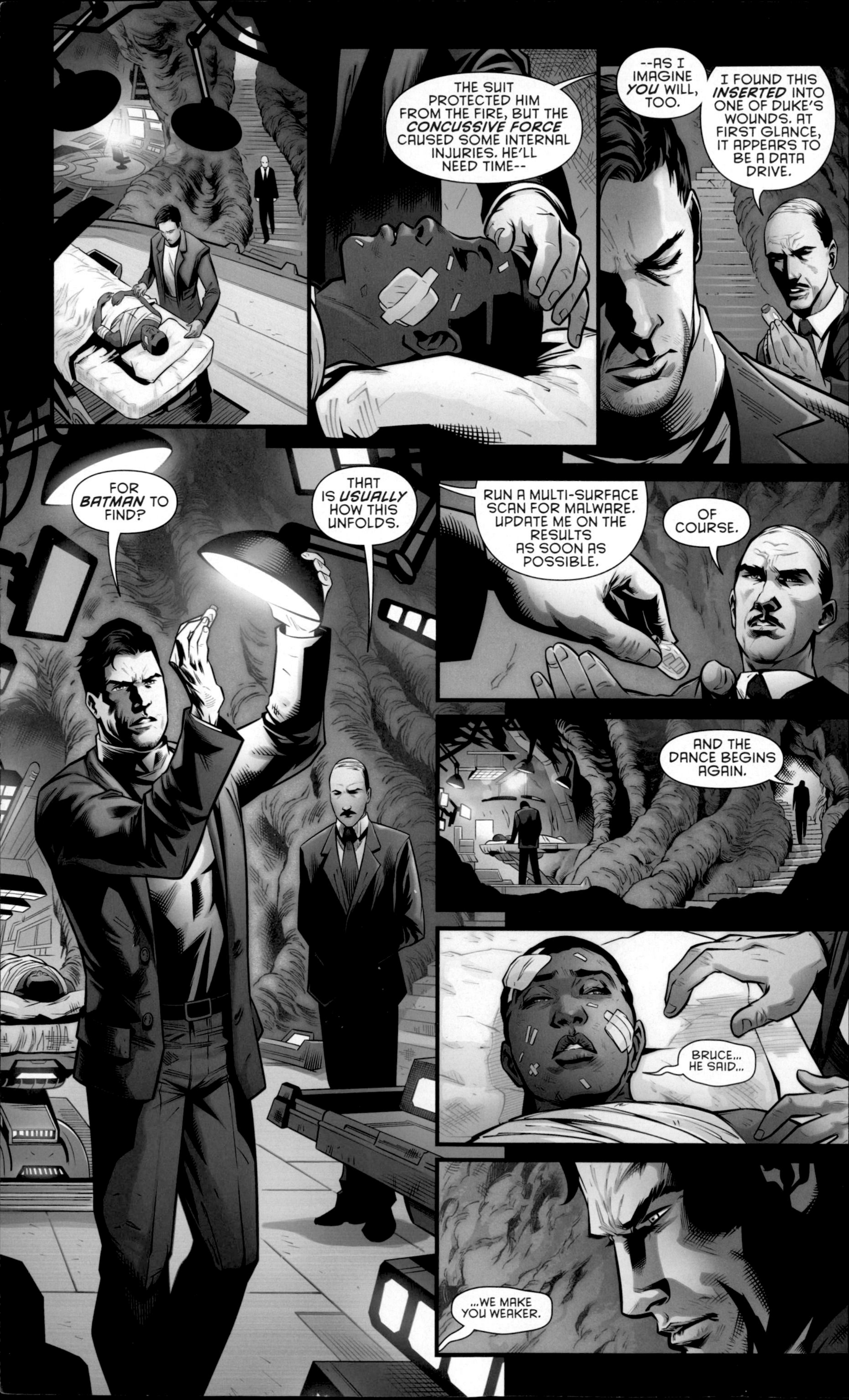
THE SUIT PROTECTED HIM FROM THE FIRE, BUT THE *CONCUSSIVE FORCE* CAUSED SOME INTERNAL INJURIES. HE'LL NEED TIME--
--AS I IMAGINE *YOU* WILL, TOO.
I FOUND THIS *INSERTED* INTO ONE OF DUKE'S WOUNDS. AT FIRST GLANCE, IT APPEARS TO BE A DATA DRIVE.
FOR *BATMAN* TO FIND?
THAT IS *USUALLY* HOW THIS UNFOLDS.
RUN A MULTI-SURFACE SCAN FOR MALWARE. UPDATE ME ON THE RESULTS AS SOON AS POSSIBLE.
OF COURSE.
AND THE DANCE BEGINS AGAIN.
BRUCE... HE SAID...
...WE MAKE YOU WEAKER.

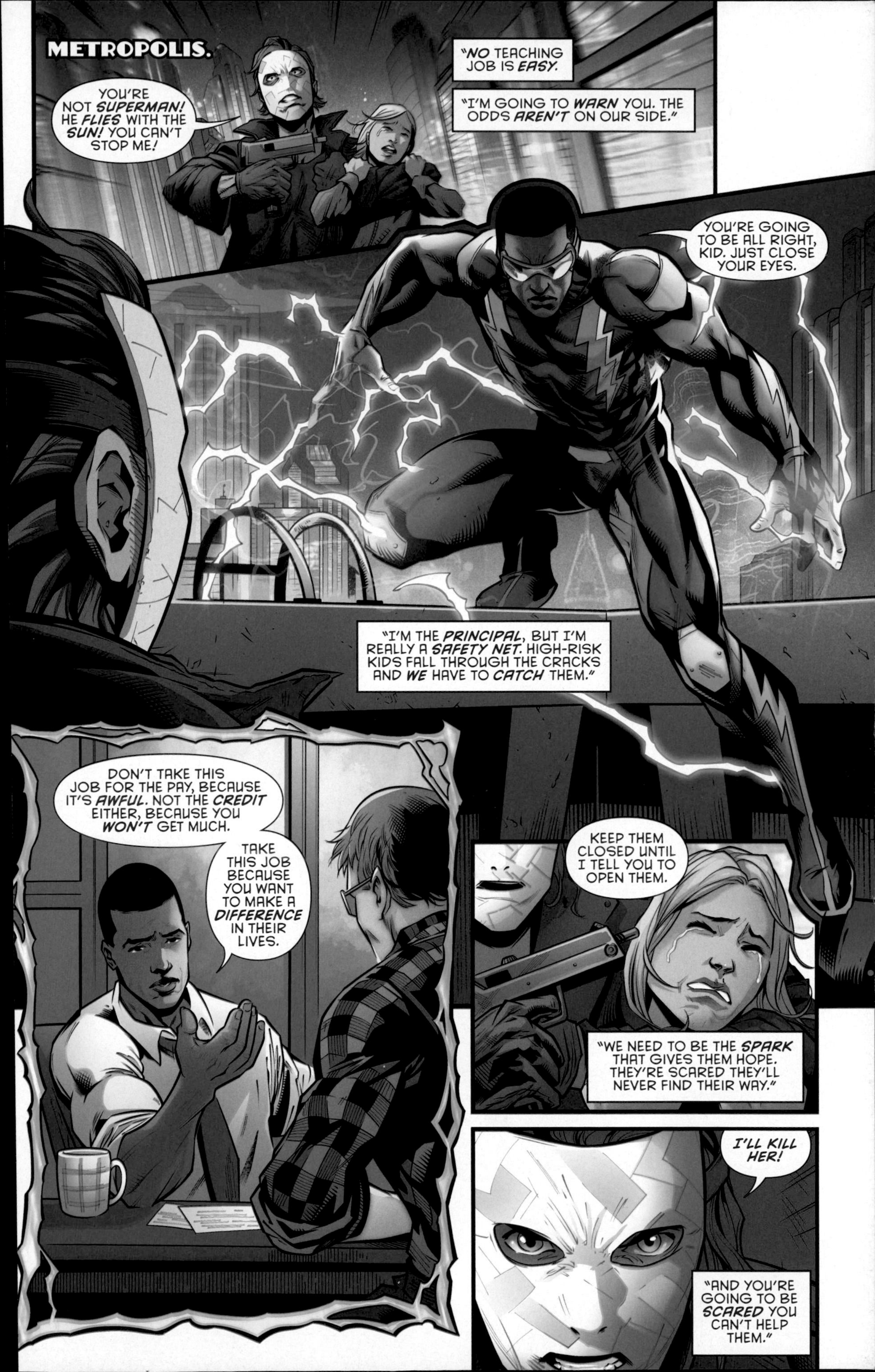
METROPOLIS.
"NO TEACHING JOB IS EASY.
"I'M GOING TO WARN YOU. THE ODDS AREN'T ON OUR SIDE."
YOU'RE NOT SUPERMAN! HE FLIES WITH THE SUN! YOU CAN'T STOP ME!
YOU'RE GOING TO BE ALL RIGHT, KID. JUST CLOSE YOUR EYES.
"I'M THE PRINCIPAL, BUT I'M REALLY A SAFETY NET. HIGH-RISK KIDS FALL THROUGH THE CRACKS AND WE HAVE TO CATCH THEM."
DON'T TAKE THIS JOB FOR THE PAY, BECAUSE IT'S AWFUL. NOT THE CREDIT EITHER, BECAUSE YOU WON'T GET MUCH.
TAKE THIS JOB BECAUSE YOU WANT TO MAKE A DIFFERENCE IN THEIR LIVES.
KEEP THEM CLOSED UNTIL I TELL YOU TO OPEN THEM.
"WE NEED TO BE THE SPARK THAT GIVES THEM HOPE. THEY'RE SCARED THEY'LL NEVER FIND THEIR WAY."
I'LL KILL HER!
"AND YOU'RE GOING TO BE SCARED YOU CAN'T HELP THEM."

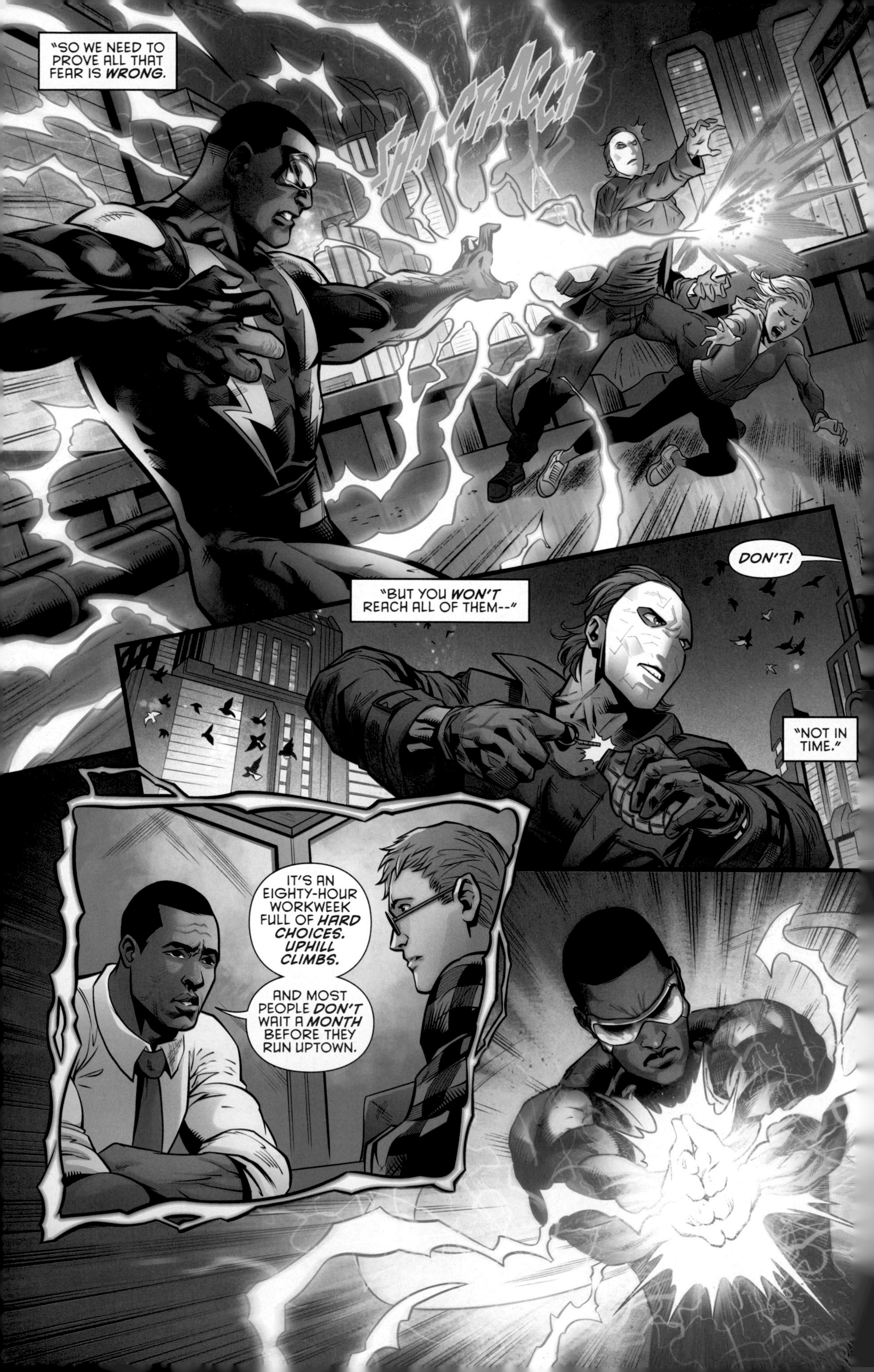
"SO WE NEED TO PROVE ALL THAT FEAR IS *WRONG*.
SHA-CRACCK
"BUT YOU *WON'T* REACH ALL OF THEM--"
DON'T!
"NOT IN TIME."
IT'S AN EIGHTY-HOUR WORKWEEK FULL OF *HARD CHOICES. UPHILL CLIMBS.*
AND MOST PEOPLE *DON'T* WAIT A *MONTH* BEFORE THEY RUN UPTOWN.

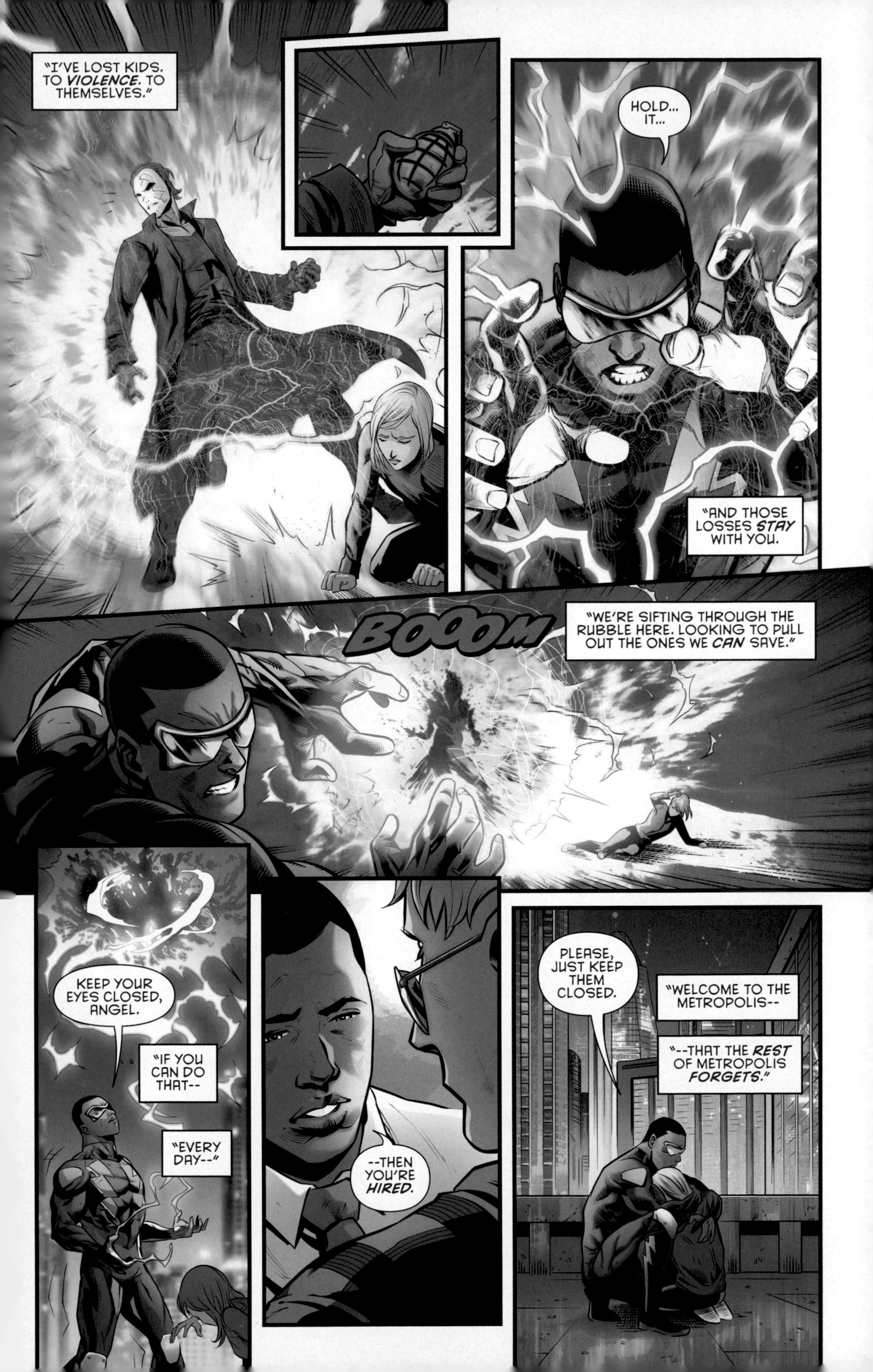
"I'VE LOST KIDS. TO *VIOLENCE*. TO THEMSELVES."
HOLD... IT...
"AND THOSE LOSSES *STAY* WITH YOU.
BOOOM
"WE'RE SIFTING THROUGH THE RUBBLE HERE. LOOKING TO PULL OUT THE ONES WE *CAN* SAVE."
KEEP YOUR EYES CLOSED, ANGEL.
"IF YOU CAN DO THAT--
"EVERY DAY--"
--THEN YOU'RE *HIRED*.
PLEASE, JUST KEEP THEM CLOSED.
"WELCOME TO THE METROPOLIS--
"--THAT THE *REST* OF METROPOLIS *FORGETS*."

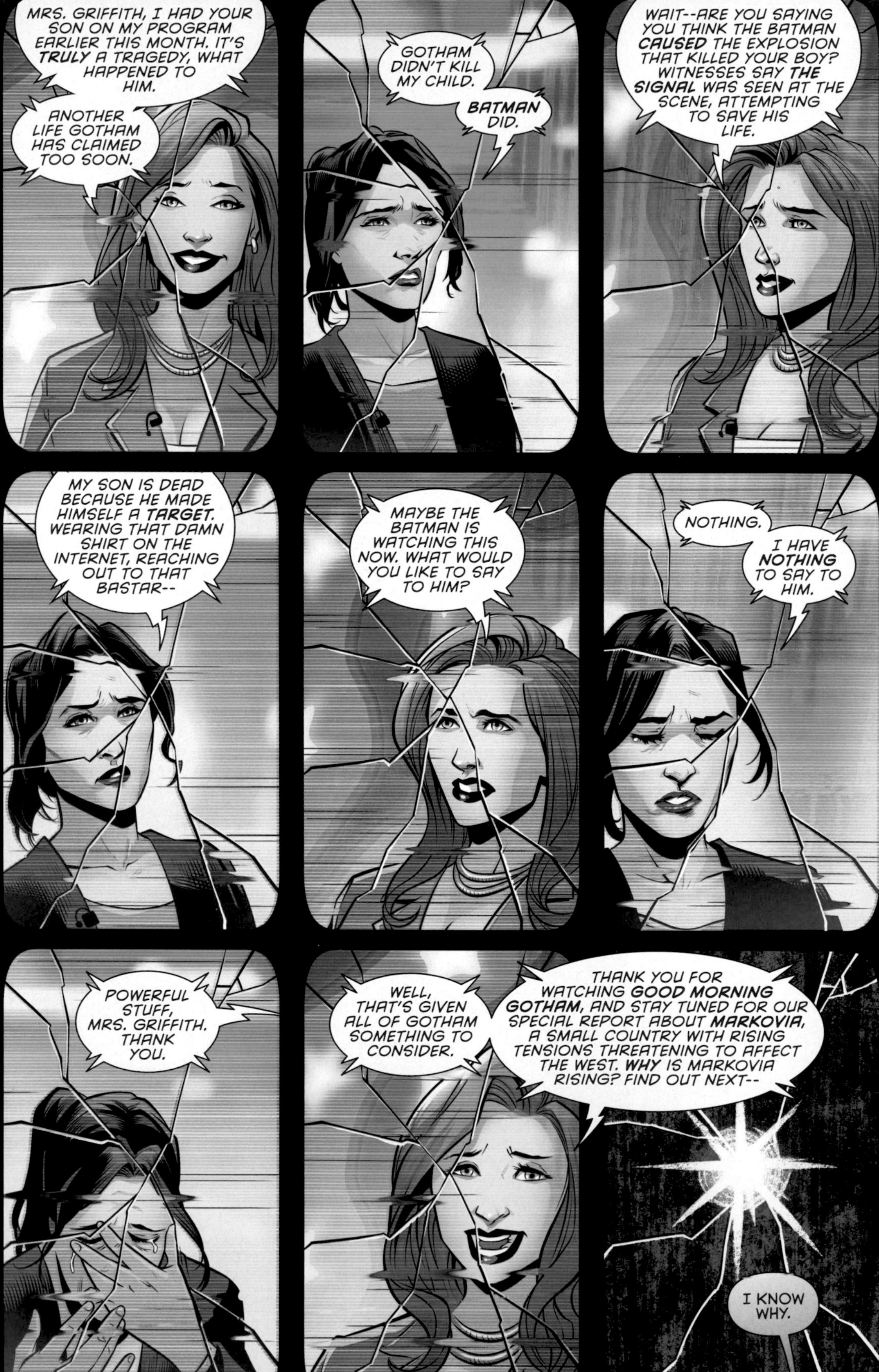
MRS. GRIFFITH, I HAD YOUR SON ON MY PROGRAM EARLIER THIS MONTH. IT'S **TRULY** A TRAGEDY, WHAT HAPPENED TO HIM.
ANOTHER LIFE GOTHAM HAS CLAIMED TOO SOON.
GOTHAM DIDN'T KILL MY CHILD.
BATMAN DID.
WAIT--ARE YOU SAYING YOU THINK THE BATMAN **CAUSED** THE EXPLOSION THAT KILLED YOUR BOY? WITNESSES SAY **THE SIGNAL** WAS SEEN AT THE SCENE, ATTEMPTING TO SAVE HIS LIFE.
MY SON IS DEAD BECAUSE HE MADE HIMSELF A **TARGET.** WEARING THAT DAMN SHIRT ON THE INTERNET, REACHING OUT TO THAT BASTAR--
MAYBE THE BATMAN IS WATCHING THIS NOW. WHAT WOULD YOU LIKE TO SAY TO HIM?
NOTHING.
I HAVE **NOTHING** TO SAY TO HIM.
POWERFUL STUFF, MRS. GRIFFITH. THANK YOU.
WELL, THAT'S GIVEN ALL OF GOTHAM SOMETHING TO CONSIDER.
THANK YOU FOR WATCHING **GOOD MORNING GOTHAM,** AND STAY TUNED FOR OUR SPECIAL REPORT ABOUT **MARKOVIA,** A SMALL COUNTRY WITH RISING TENSIONS THREATENING TO AFFECT THE WEST. **WHY** IS MARKOVIA RISING? FIND OUT NEXT--
I KNOW WHY.

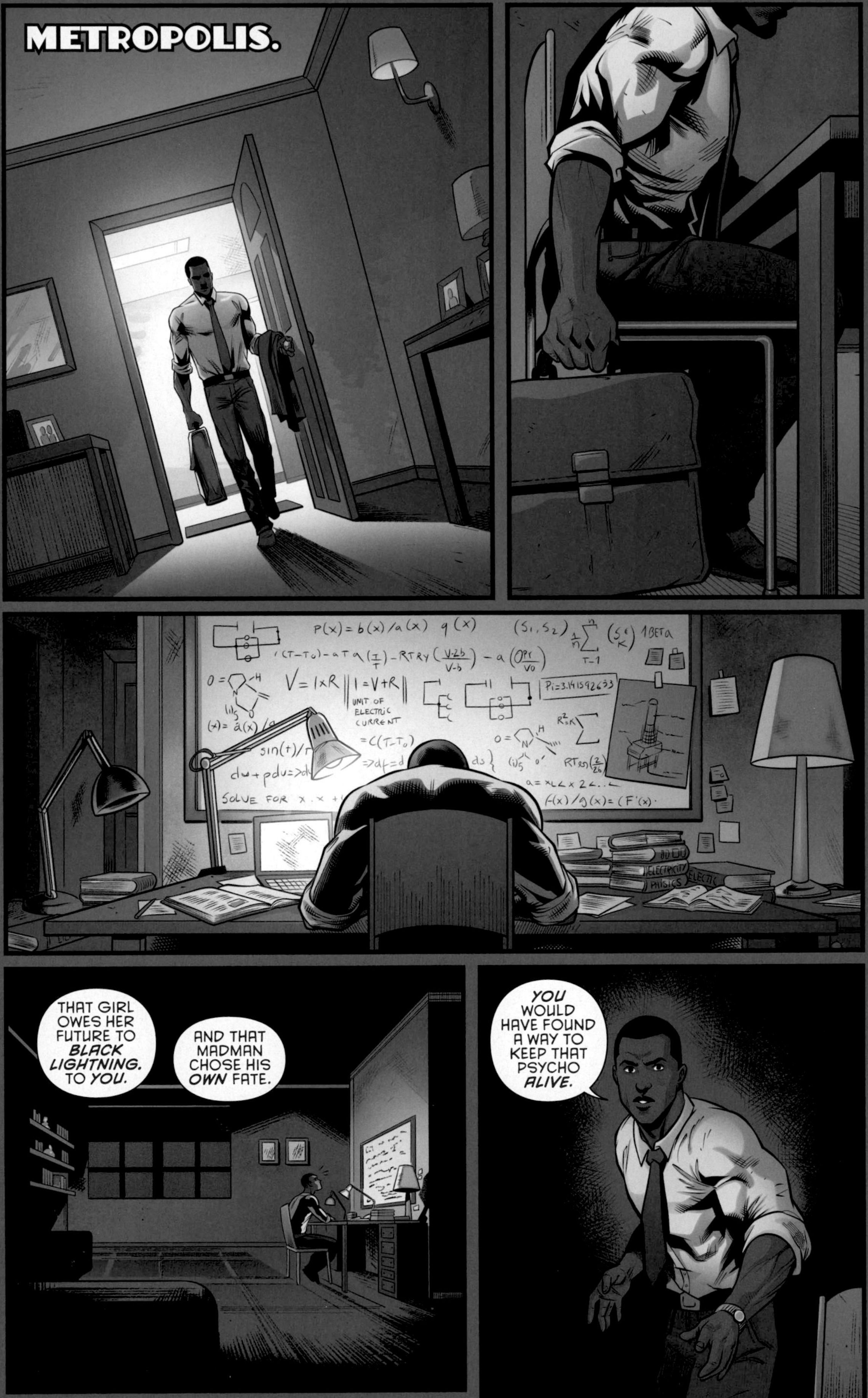
METROPOLIS.
THAT GIRL OWES HER FUTURE TO *BLACK LIGHTNING.* TO *YOU.*
AND THAT MADMAN CHOSE HIS *OWN* FATE.
YOU WOULD HAVE FOUND A WAY TO KEEP THAT PSYCHO *ALIVE.*

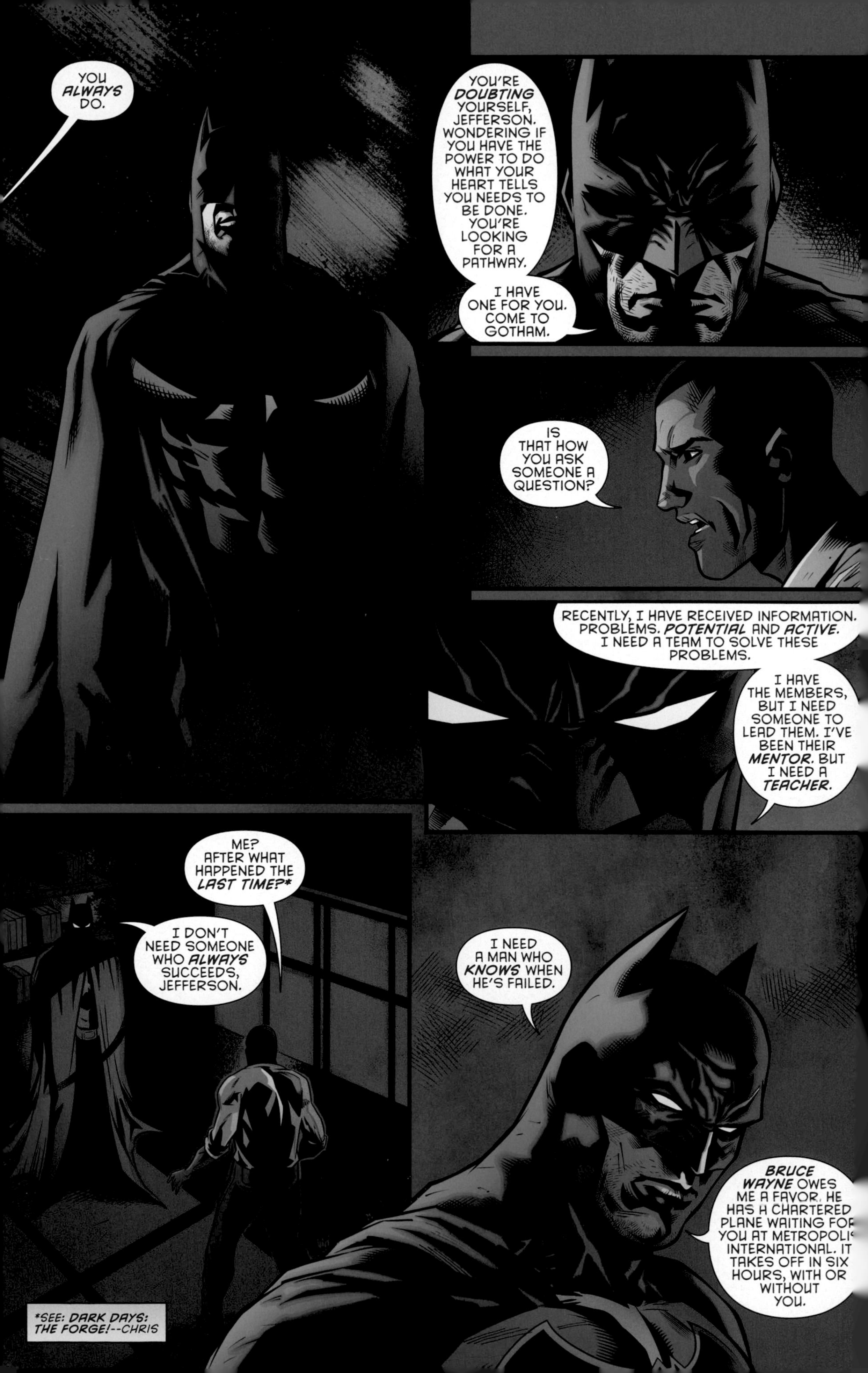
YOU ALWAYS DO.
YOU'RE DOUBTING YOURSELF, JEFFERSON. WONDERING IF YOU HAVE THE POWER TO DO WHAT YOUR HEART TELLS YOU NEEDS TO BE DONE. YOU'RE LOOKING FOR A PATHWAY.
I HAVE ONE FOR YOU. COME TO GOTHAM.
IS THAT HOW YOU ASK SOMEONE A QUESTION?
RECENTLY, I HAVE RECEIVED INFORMATION. PROBLEMS. POTENTIAL AND ACTIVE. I NEED A TEAM TO SOLVE THESE PROBLEMS.
I HAVE THE MEMBERS, BUT I NEED SOMEONE TO LEAD THEM. I'VE BEEN THEIR MENTOR. BUT I NEED A TEACHER.
ME? AFTER WHAT HAPPENED THE LAST TIME?*
I DON'T NEED SOMEONE WHO ALWAYS SUCCEEDS, JEFFERSON.
I NEED A MAN WHO KNOWS WHEN HE'S FAILED.
BRUCE WAYNE OWES ME A FAVOR. HE HAS A CHARTERED PLANE WAITING FOR YOU AT METROPOLIS INTERNATIONAL. IT TAKES OFF IN SIX HOURS, WITH OR WITHOUT YOU.
*SEE: DARK DAYS: THE FORGE!--CHRIS

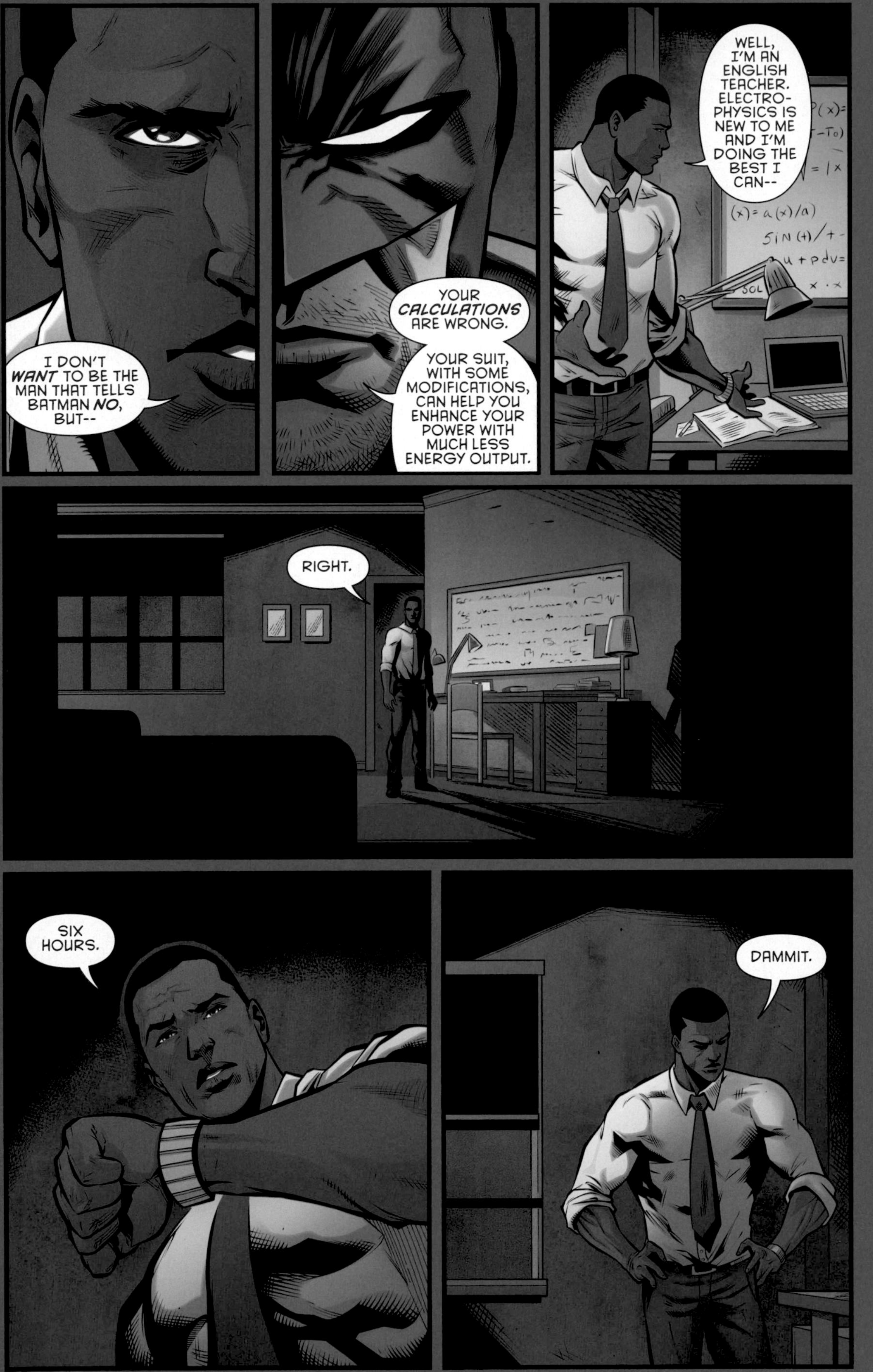

I DON'T *WANT* TO BE THE MAN THAT TELLS BATMAN *NO*, BUT--
YOUR *CALCULATIONS* ARE WRONG.
YOUR SUIT, WITH SOME MODIFICATIONS, CAN HELP YOU ENHANCE YOUR POWER WITH MUCH LESS ENERGY OUTPUT.
WELL, I'M AN ENGLISH TEACHER. ELECTRO-PHYSICS IS NEW TO ME AND I'M DOING THE BEST I CAN--
RIGHT.
SIX HOURS.
DAMMIT.

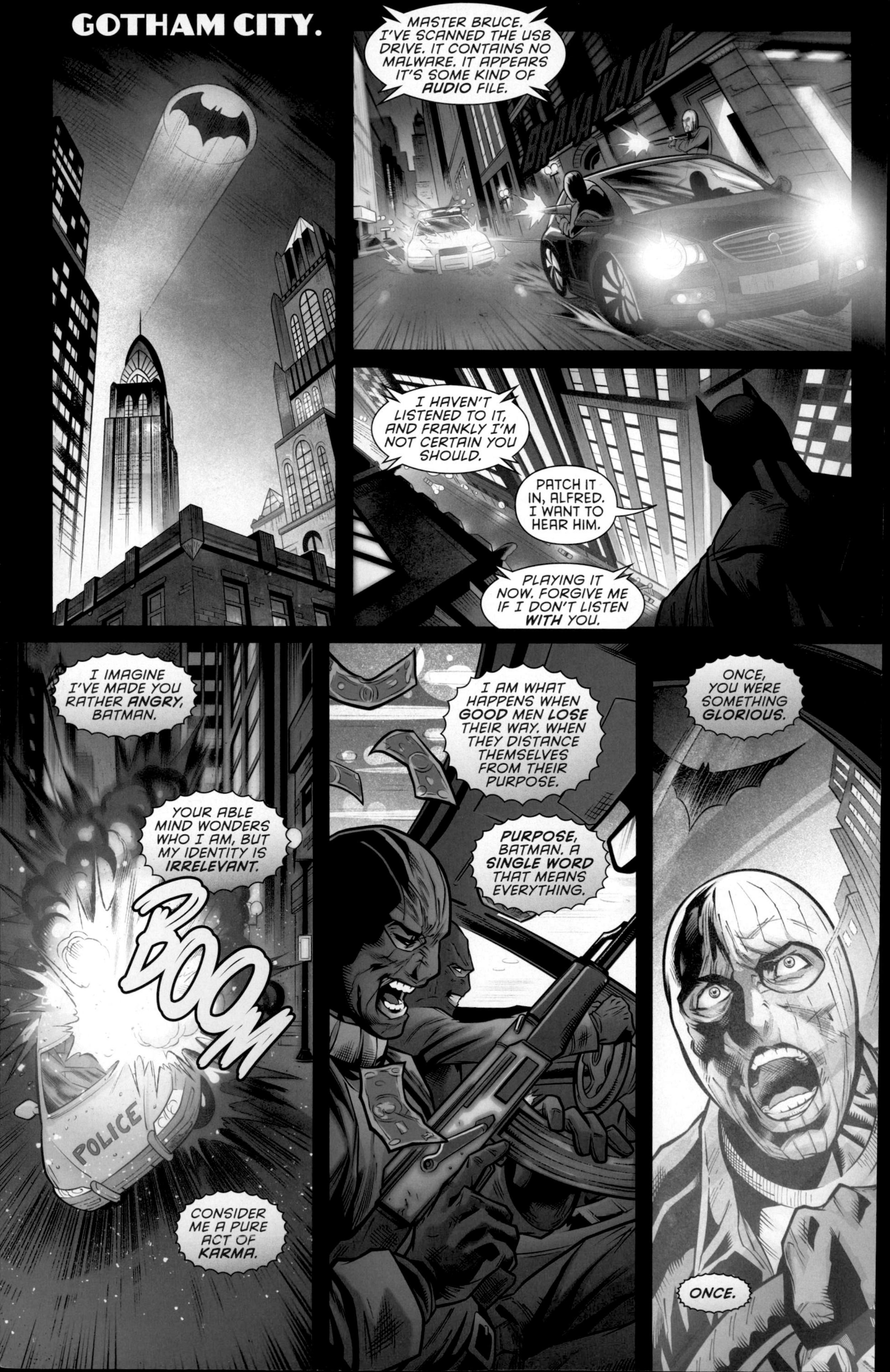
GOTHAM CITY.
MASTER BRUCE. I'VE SCANNED THE USB DRIVE. IT CONTAINS NO MALWARE. IT APPEARS IT'S SOME KIND OF AUDIO FILE.
BRAKAKAKA
I HAVEN'T LISTENED TO IT, AND FRANKLY I'M NOT CERTAIN YOU SHOULD.
PATCH IT IN, ALFRED. I WANT TO HEAR HIM.
PLAYING IT NOW. FORGIVE ME IF I DON'T LISTEN WITH YOU.
I IMAGINE I'VE MADE YOU RATHER ANGRY, BATMAN.
YOUR ABLE MIND WONDERS WHO I AM, BUT MY IDENTITY IS IRRELEVANT.
BOOM
POLICE
CONSIDER ME A PURE ACT OF KARMA.
I AM WHAT HAPPENS WHEN GOOD MEN LOSE THEIR WAY. WHEN THEY DISTANCE THEMSELVES FROM THEIR PURPOSE.
PURPOSE, BATMAN. A SINGLE WORD THAT MEANS EVERYTHING.
ONCE, YOU WERE SOMETHING GLORIOUS.
ONCE.

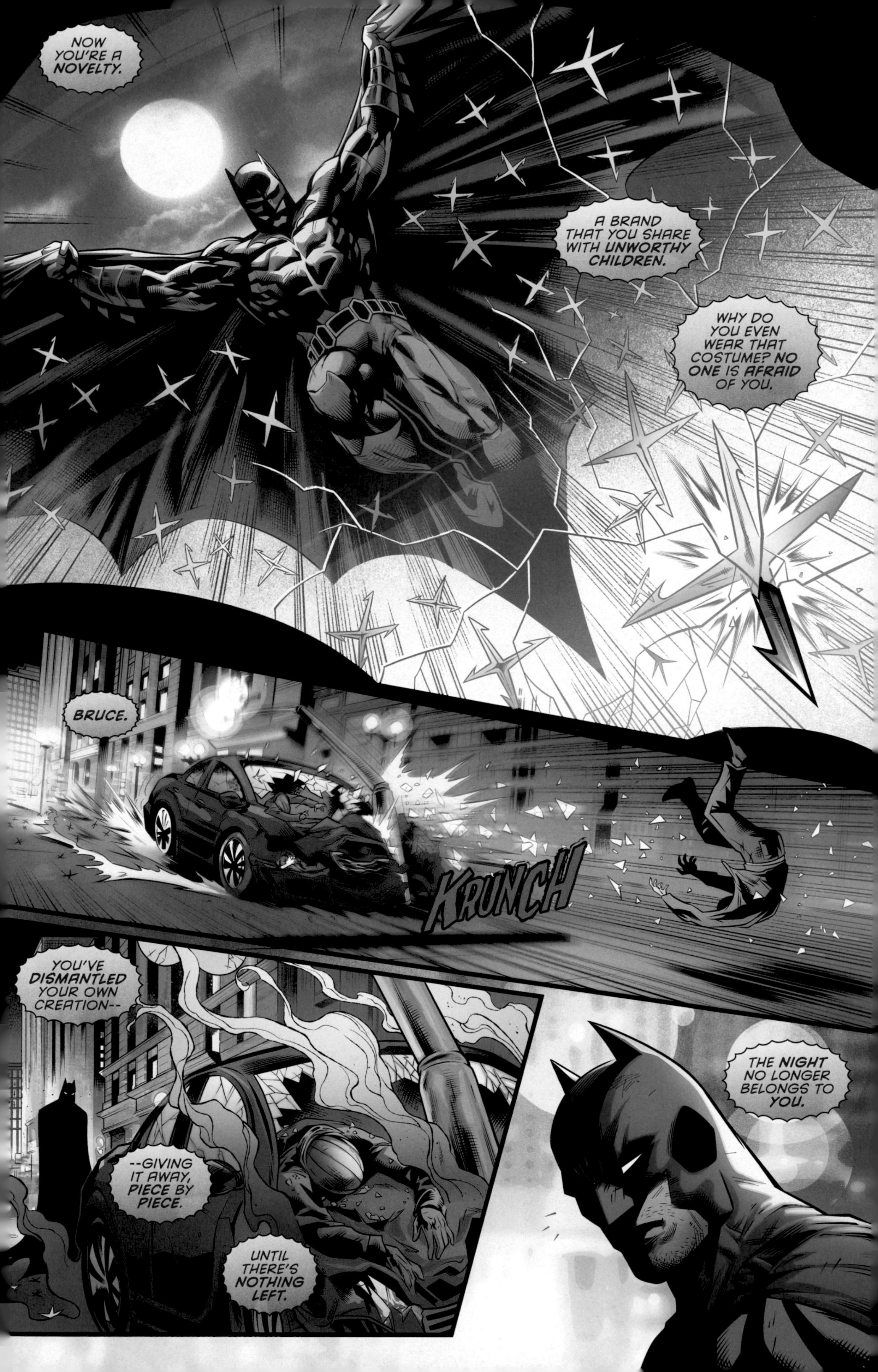
NOW YOU'RE A NOVELTY.
A BRAND THAT YOU SHARE WITH UNWORTHY CHILDREN.
WHY DO YOU EVEN WEAR THAT COSTUME? NO ONE IS AFRAID OF YOU.
BRUCE.
KRUNCH
YOU'VE DISMANTLED YOUR OWN CREATION--
--GIVING IT AWAY, PIECE BY PIECE.
UNTIL THERE'S NOTHING LEFT.
THE NIGHT NO LONGER BELONGS TO YOU.

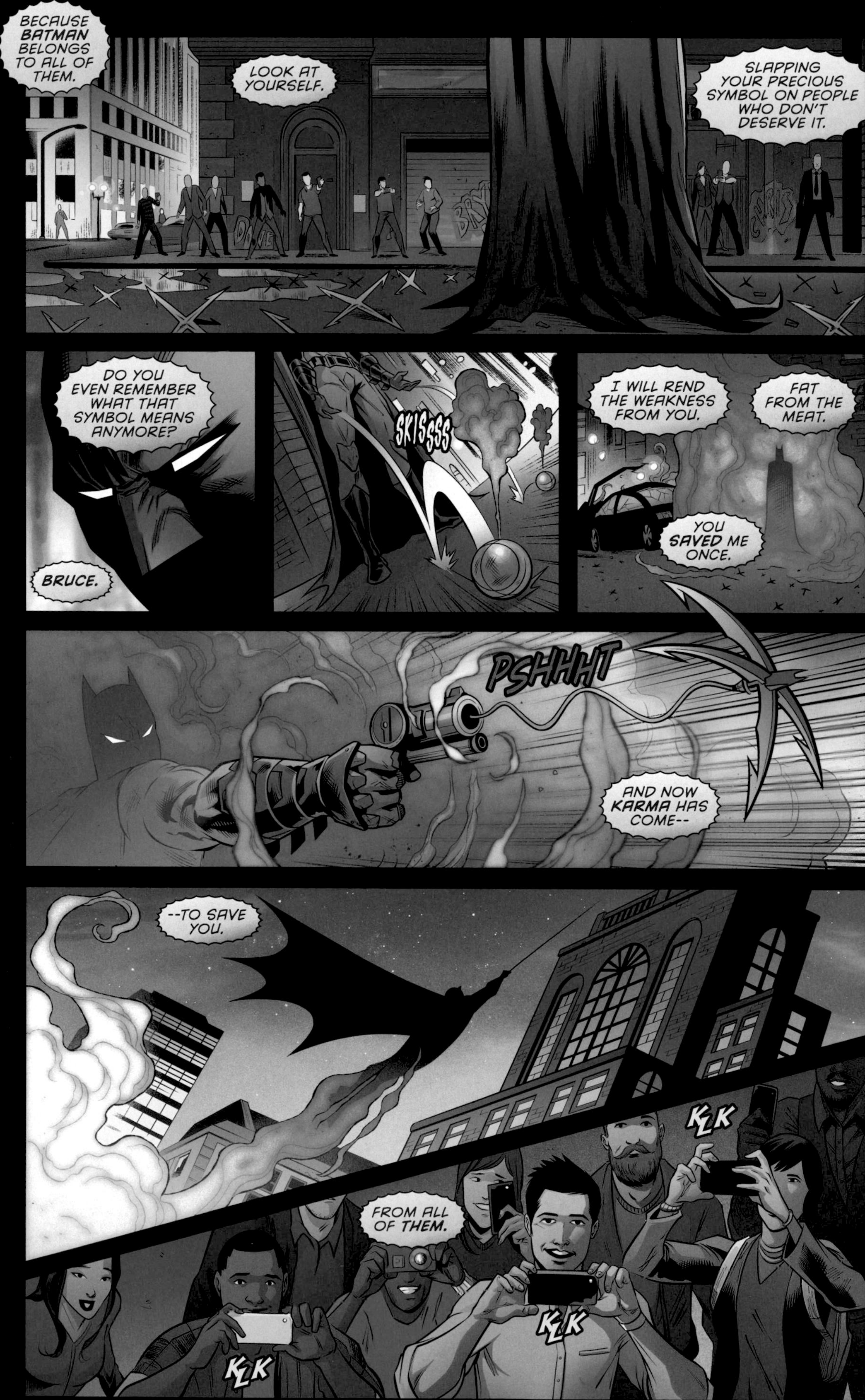
BECAUSE BATMAN BELONGS TO ALL OF THEM.
LOOK AT YOURSELF.
SLAPPING YOUR PRECIOUS SYMBOL ON PEOPLE WHO DON'T DESERVE IT.
DO YOU EVEN REMEMBER WHAT THAT SYMBOL MEANS ANYMORE?
BRUCE.
SKISSSS
I WILL REND THE WEAKNESS FROM YOU.
FAT FROM THE MEAT.
YOU SAVED ME ONCE.
PSHHHT
AND NOW KARMA HAS COME--
--TO SAVE YOU.
KLK
FROM ALL OF THEM.
KLK
KLK

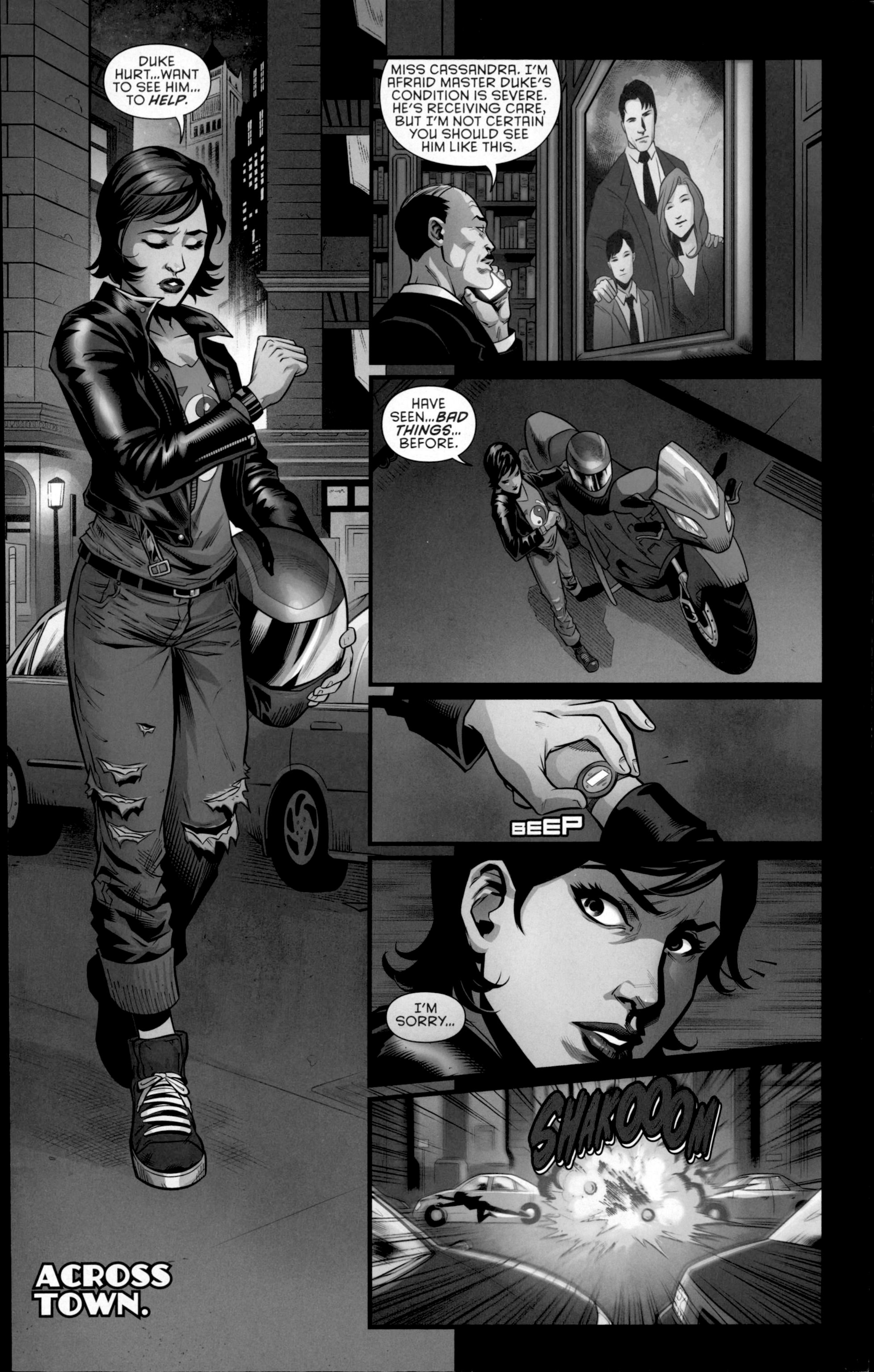
ACROSS TOWN.
DUKE HURT...WANT TO SEE HIM... TO *HELP*.
MISS CASSANDRA. I'M AFRAID MASTER DUKE'S CONDITION IS SEVERE. HE'S RECEIVING CARE, BUT I'M NOT CERTAIN YOU SHOULD SEE HIM LIKE THIS.
HAVE SEEN...*BAD THINGS*... BEFORE.
BEEP
I'M SORRY...
SHAKOOOM

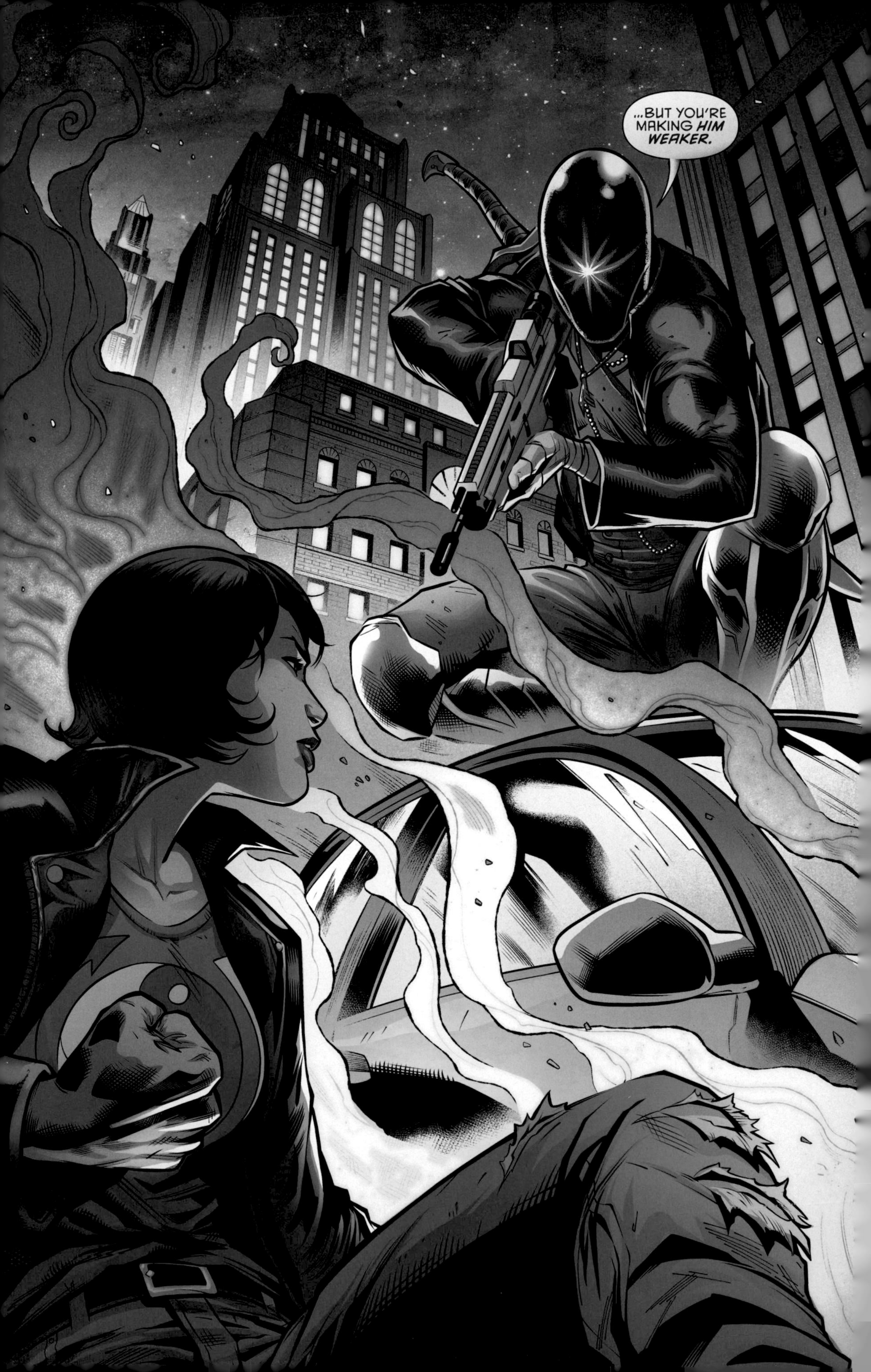
...BUT YOU'RE MAKING *HIM* WEAKER.

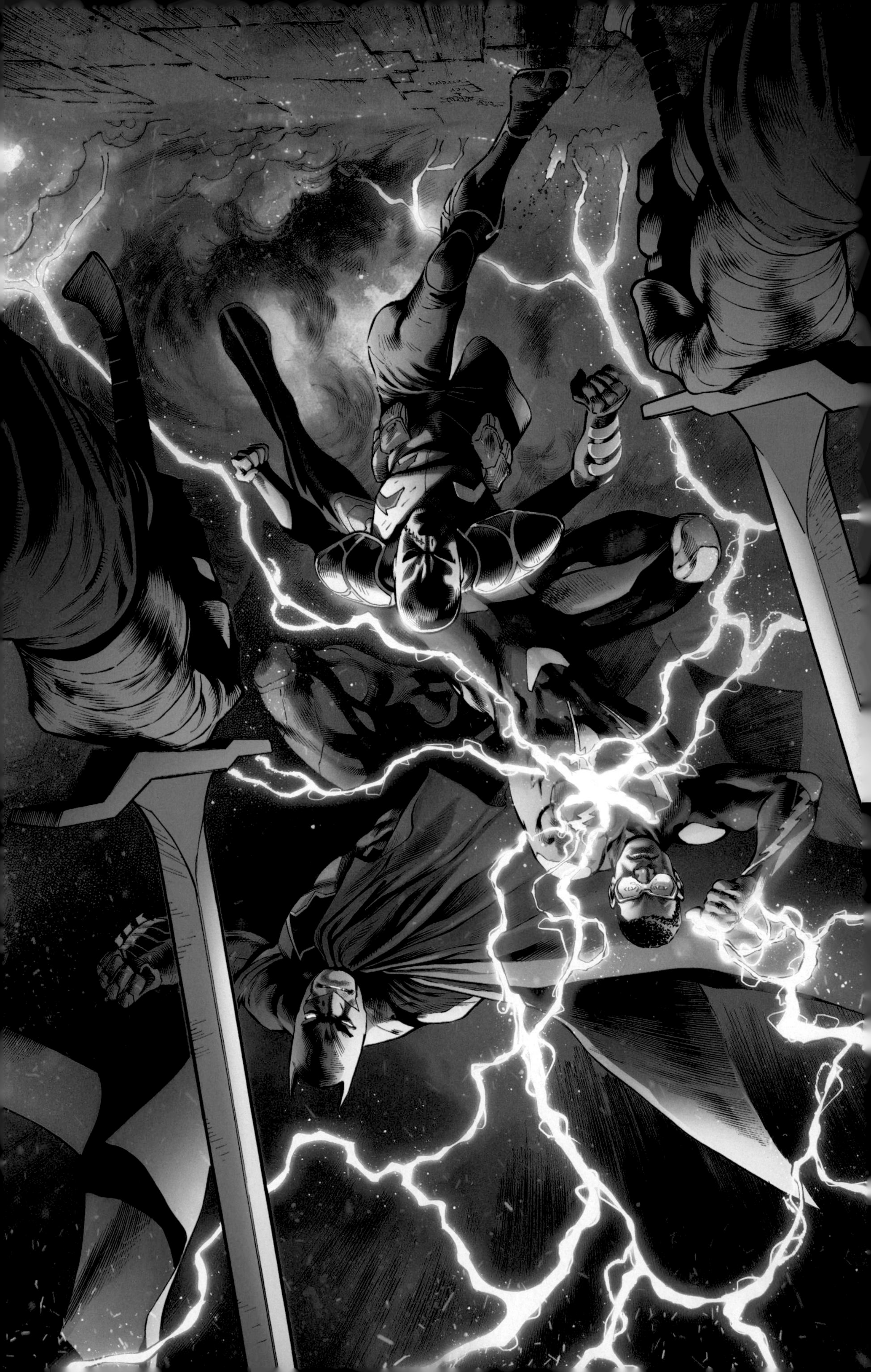

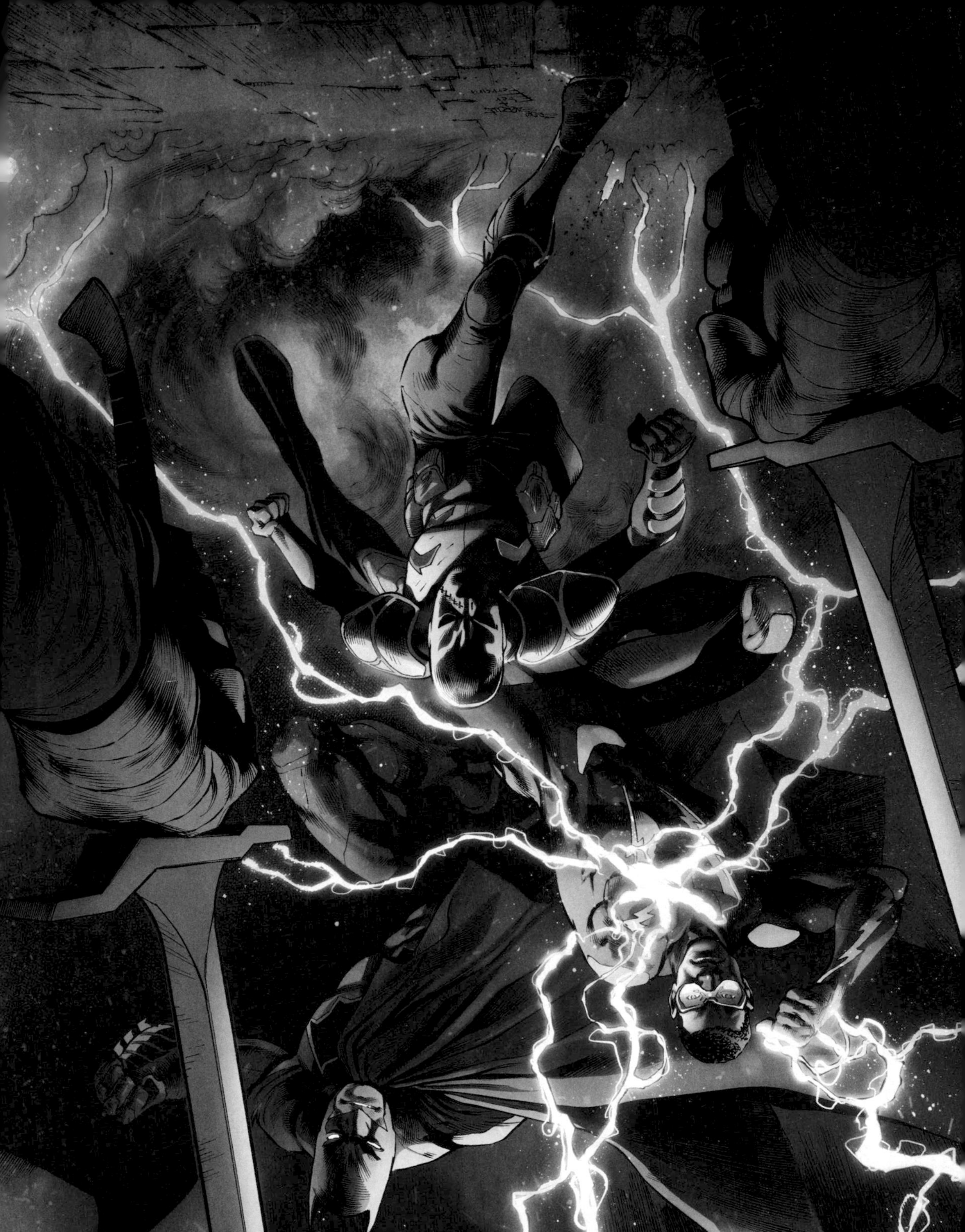

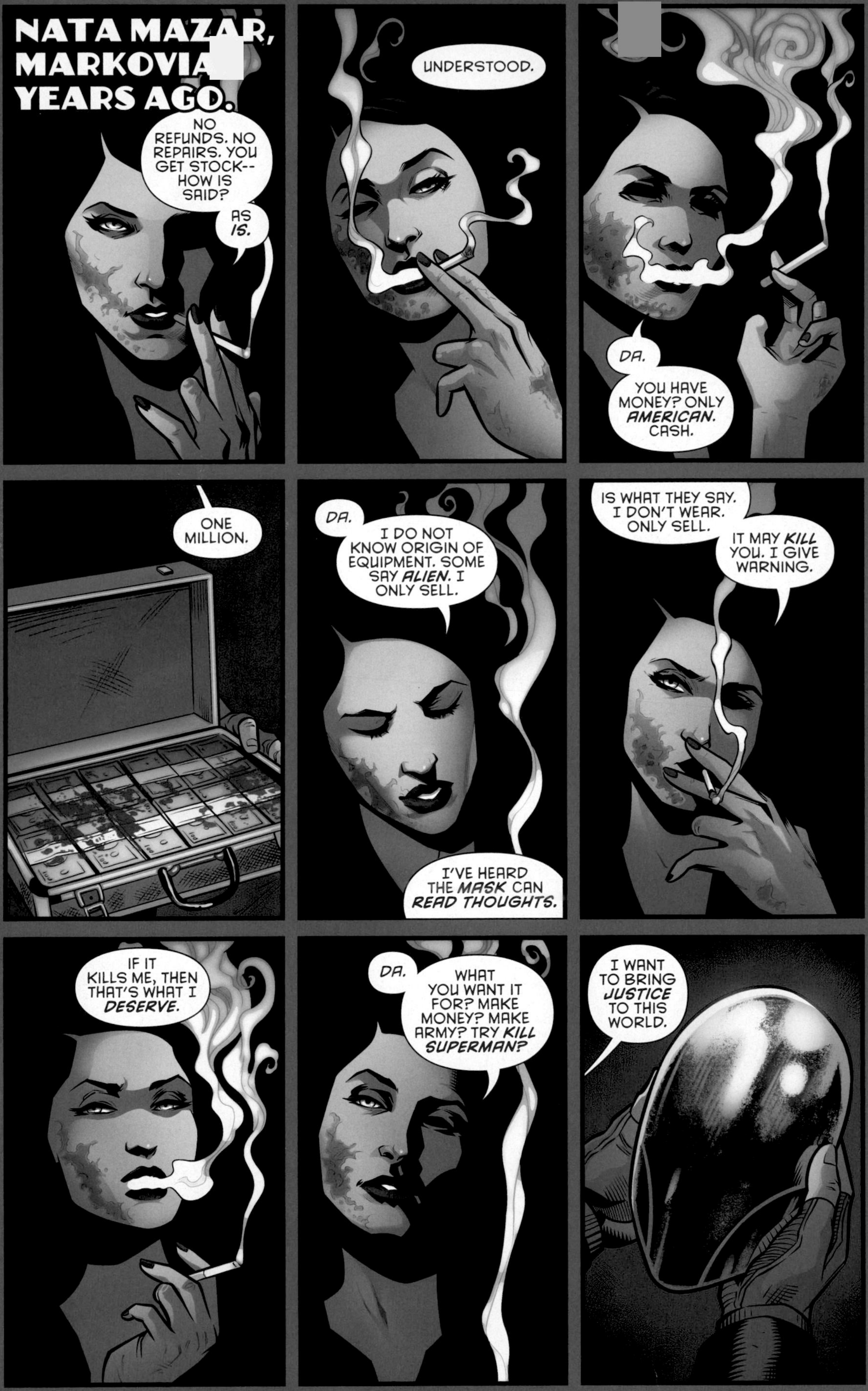

NATA MAZAR, MARKOVIA YEARS AGO.
NO REFUNDS. NO REPAIRS. YOU GET STOCK-- HOW IS SAID?
AS *IS.*
UNDERSTOOD.
DA.
YOU HAVE MONEY? ONLY ***AMERICAN.*** CASH.
ONE MILLION.
DA.
I DO NOT KNOW ORIGIN OF EQUIPMENT. SOME SAY ***ALIEN.*** I ONLY SELL.
I'VE HEARD THE ***MASK*** CAN ***READ THOUGHTS.***
IS WHAT THEY SAY. I DON'T WEAR. ONLY SELL.
IT MAY ***KILL*** YOU. I GIVE WARNING.
IF IT KILLS ME, THEN THAT'S WHAT I ***DESERVE.***
DA.
WHAT YOU WANT IT FOR? MAKE MONEY? MAKE ARMY? TRY ***KILL SUPERMAN?***
I WANT TO BRING ***JUSTICE*** TO THIS WORLD.

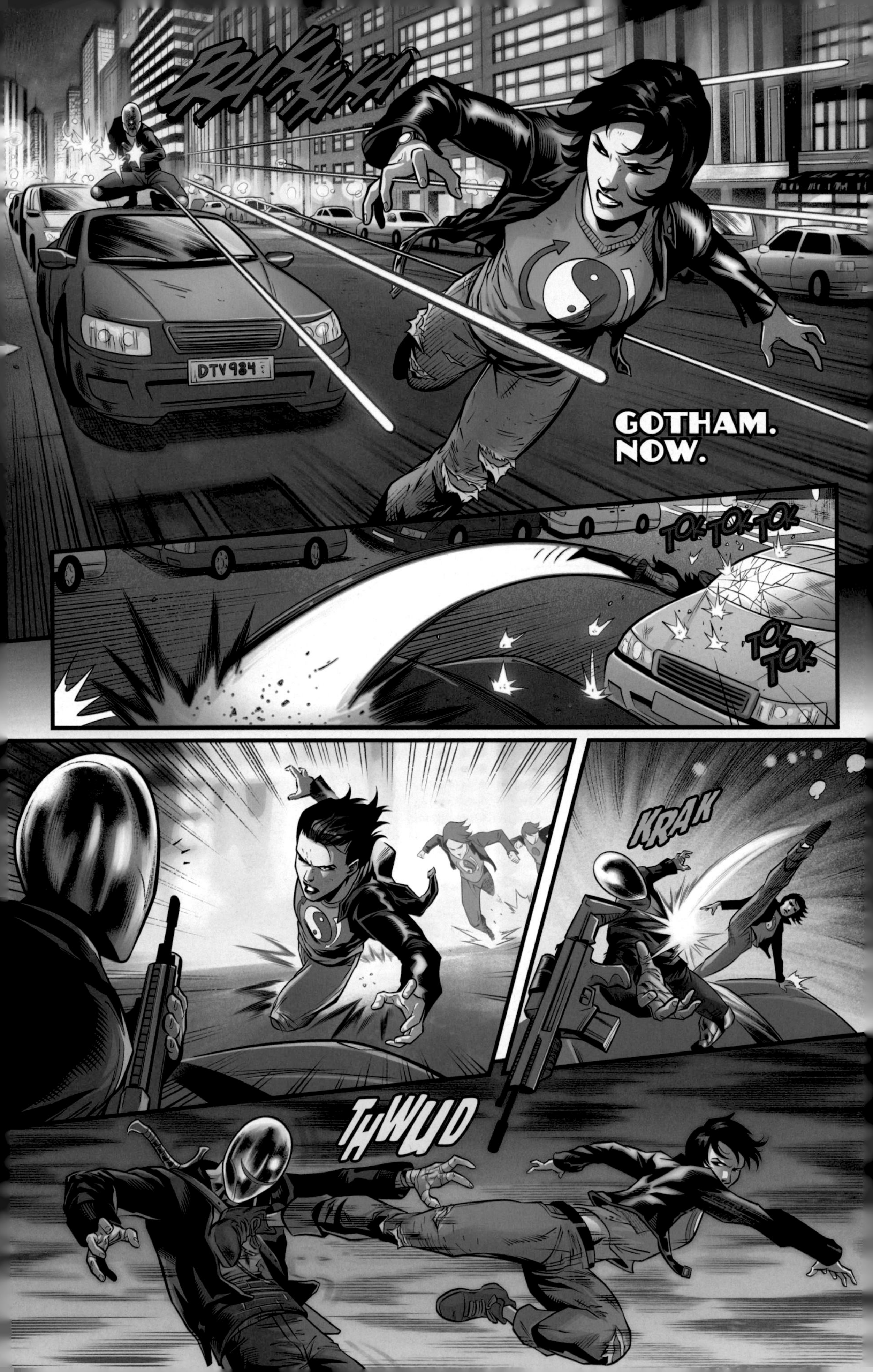
GOTHAM.
NOW.
TOK TOK TOK
TOK TOK
KRAK
THWUD

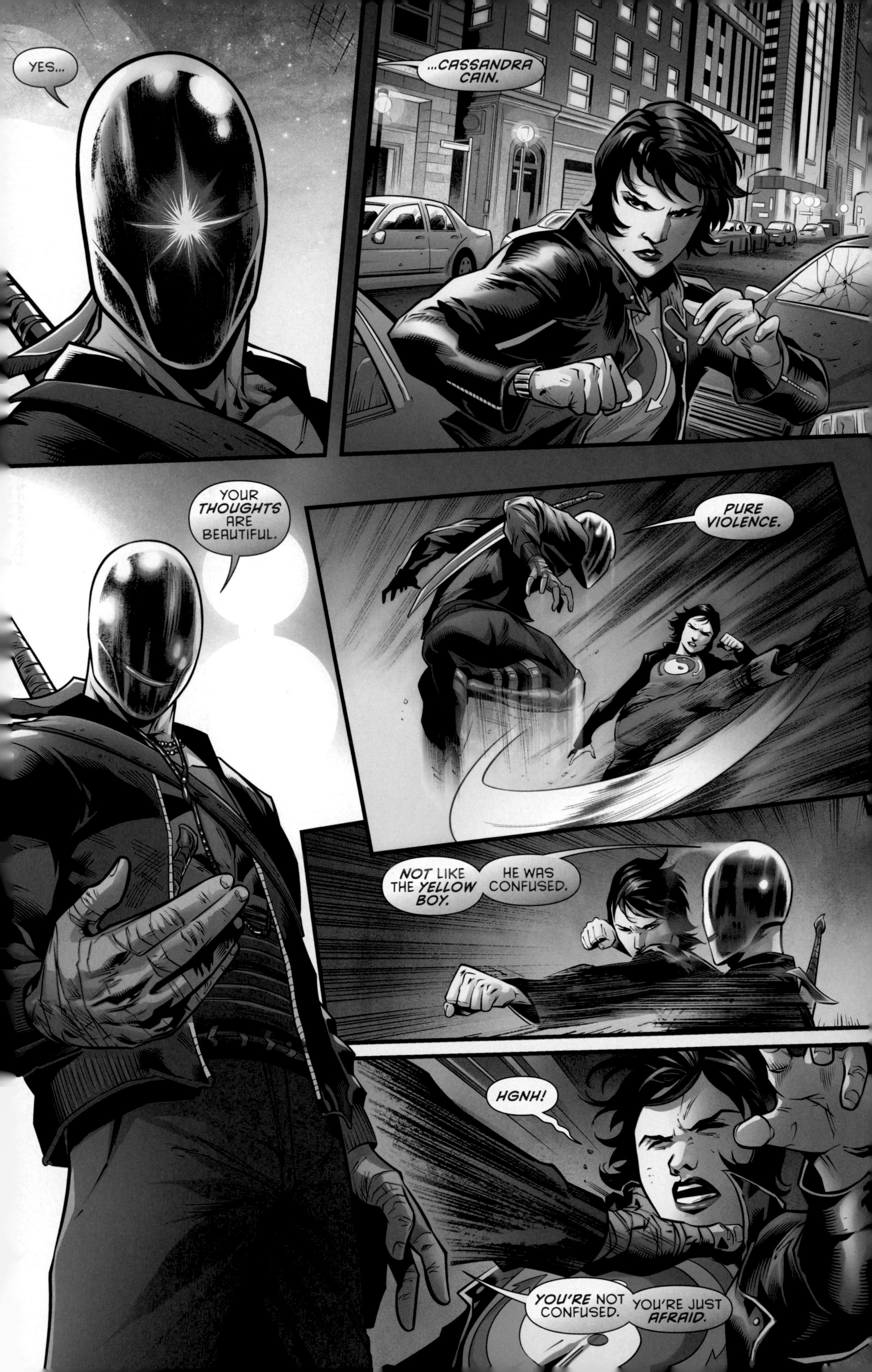
YES...
...CASSANDRA CAIN.
YOUR THOUGHTS ARE BEAUTIFUL.
PURE VIOLENCE.
NOT LIKE THE YELLOW BOY.
HE WAS CONFUSED.
HGNH!
YOU'RE NOT CONFUSED.
YOU'RE JUST AFRAID.

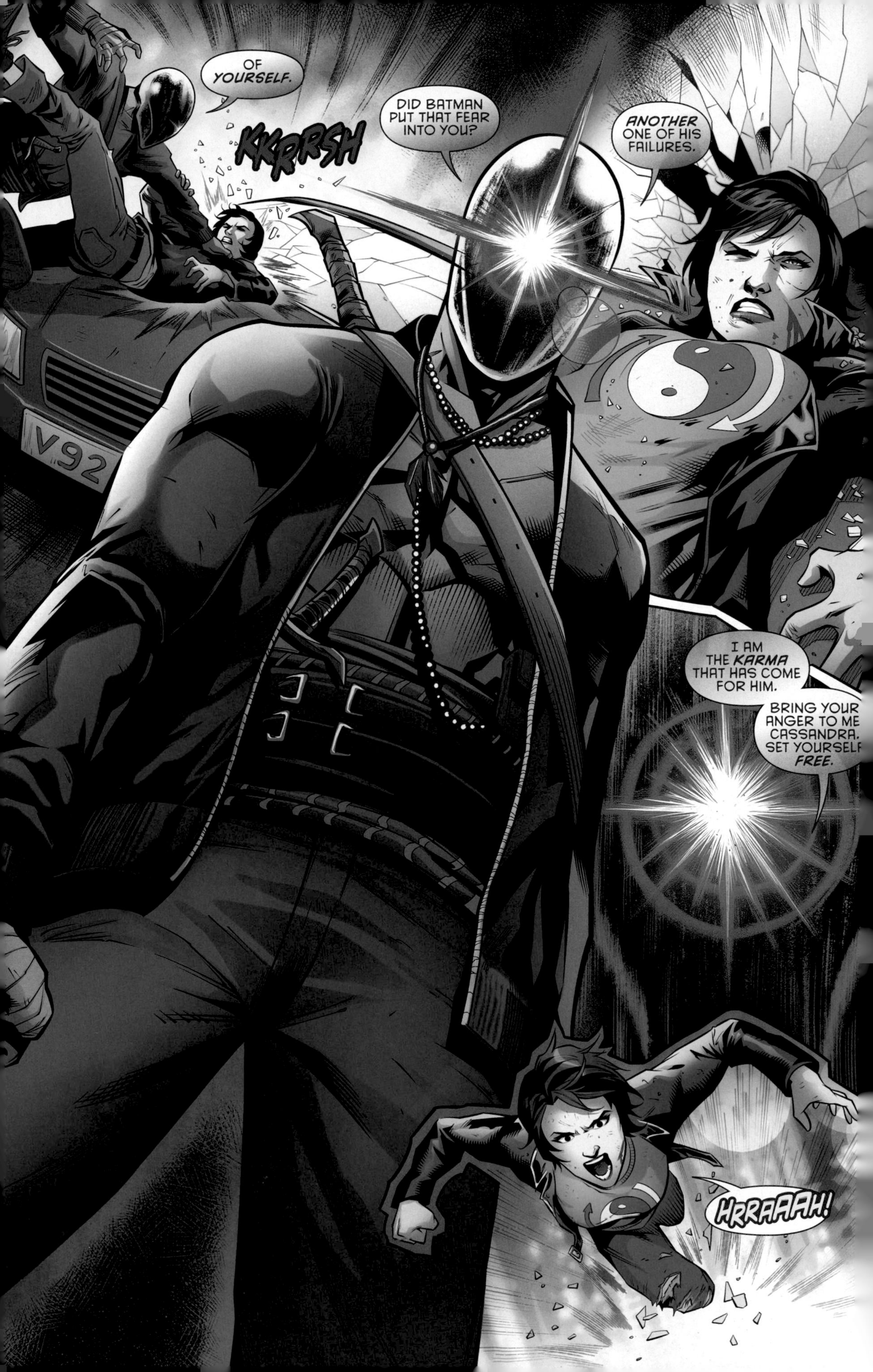
OF YOURSELF.
KKRRSH
DID BATMAN PUT THAT FEAR INTO YOU?
ANOTHER ONE OF HIS FAILURES.
I AM THE KARMA THAT HAS COME FOR HIM.
BRING YOUR ANGER TO ME CASSANDRA. SET YOURSELF FREE.
HRRAAAH!

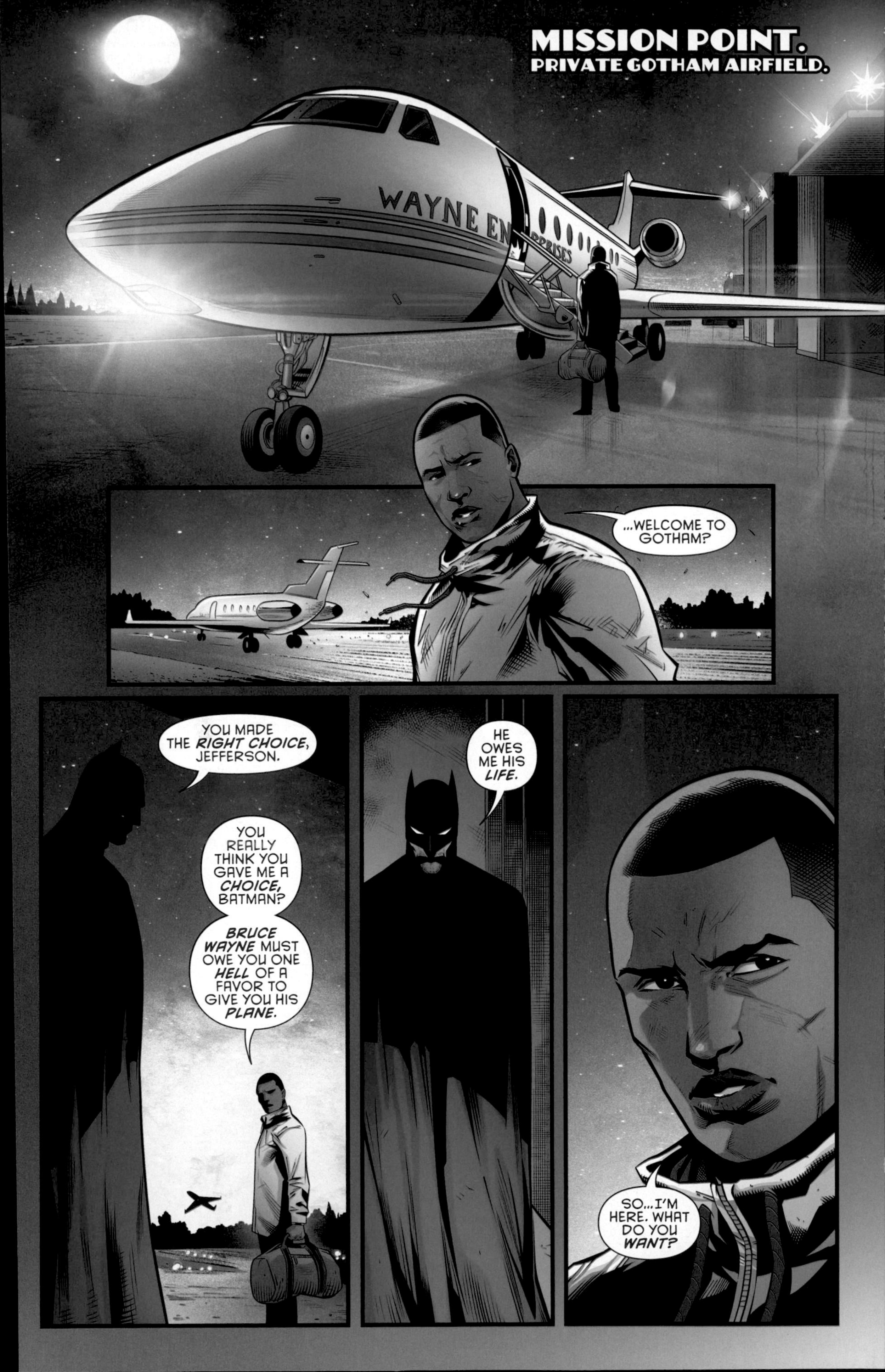
MISSION POINT.
PRIVATE GOTHAM AIRFIELD.
WAYNE EN PRISES
...WELCOME TO GOTHAM?
YOU MADE THE *RIGHT CHOICE*, JEFFERSON.
YOU REALLY THINK YOU GAVE ME A *CHOICE*, BATMAN?
BRUCE WAYNE MUST OWE YOU ONE *HELL* OF A FAVOR TO GIVE YOU HIS *PLANE*.
HE OWES ME HIS *LIFE*.
SO...I'M HERE. WHAT DO YOU *WANT*?

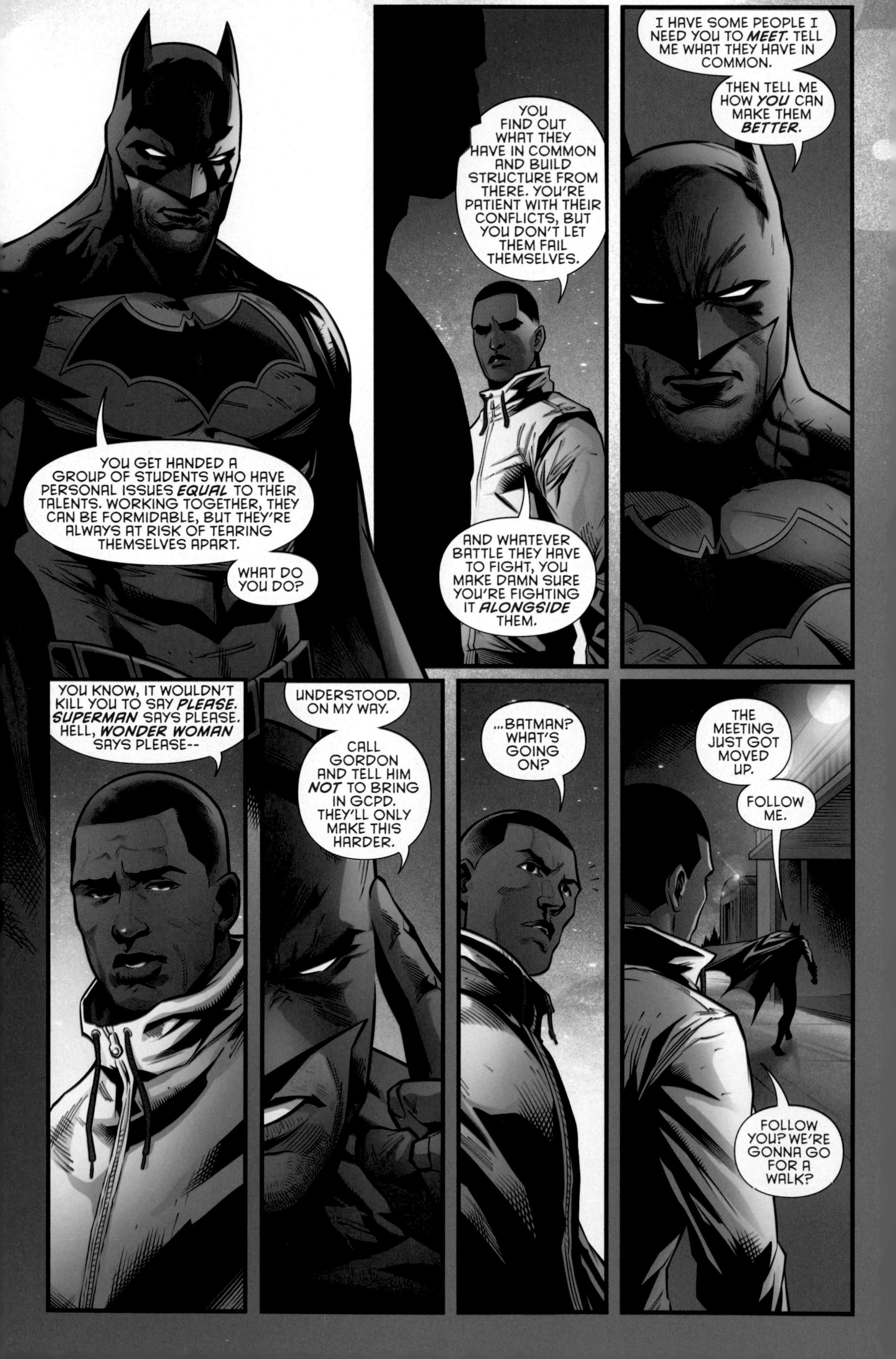
YOU GET HANDED A GROUP OF STUDENTS WHO HAVE PERSONAL ISSUES EQUAL TO THEIR TALENTS. WORKING TOGETHER, THEY CAN BE FORMIDABLE, BUT THEY'RE ALWAYS AT RISK OF TEARING THEMSELVES APART.
WHAT DO YOU DO?
YOU FIND OUT WHAT THEY HAVE IN COMMON AND BUILD STRUCTURE FROM THERE. YOU'RE PATIENT WITH THEIR CONFLICTS, BUT YOU DON'T LET THEM FAIL THEMSELVES.
AND WHATEVER BATTLE THEY HAVE TO FIGHT, YOU MAKE DAMN SURE YOU'RE FIGHTING IT ALONGSIDE THEM.
I HAVE SOME PEOPLE I NEED YOU TO MEET. TELL ME WHAT THEY HAVE IN COMMON.
THEN TELL ME HOW YOU CAN MAKE THEM BETTER.
YOU KNOW, IT WOULDN'T KILL YOU TO SAY PLEASE. SUPERMAN SAYS PLEASE. HELL, WONDER WOMAN SAYS PLEASE--
UNDERSTOOD. ON MY WAY.
CALL GORDON AND TELL HIM NOT TO BRING IN GCPD. THEY'LL ONLY MAKE THIS HARDER.
...BATMAN? WHAT'S GOING ON?
THE MEETING JUST GOT MOVED UP.
FOLLOW ME.
FOLLOW YOU? WE'RE GONNA GO FOR A WALK?

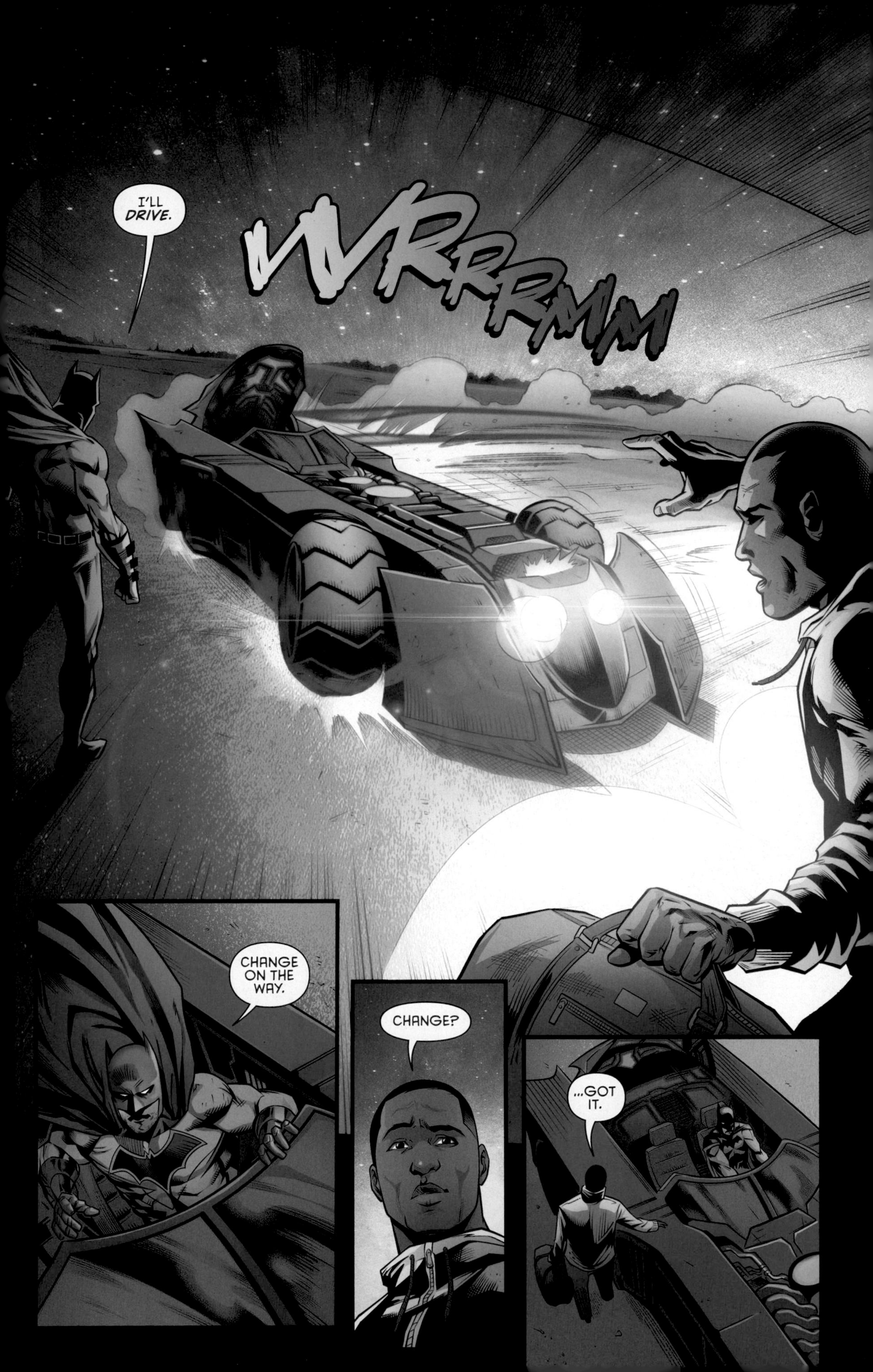
I'LL DRIVE.
VVRRRMMM
CHANGE ON THE WAY.
CHANGE?
...GOT IT.

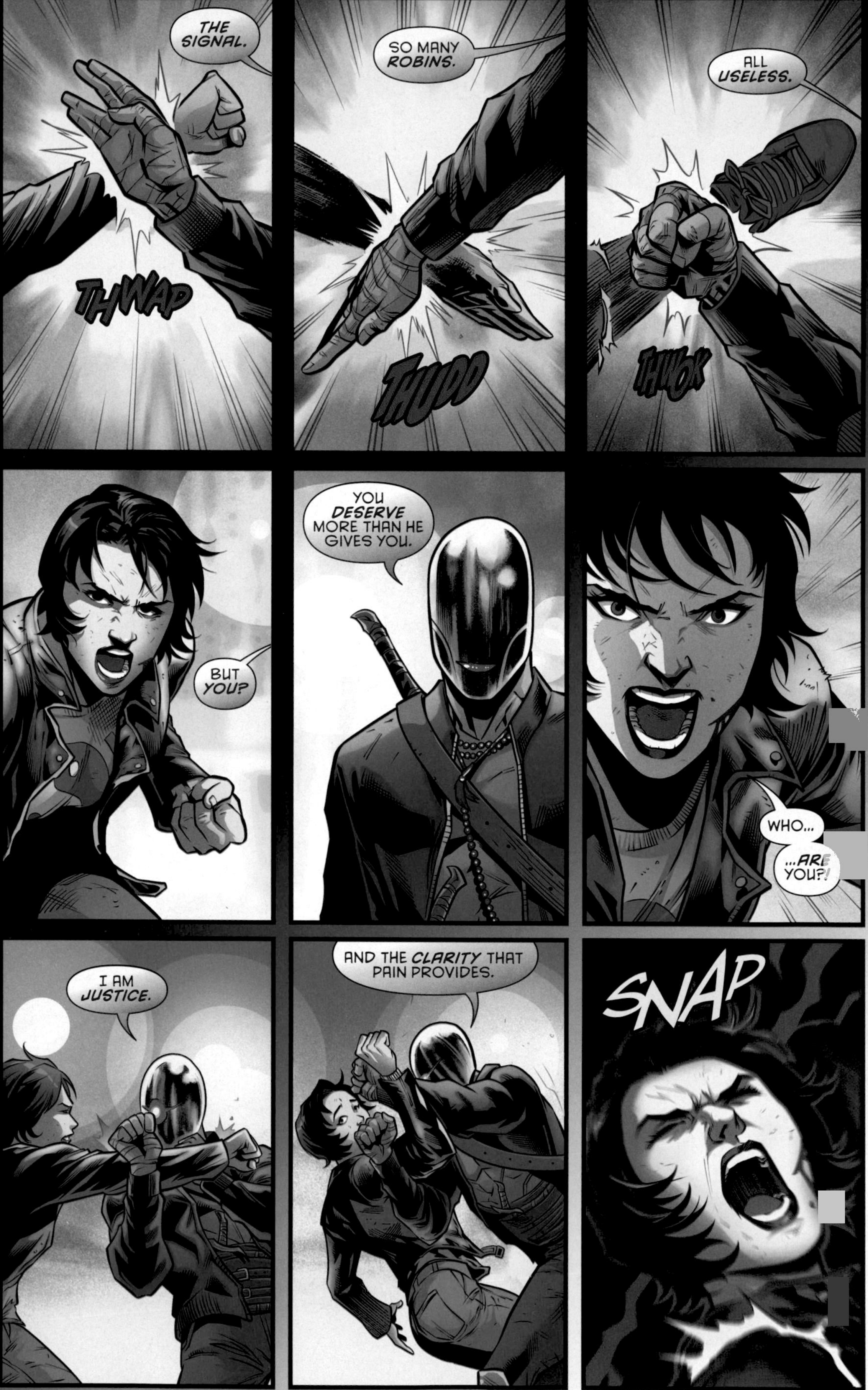
THE SIGNAL.
THWAP
SO MANY ROBINS.
THUDD
ALL USELESS.
THWOK
BUT YOU?
YOU DESERVE MORE THAN HE GIVES YOU.
WHO...
...ARE YOU?!
I AM JUSTICE.
AND THE CLARITY THAT PAIN PROVIDES.
SNAP

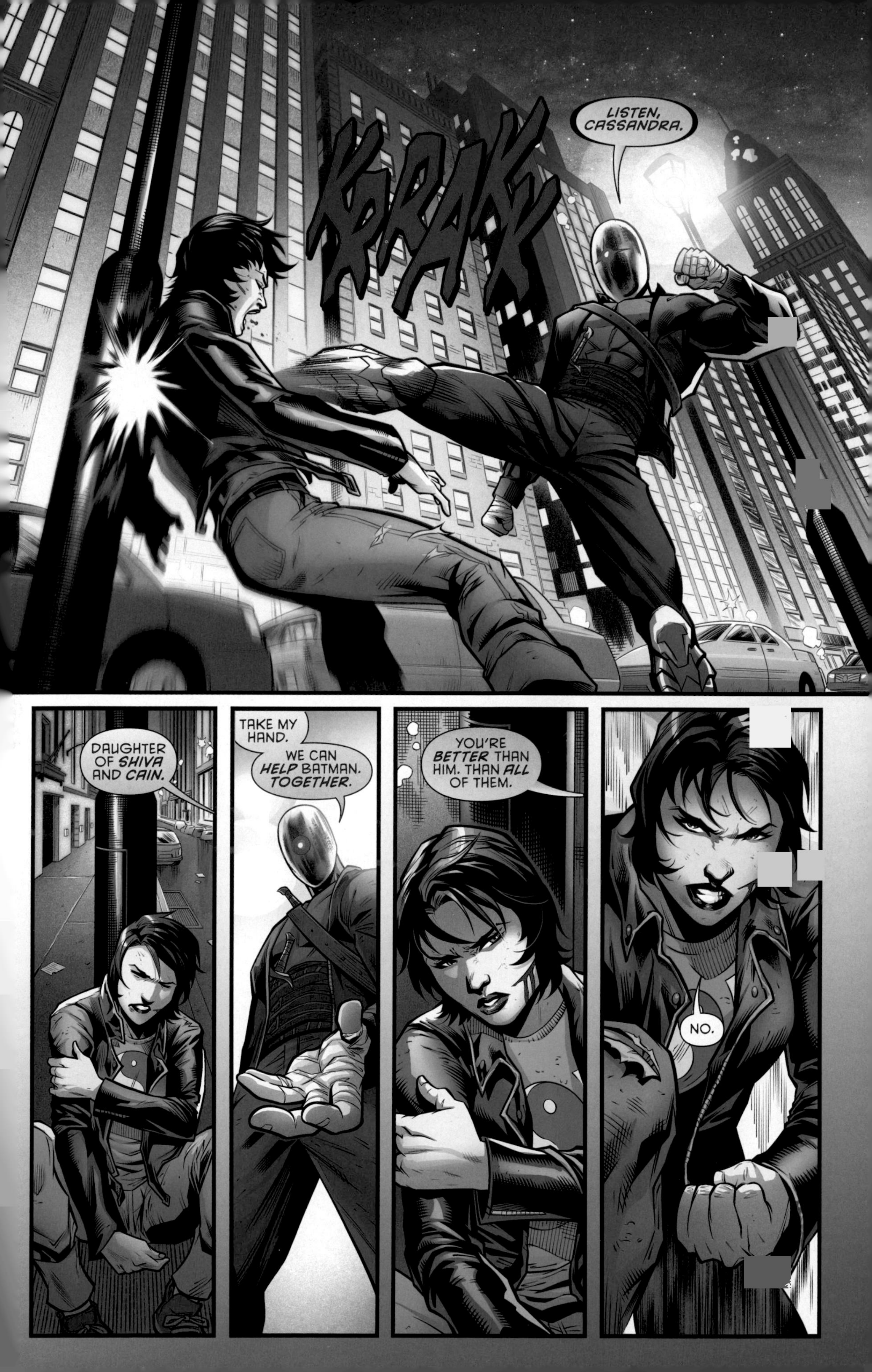
LISTEN, CASSANDRA.
KRAK
DAUGHTER OF SHIVA AND CAIN.
TAKE MY HAND.
WE CAN HELP BATMAN. TOGETHER.
YOU'RE BETTER THAN HIM. THAN ALL OF THEM.
NO.

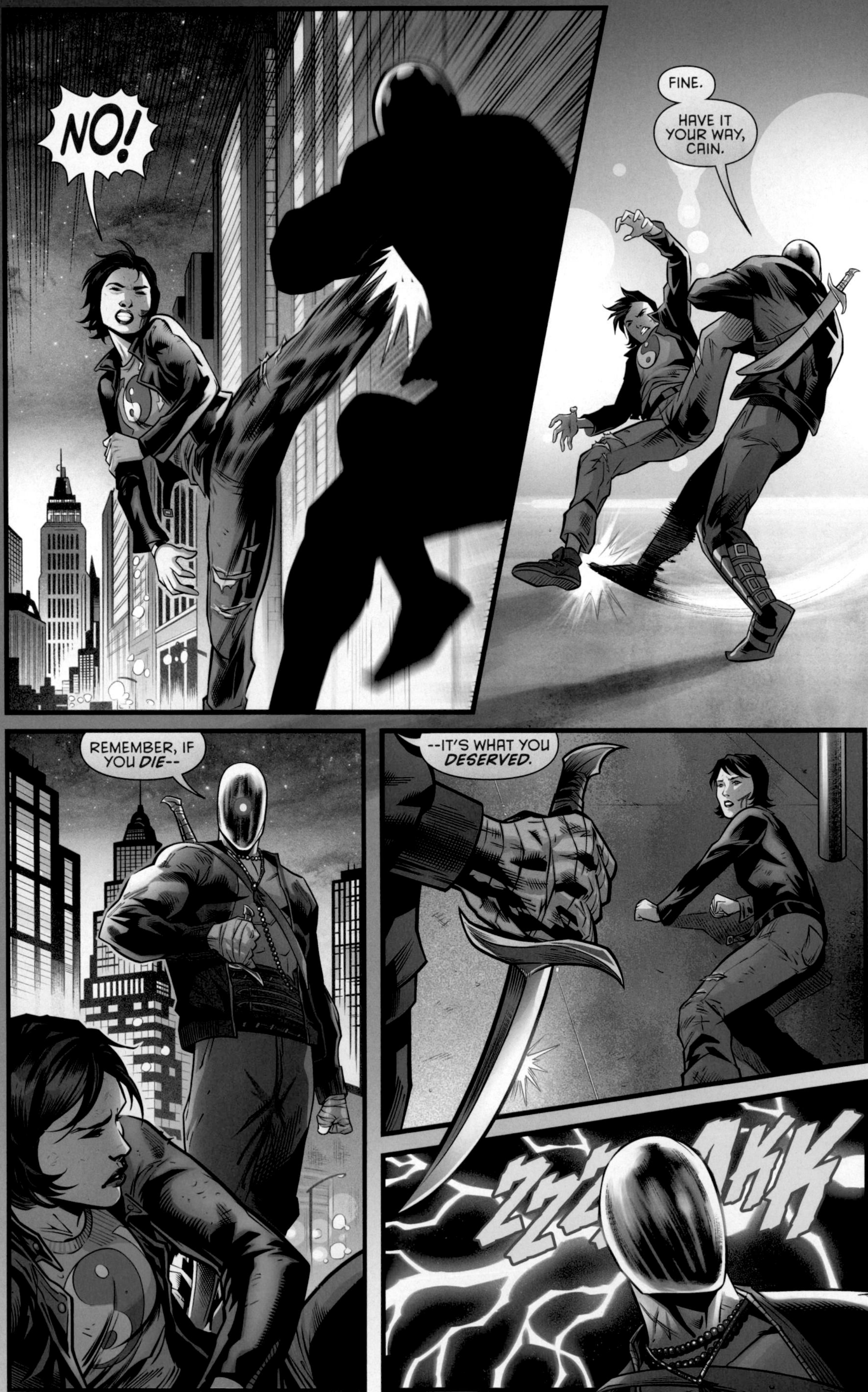
NO!
FINE.
HAVE IT YOUR WAY, CAIN.
REMEMBER, IF YOU *DIE*--
--IT'S WHAT YOU *DESERVED.*

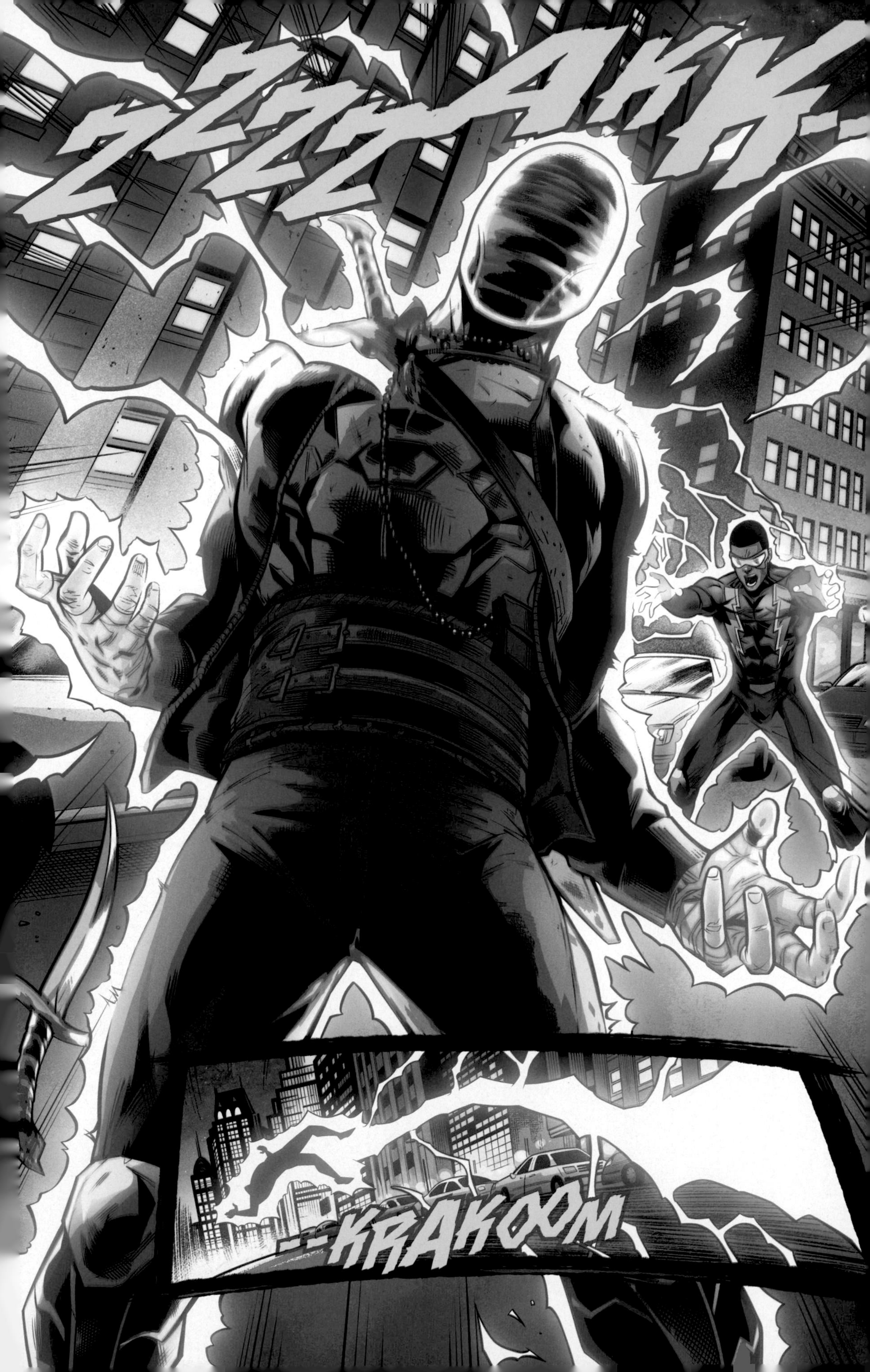
--KRAKOOM

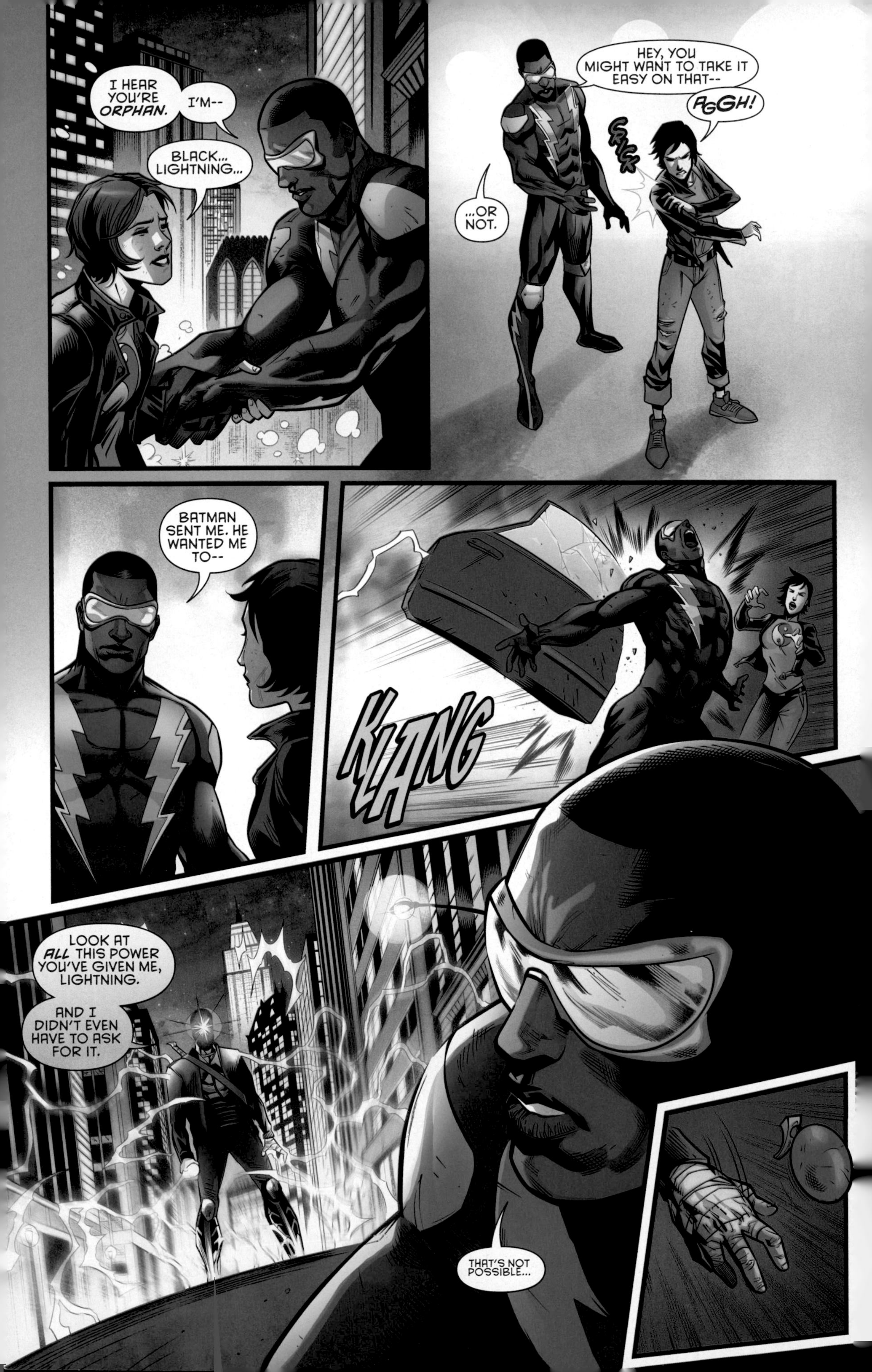
I HEAR YOU'RE *ORPHAN.*
I'M--
BLACK... LIGHTNING...
HEY, YOU MIGHT WANT TO TAKE IT EASY ON THAT--
CRICK
AGGH!
...OR NOT.
BATMAN SENT ME. HE WANTED ME TO--
KLANG
LOOK AT *ALL* THIS POWER YOU'VE GIVEN ME, LIGHTNING.
AND I DIDN'T EVEN HAVE TO ASK FOR IT.
THAT'S NOT POSSIBLE...

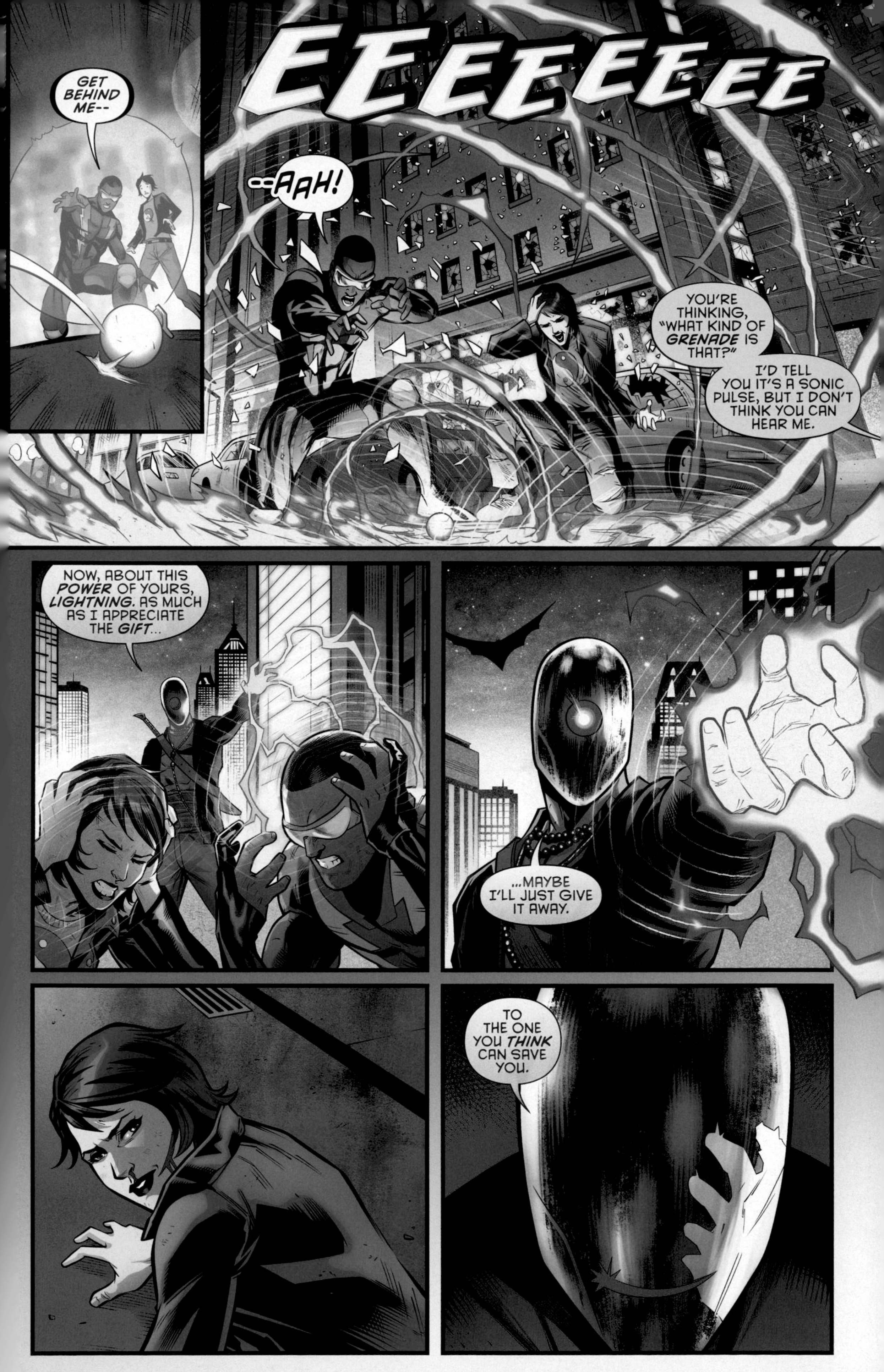
GET BEHIND ME--
EEEEEEEE
--AAH!
YOU'RE THINKING, "WHAT KIND OF GRENADE IS THAT?"
I'D TELL YOU IT'S A SONIC PULSE, BUT I DON'T THINK YOU CAN HEAR ME.
NOW, ABOUT THIS POWER OF YOURS, LIGHTNING. AS MUCH AS I APPRECIATE THE GIFT...
...MAYBE I'LL JUST GIVE IT AWAY.
TO THE ONE YOU THINK CAN SAVE YOU.

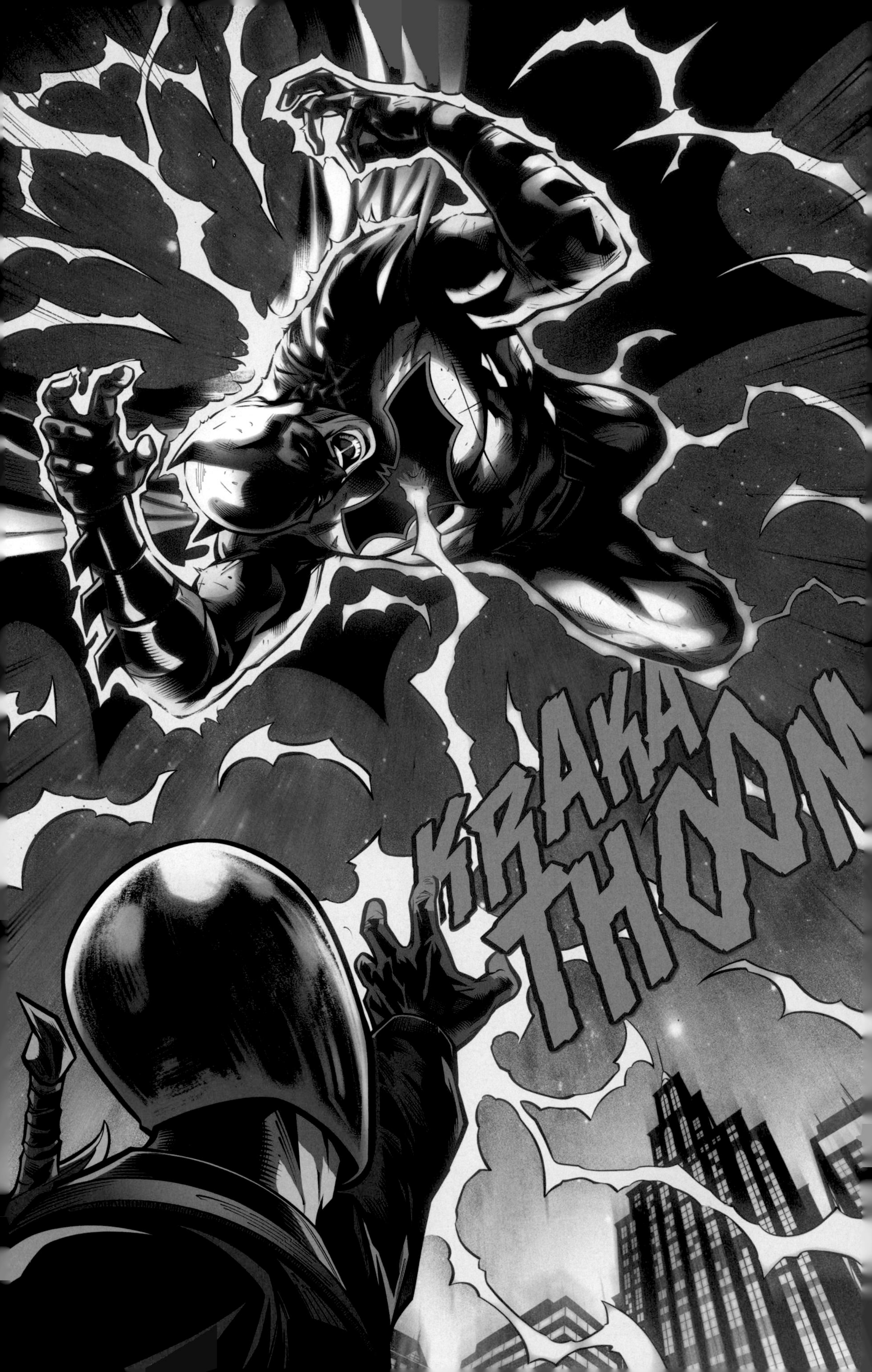
KRAKA THOOM

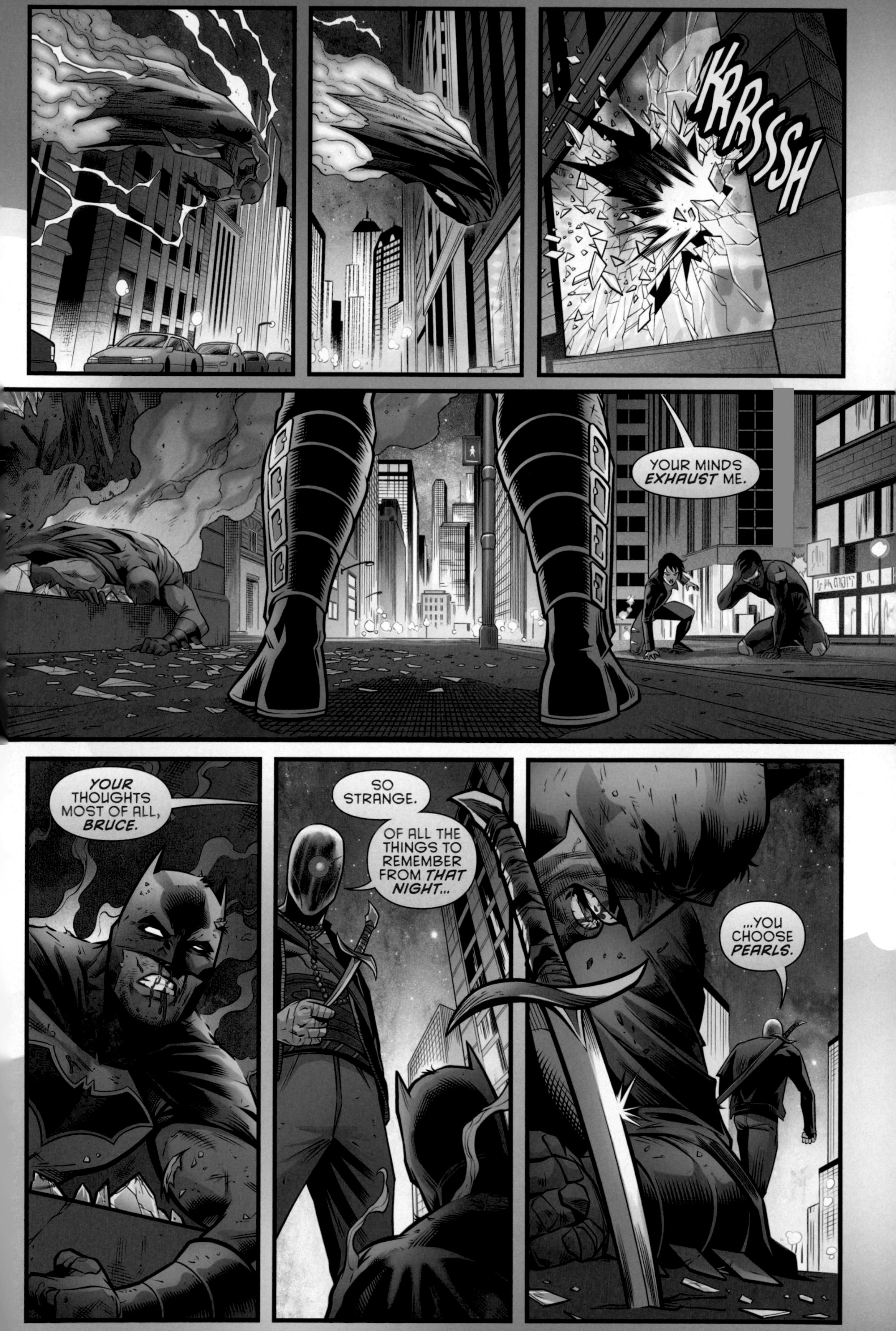
KRRSSSH
YOUR MINDS *EXHAUST* ME.
YOUR THOUGHTS MOST OF ALL, *BRUCE*.
SO STRANGE.
OF ALL THE THINGS TO REMEMBER FROM *THAT* NIGHT...
...YOU CHOOSE *PEARLS*.

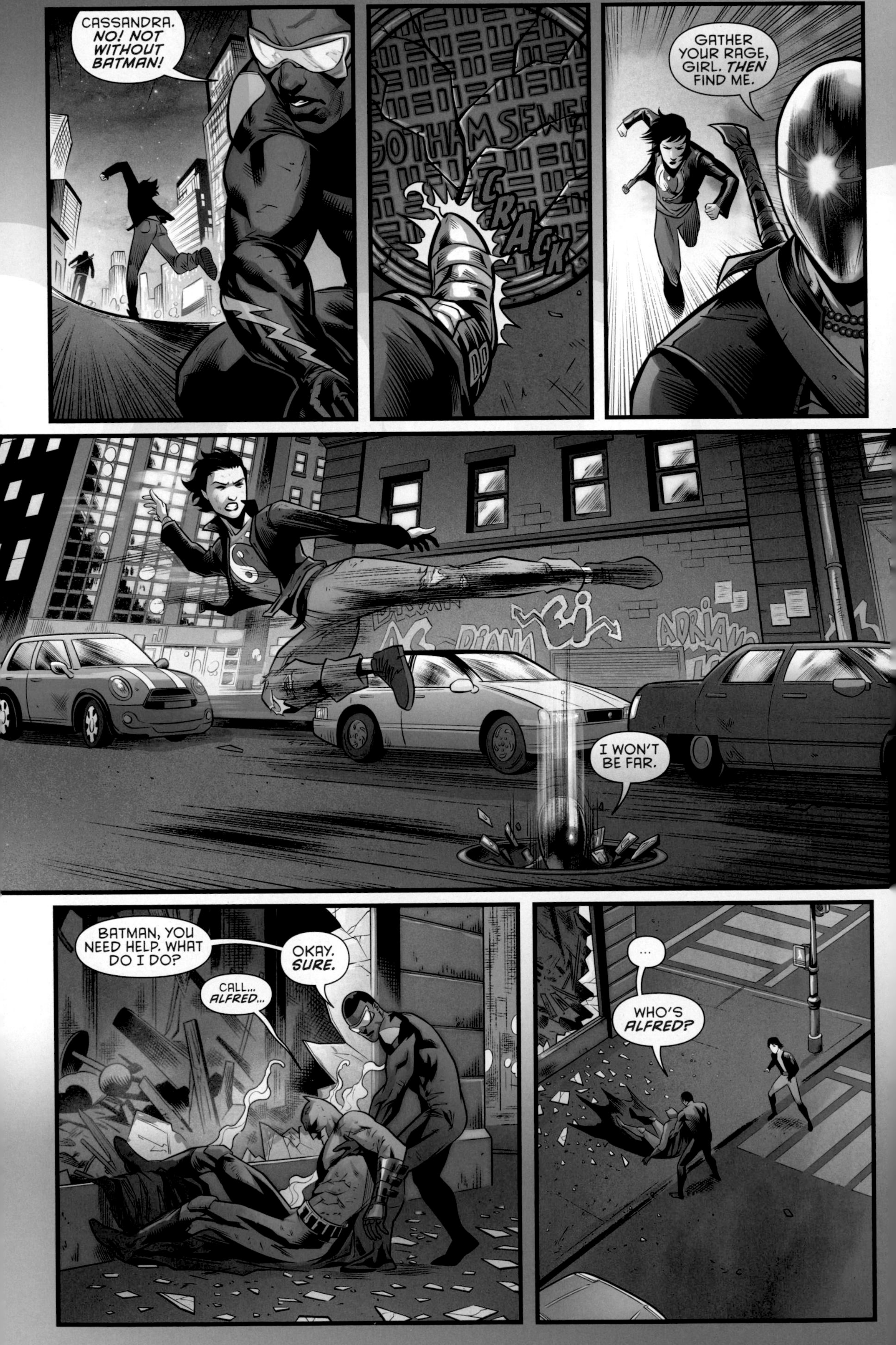
CASSANDRA. NO! NOT WITHOUT BATMAN!
GOTHAM SEWE
CRACK
GATHER YOUR RAGE, GIRL. THEN FIND ME.
I WON'T BE FAR.
BATMAN, YOU NEED HELP. WHAT DO I DO?
CALL... ALFRED...
OKAY. SURE.
...
WHO'S ALFRED?

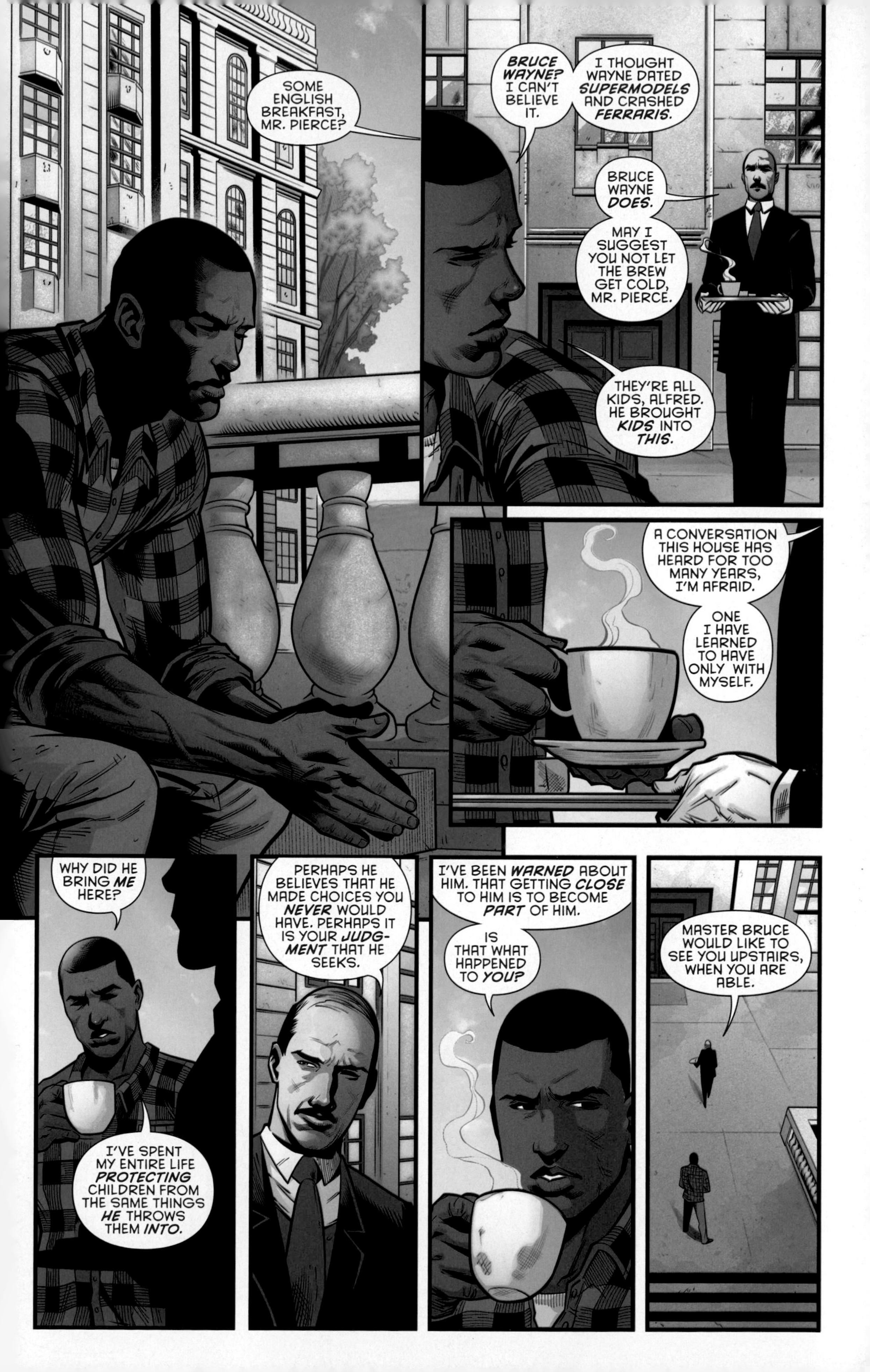
SOME ENGLISH BREAKFAST, MR. PIERCE?
BRUCE WAYNE? I CAN'T BELIEVE IT.
I THOUGHT WAYNE DATED SUPERMODELS AND CRASHED FERRARIS.
BRUCE WAYNE DOES.
MAY I SUGGEST YOU NOT LET THE BREW GET COLD, MR. PIERCE.
THEY'RE ALL KIDS, ALFRED. HE BROUGHT KIDS INTO THIS.
A CONVERSATION THIS HOUSE HAS HEARD FOR TOO MANY YEARS, I'M AFRAID.
ONE I HAVE LEARNED TO HAVE ONLY WITH MYSELF.
WHY DID HE BRING ME HERE?
I'VE SPENT MY ENTIRE LIFE PROTECTING CHILDREN FROM THE SAME THINGS HE THROWS THEM INTO.
PERHAPS HE BELIEVES THAT HE MADE CHOICES YOU NEVER WOULD HAVE. PERHAPS IT IS YOUR JUDGMENT THAT HE SEEKS.
I'VE BEEN WARNED ABOUT HIM. THAT GETTING CLOSE TO HIM IS TO BECOME PART OF HIM.
IS THAT WHAT HAPPENED TO YOU?
MASTER BRUCE WOULD LIKE TO SEE YOU UPSTAIRS, WHEN YOU ARE ABLE.

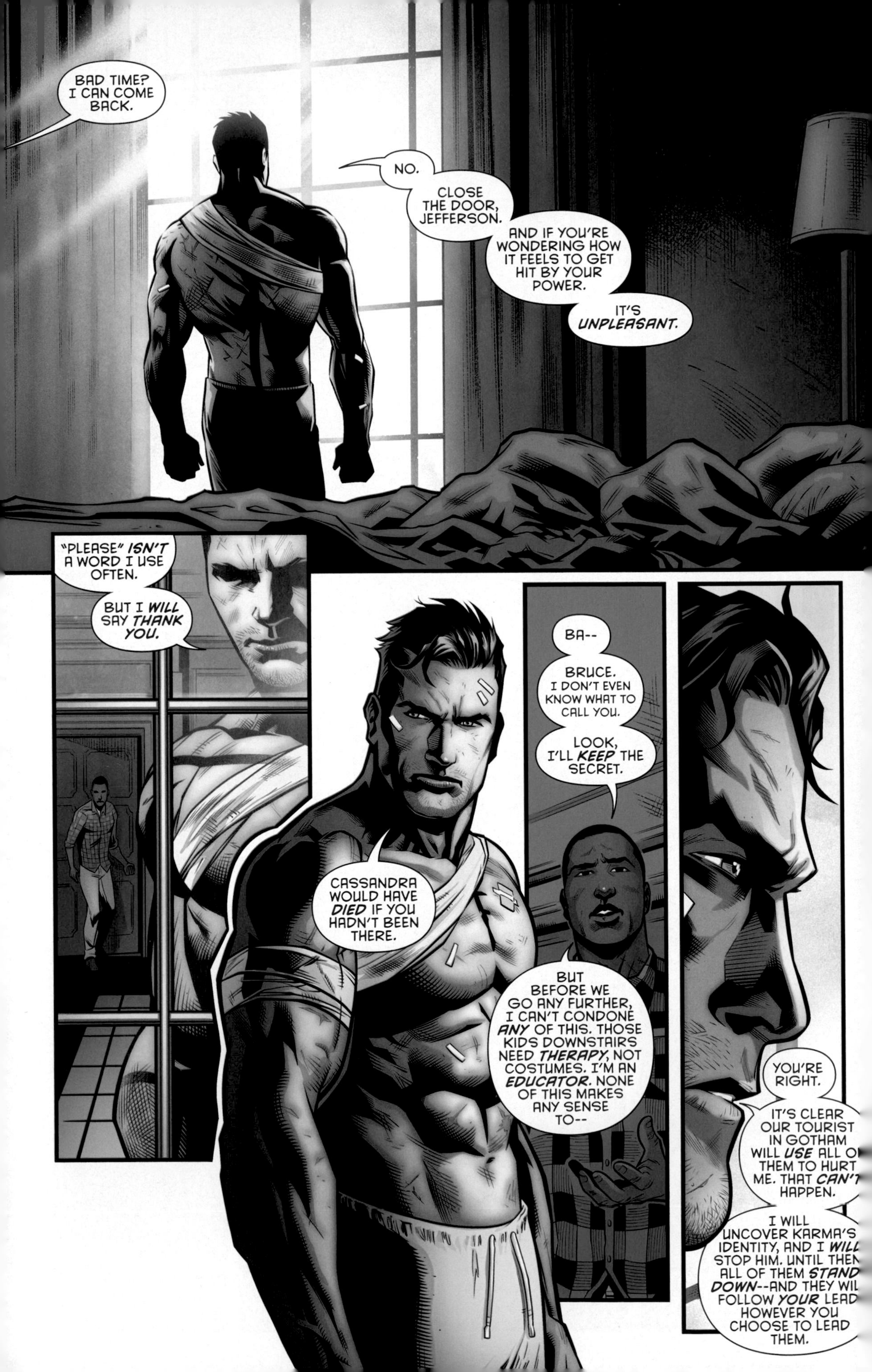
BAD TIME? I CAN COME BACK.
NO.
CLOSE THE DOOR, JEFFERSON.
AND IF YOU'RE WONDERING HOW IT FEELS TO GET HIT BY YOUR POWER.
IT'S *UNPLEASANT.*
"PLEASE" *ISN'T* A WORD I USE OFTEN.
BUT I *WILL* SAY *THANK YOU.*
CASSANDRA WOULD HAVE *DIED* IF YOU HADN'T BEEN THERE.
BA--
BRUCE. I DON'T EVEN KNOW WHAT TO CALL YOU.
LOOK, I'LL *KEEP* THE SECRET.
BUT BEFORE WE GO ANY FURTHER, I CAN'T CONDONE *ANY* OF THIS. THOSE KIDS DOWNSTAIRS NEED *THERAPY*, NOT COSTUMES. I'M AN *EDUCATOR*. NONE OF THIS MAKES ANY SENSE TO--
YOU'RE RIGHT.
IT'S CLEAR OUR TOURIST IN GOTHAM WILL *USE* ALL O[F] THEM TO HURT ME. THAT *CAN'T* HAPPEN.
I WILL UNCOVER KARMA'S IDENTITY, AND I *WILL* STOP HIM. UNTIL THEN ALL OF THEM *STAND DOWN*--AND THEY WIL[L] FOLLOW *YOUR* LEAD HOWEVER YOU CHOOSE TO LEAD THEM.

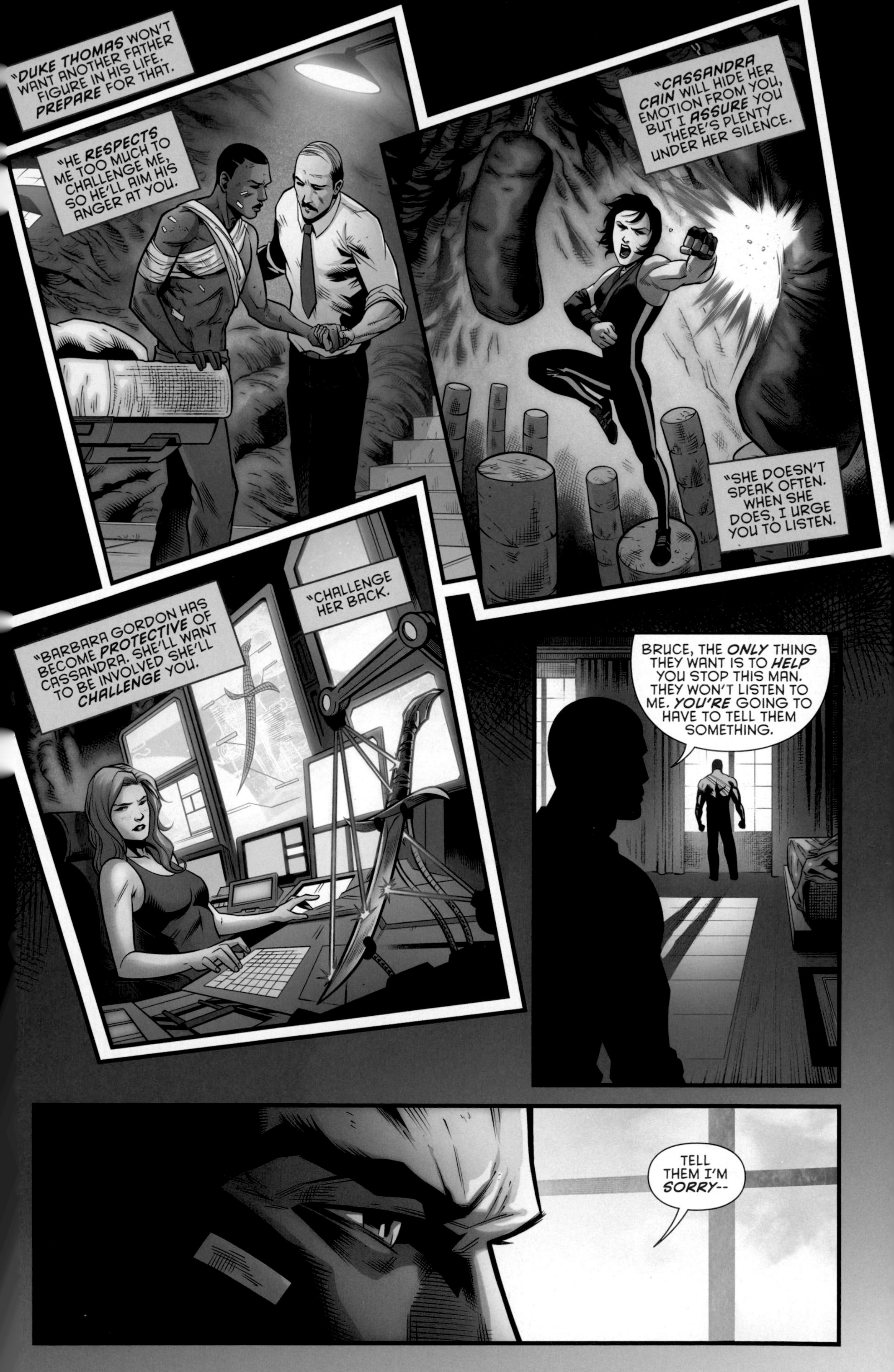
"DUKE THOMAS WON'T WANT ANOTHER FATHER FIGURE IN HIS LIFE. PREPARE FOR THAT.
"HE RESPECTS ME TOO MUCH TO CHALLENGE ME, SO HE'LL AIM HIS ANGER AT YOU.
"CASSANDRA CAIN WILL HIDE HER EMOTION FROM YOU, BUT I ASSURE YOU THERE'S PLENTY UNDER HER SILENCE.
"SHE DOESN'T SPEAK OFTEN. WHEN SHE DOES, I URGE YOU TO LISTEN.
"BARBARA GORDON HAS BECOME PROTECTIVE OF CASSANDRA. SHE'LL WANT TO BE INVOLVED SHE'LL CHALLENGE YOU.
"CHALLENGE HER BACK.
BRUCE, THE ONLY THING THEY WANT IS TO HELP YOU STOP THIS MAN. THEY WON'T LISTEN TO ME. YOU'RE GOING TO HAVE TO TELL THEM SOMETHING.
TELL THEM I'M SORRY--

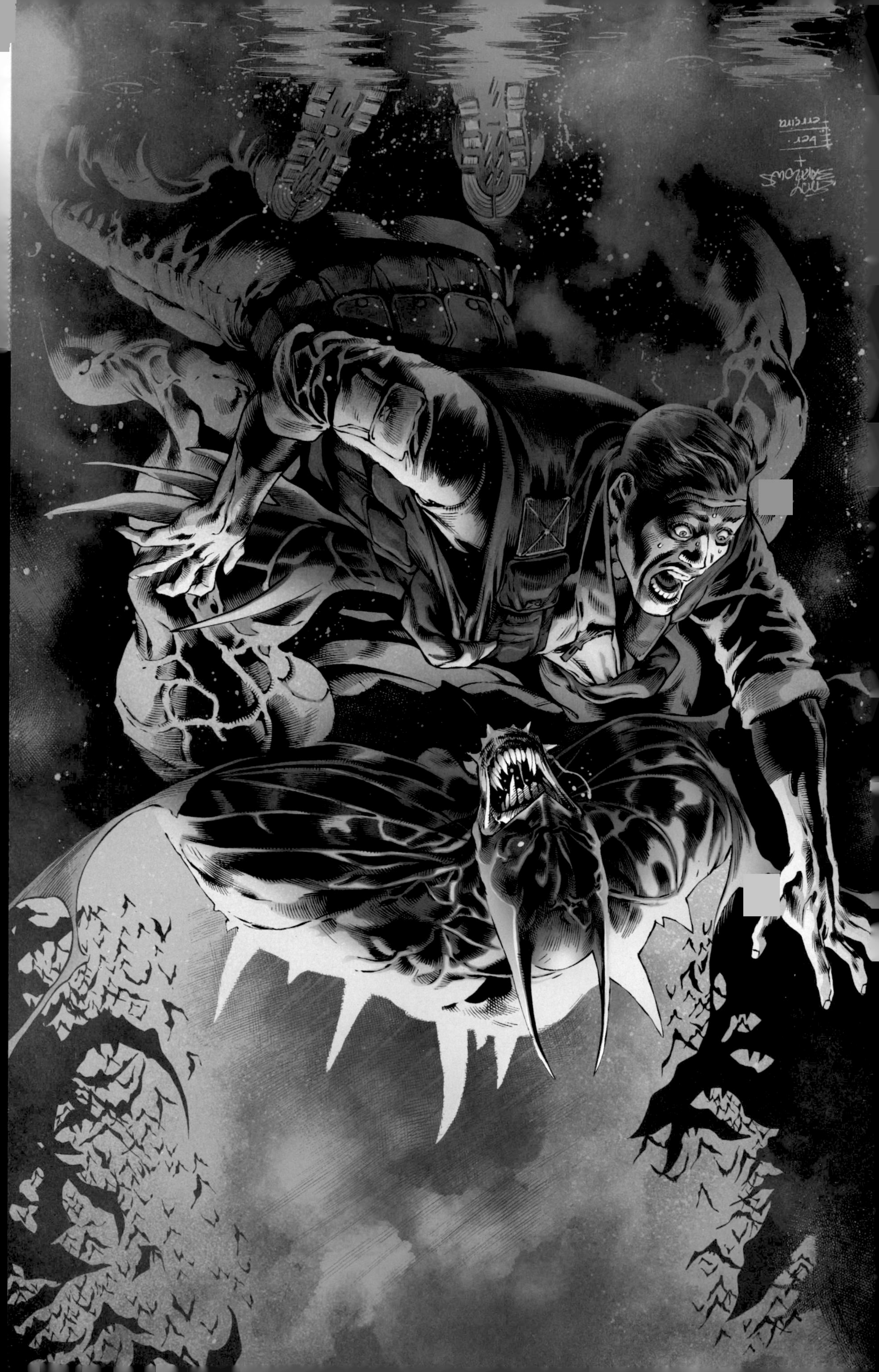

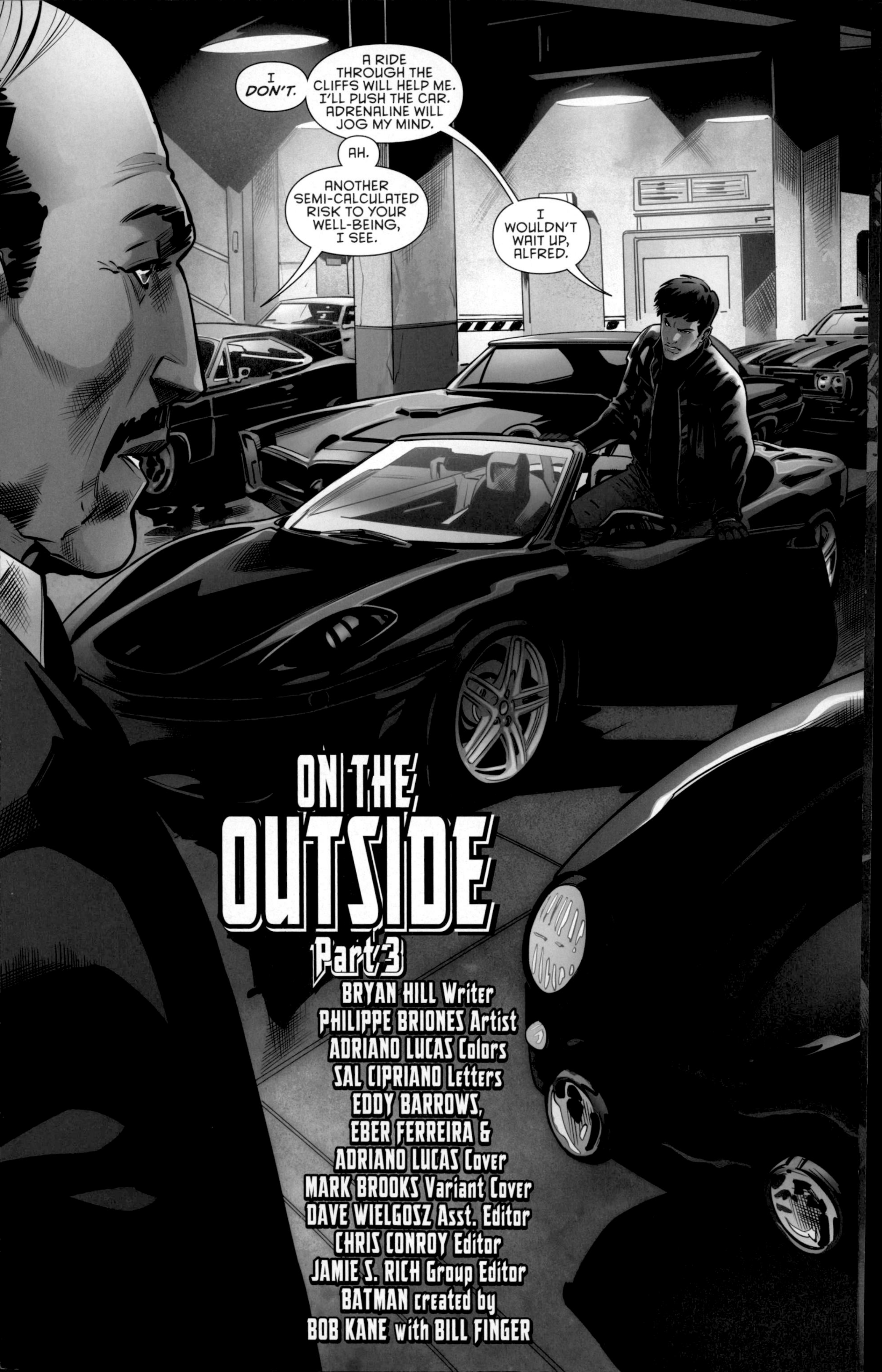
I DON'T.
A RIDE THROUGH THE CLIFFS WILL HELP ME. I'LL PUSH THE CAR. ADRENALINE WILL JOG MY MIND.
AH.
ANOTHER SEMI-CALCULATED RISK TO YOUR WELL-BEING, I SEE.
I WOULDN'T WAIT UP, ALFRED.
ON THE OUTSIDE
Part 3
BRYAN HILL Writer
PHILIPPE BRIONES Artist
ADRIANO LUCAS Colors
SAL CIPRIANO Letters
EDDY BARROWS, EBER FERREIRA & ADRIANO LUCAS Cover
MARK BROOKS Variant Cover
DAVE WIELGOSZ Asst. Editor
CHRIS CONROY Editor
JAMIE S. RICH Group Editor
BATMAN created by BOB KANE with BILL FINGER

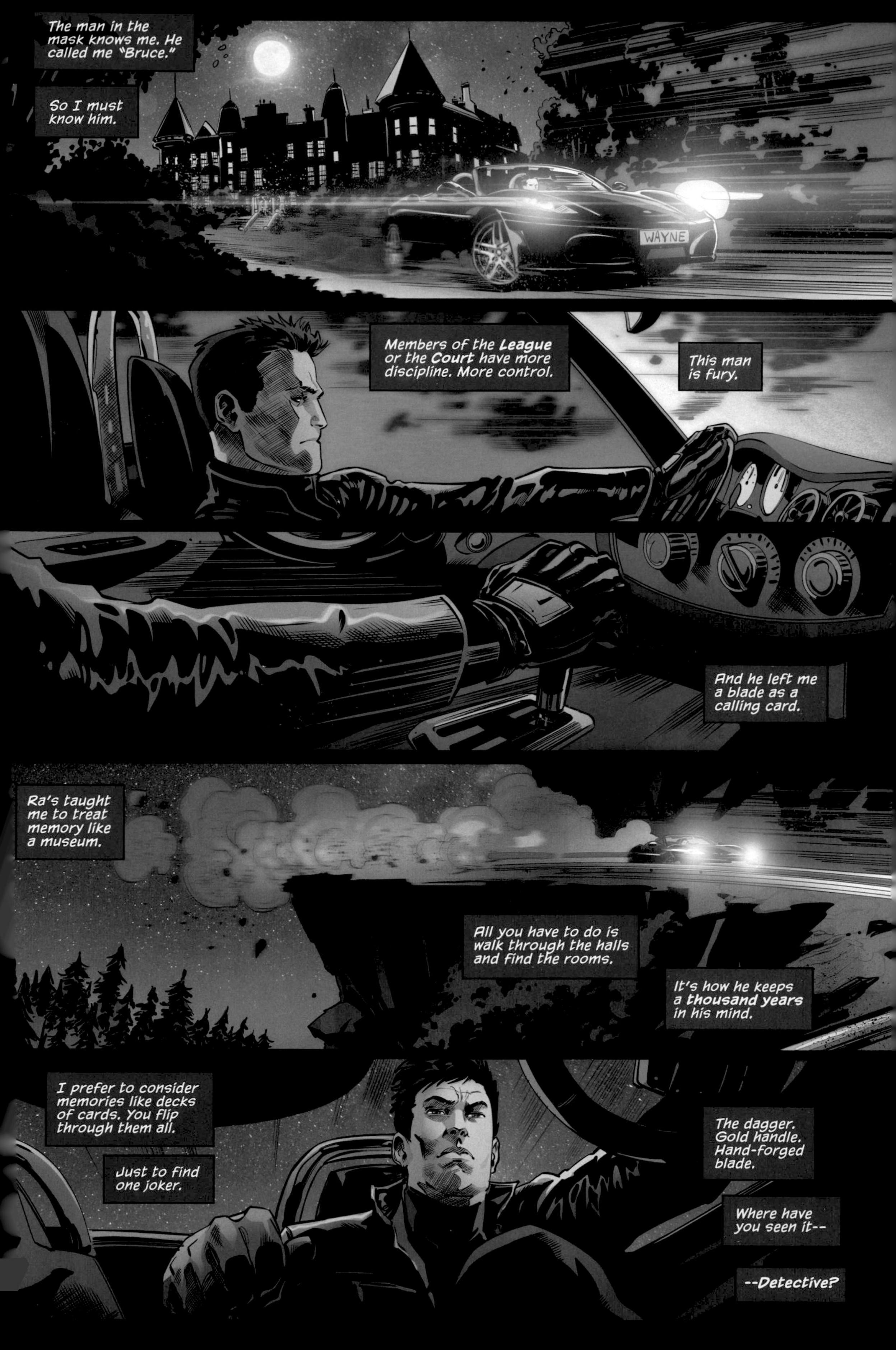
The man in the mask knows me. He called me "Bruce."
So I must know him.
WAYNE
Members of the **League** or the **Court** have more discipline. More control.
This man is fury.
And he left me a blade as a calling card.
Ra's taught me to treat memory like a museum.
All you have to do is walk through the halls and find the rooms.
It's how he keeps a **thousand years** in his mind.
I prefer to consider memories like decks of cards. You flip through them all.
Just to find one joker.
The dagger. Gold handle. Hand-forged blade.
Where have you seen it--
--Detective?

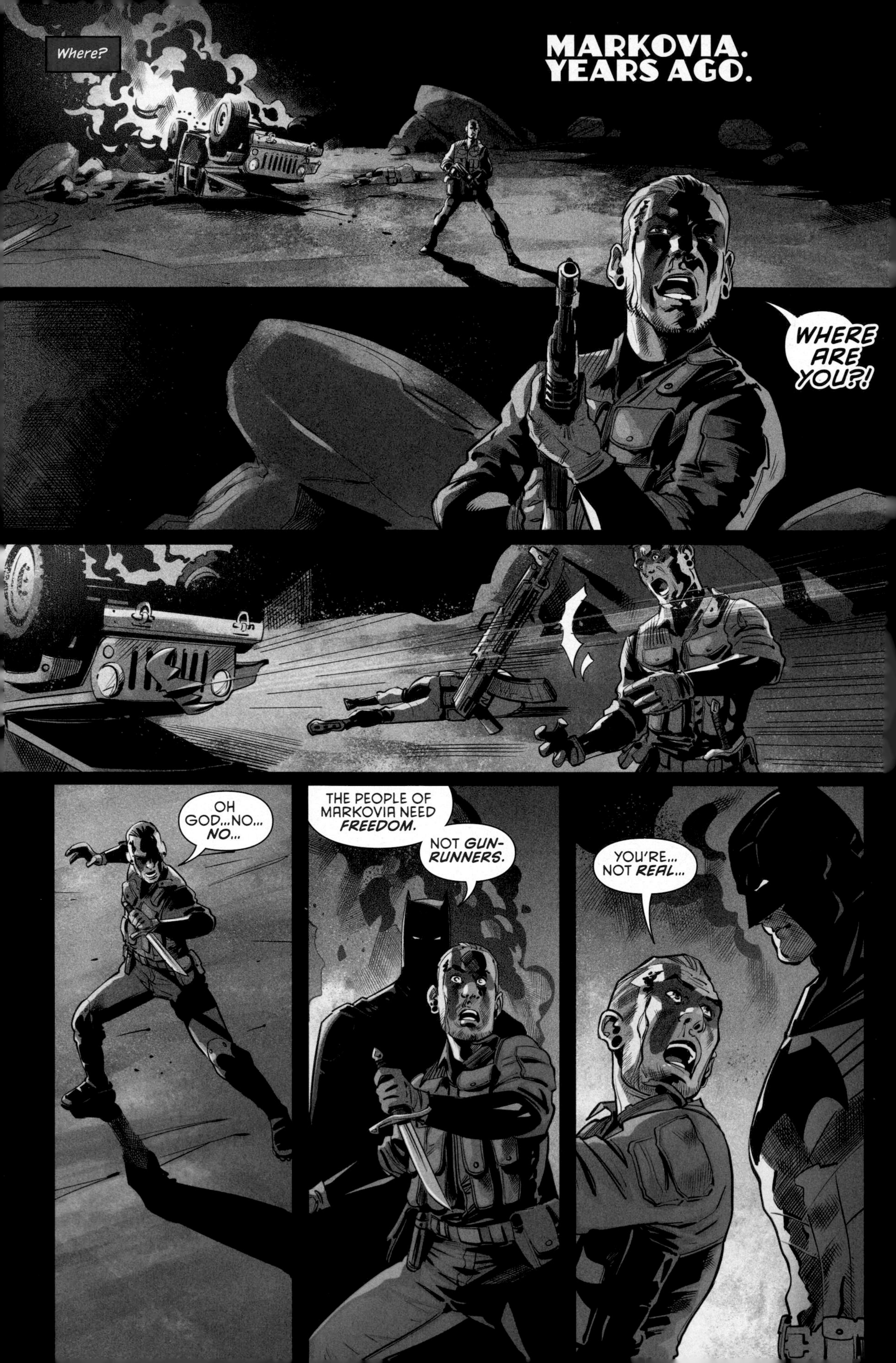
Where?
MARKOVIA. YEARS AGO.
WHERE ARE YOU?!
OH GOD...NO... NO...
THE PEOPLE OF MARKOVIA NEED FREEDOM.
NOT GUN-RUNNERS.
YOU'RE... NOT REAL...

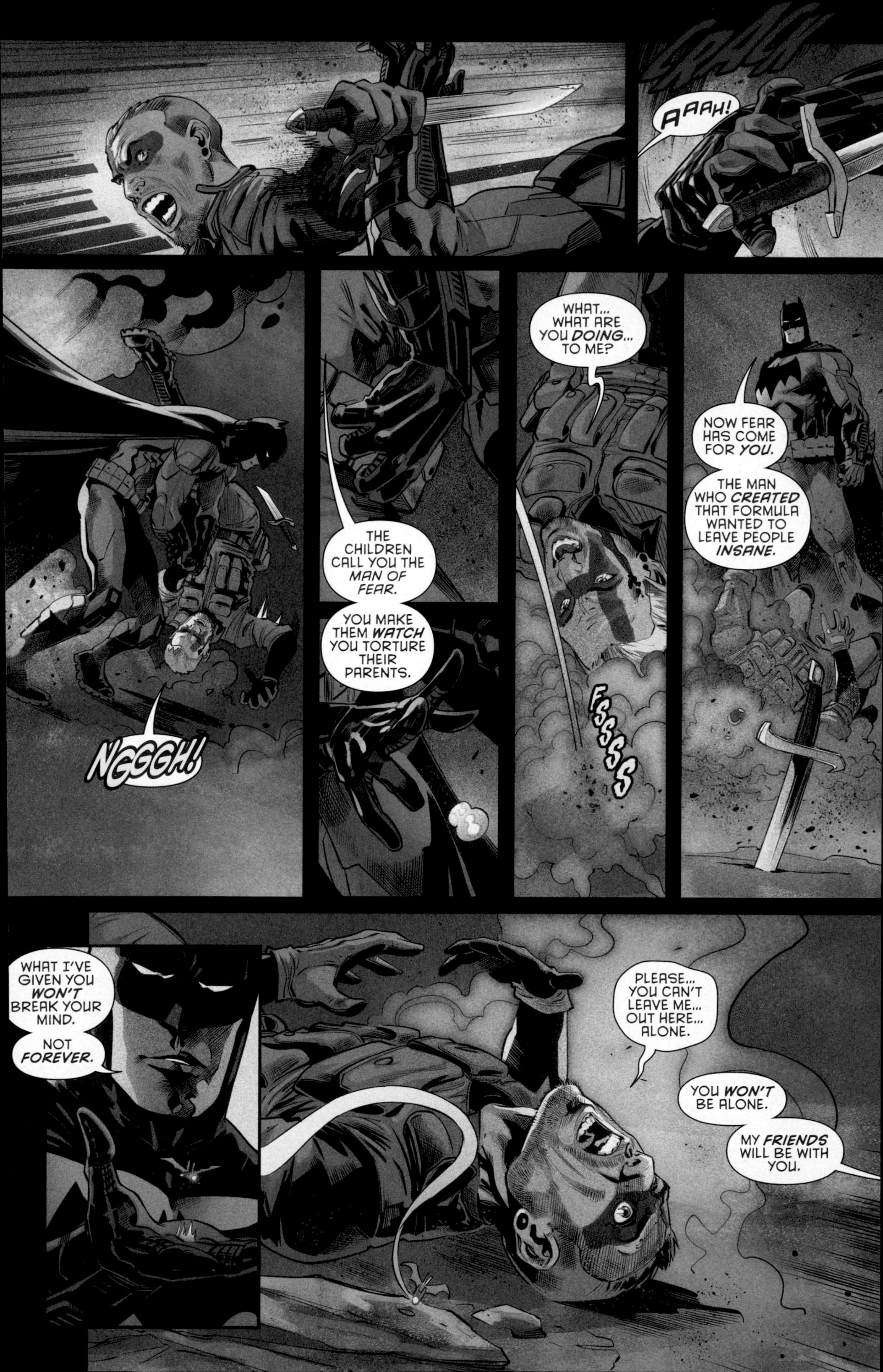
AAAH!
NGGGH!
THE CHILDREN CALL YOU THE *MAN OF FEAR.*
YOU MAKE THEM *WATCH* YOU TORTURE THEIR PARENTS.
WHAT... WHAT ARE YOU *DOING*... TO ME?
FSSSS
NOW FEAR HAS COME FOR *YOU.*
THE MAN WHO *CREATED* THAT FORMULA WANTED TO LEAVE PEOPLE *INSANE.*
WHAT I'VE GIVEN YOU *WON'T* BREAK YOUR MIND.
NOT *FOREVER.*
PLEASE... YOU CAN'T LEAVE ME... OUT HERE... ALONE.
YOU *WON'T* BE ALONE.
MY *FRIENDS* WILL BE WITH YOU.

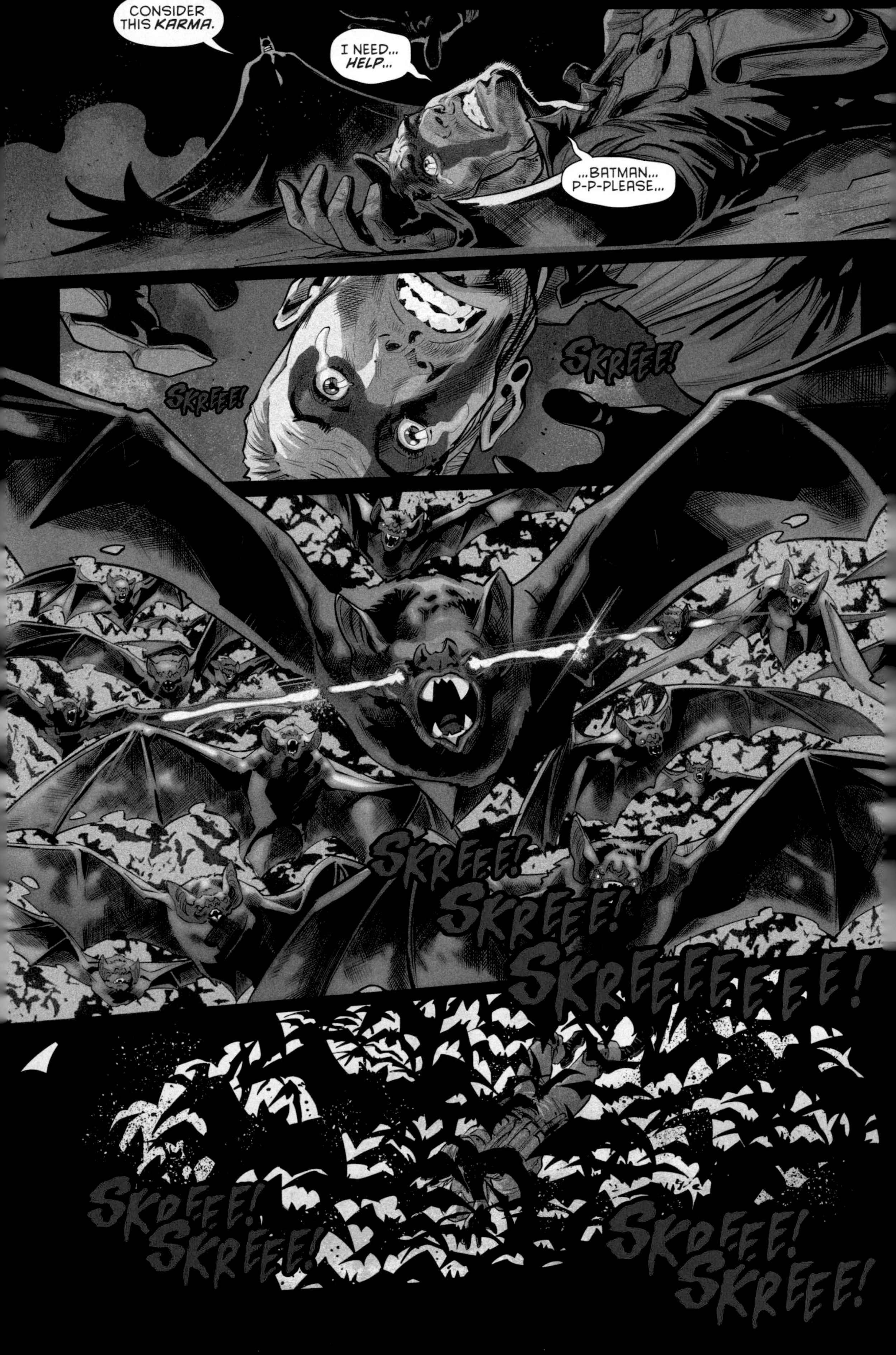
CONSIDER THIS *KARMA.*
I NEED... *HELP*...
...BATMAN... P-P-PLEASE...
SKREEE!
SKREEE!
SKREEE!
SKREEE!
SKREEEEEEEE!
SKDEEE!
SKREEE!
SKDEEE!
SKREEE!

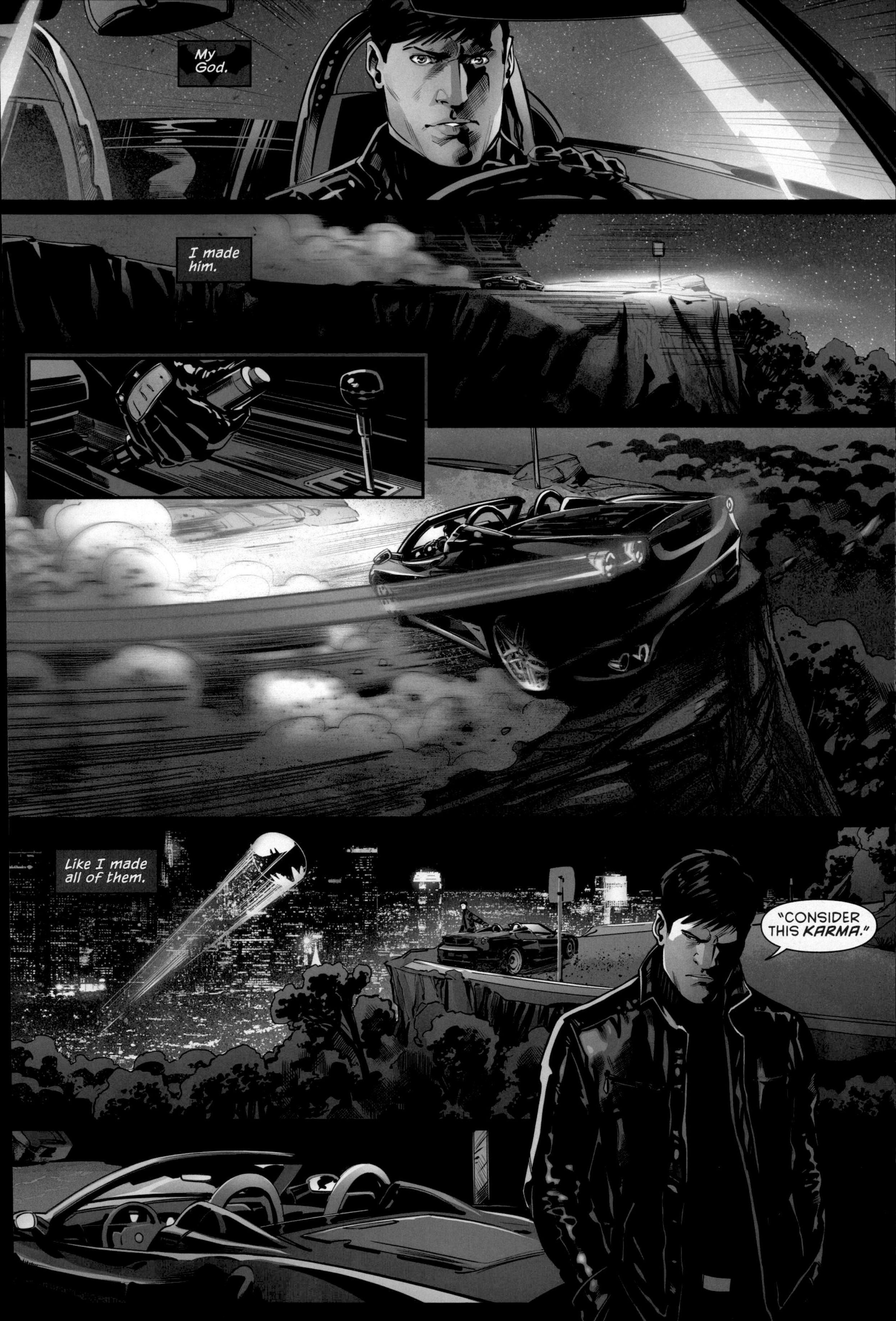
My God.
I made him.
Like I made all of them.
"CONSIDER THIS KARMA."

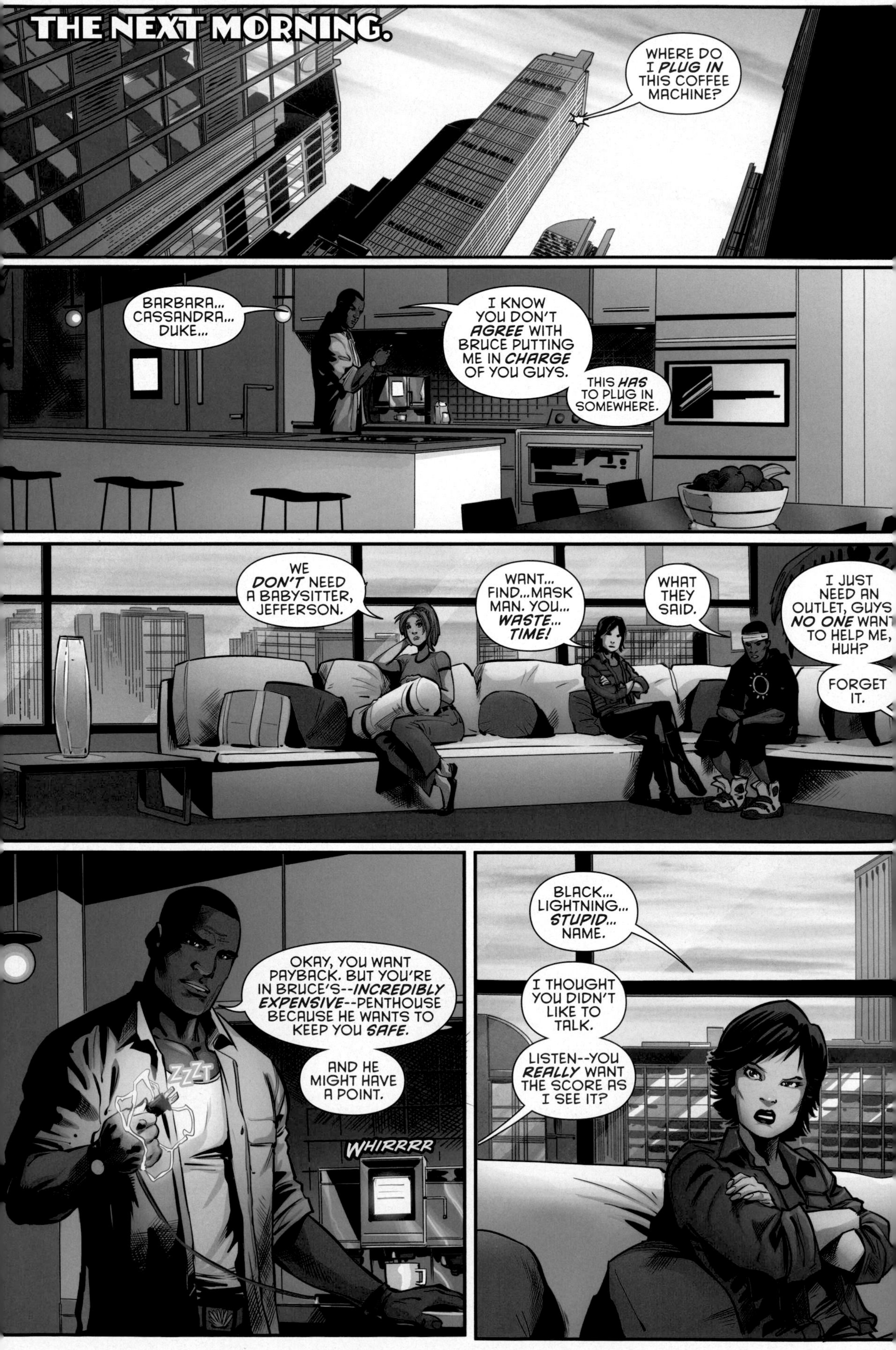
THE NEXT MORNING.
WHERE DO I PLUG IN THIS COFFEE MACHINE?
BARBARA... CASSANDRA... DUKE...
I KNOW YOU DON'T AGREE WITH BRUCE PUTTING ME IN CHARGE OF YOU GUYS.
THIS HAS TO PLUG IN SOMEWHERE.
WE DON'T NEED A BABYSITTER, JEFFERSON.
WANT... FIND...MASK MAN. YOU... WASTE... TIME!
WHAT THEY SAID.
I JUST NEED AN OUTLET, GUYS. NO ONE WANTS TO HELP ME, HUH?
FORGET IT.
OKAY, YOU WANT PAYBACK. BUT YOU'RE IN BRUCE'S--INCREDIBLY EXPENSIVE--PENTHOUSE BECAUSE HE WANTS TO KEEP YOU SAFE.
AND HE MIGHT HAVE A POINT.
ZZZT
WHIRRRR
BLACK... LIGHTNING... STUPID... NAME.
I THOUGHT YOU DIDN'T LIKE TO TALK.
LISTEN--YOU REALLY WANT THE SCORE AS I SEE IT?

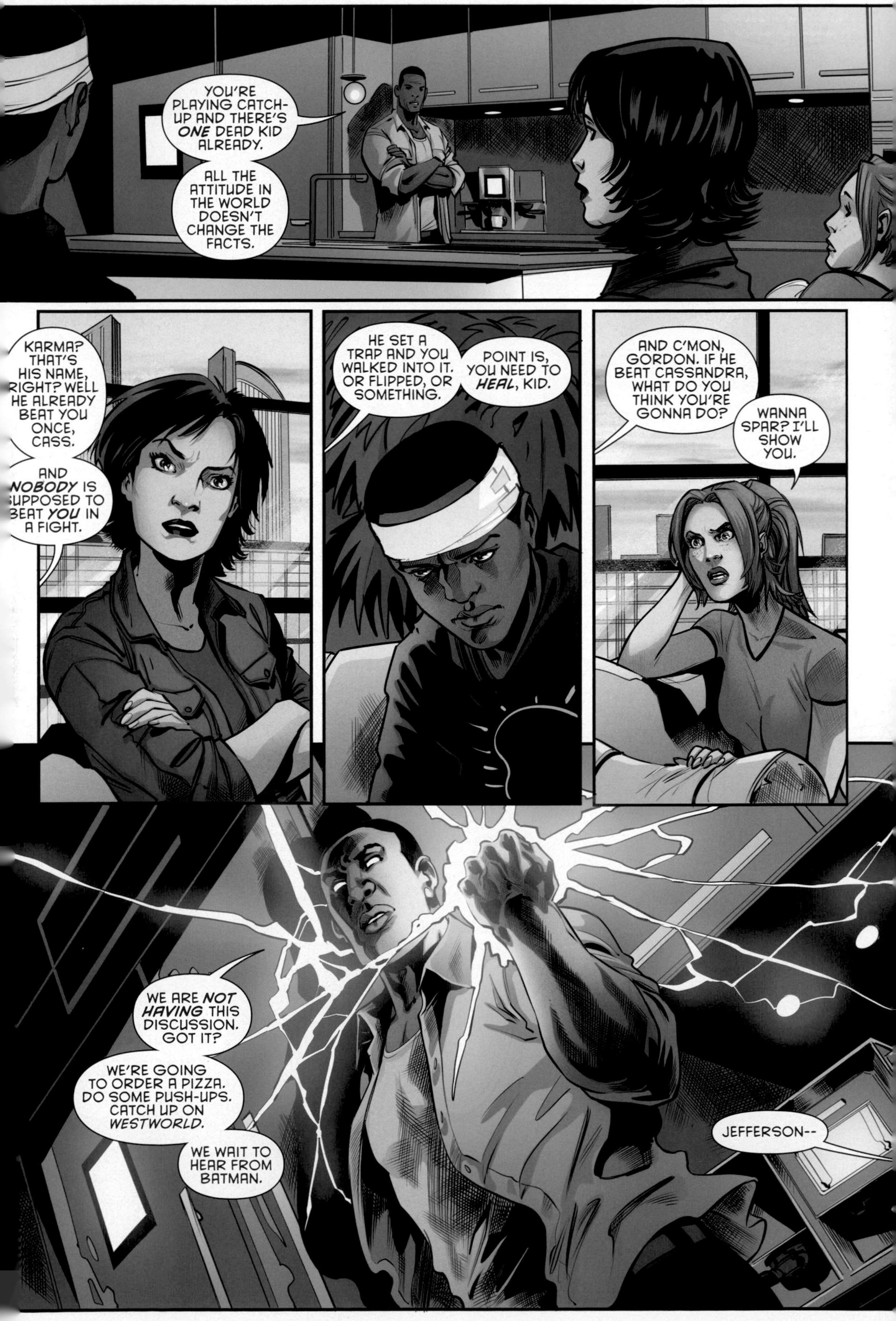
YOU'RE PLAYING CATCH-UP AND THERE'S *ONE* DEAD KID ALREADY.
ALL THE ATTITUDE IN THE WORLD DOESN'T CHANGE THE FACTS.
KARMA? THAT'S HIS NAME, RIGHT? WELL HE ALREADY BEAT YOU ONCE, CASS.
AND *NOBODY* IS SUPPOSED TO BEAT *YOU* IN A FIGHT.
HE SET A TRAP AND YOU WALKED INTO IT. OR FLIPPED, OR SOMETHING.
POINT IS, YOU NEED TO *HEAL*, KID.
AND C'MON, GORDON. IF HE BEAT CASSANDRA, WHAT DO YOU THINK YOU'RE GONNA DO?
WANNA SPAR? I'LL SHOW YOU.
WE ARE *NOT HAVING* THIS DISCUSSION. GOT IT?
WE'RE GOING TO ORDER A PIZZA. DO SOME PUSH-UPS. CATCH UP ON *WESTWORLD.*
WE WAIT TO HEAR FROM BATMAN.
JEFFERSON--

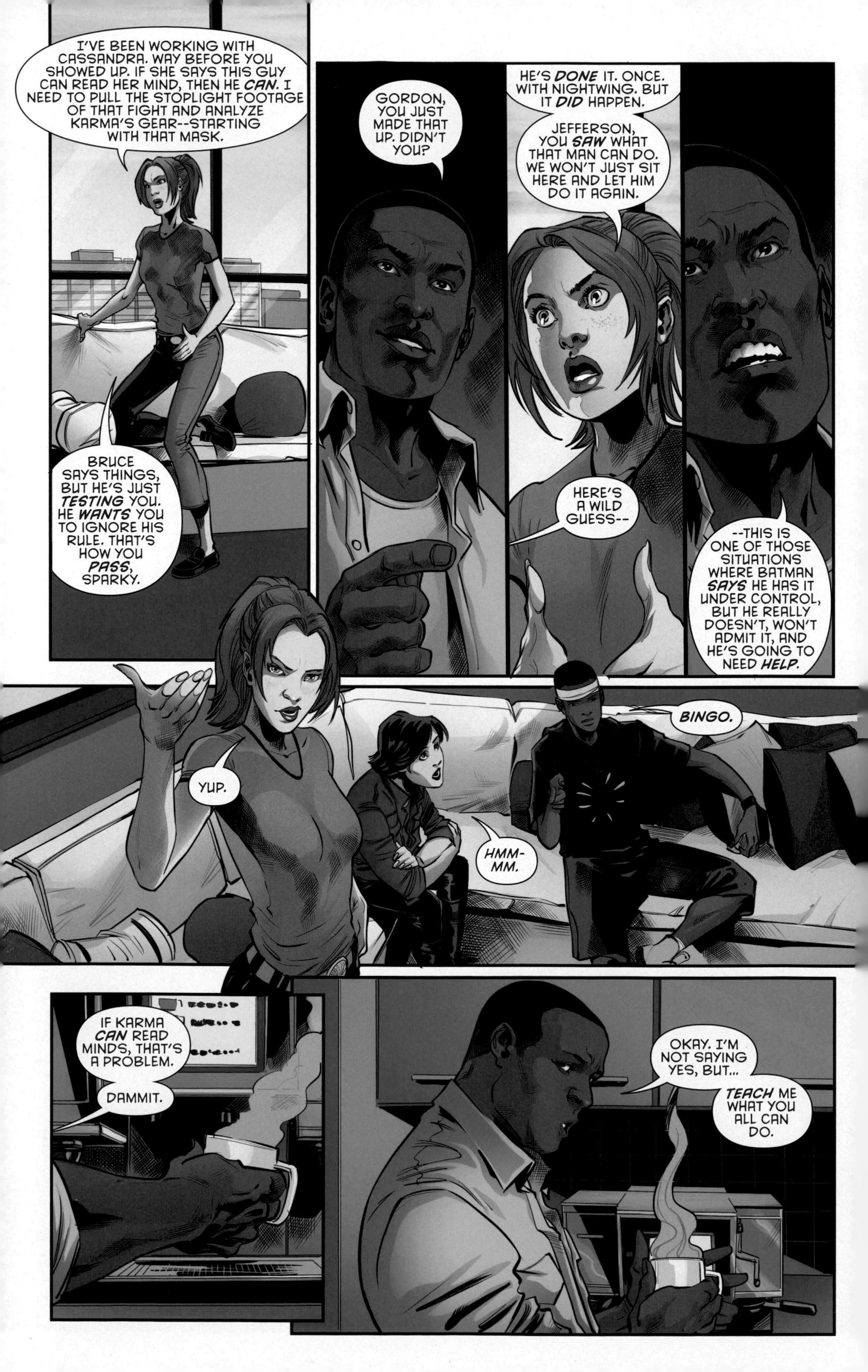
I'VE BEEN WORKING WITH CASSANDRA. WAY BEFORE YOU SHOWED UP. IF SHE SAYS THIS GUY CAN READ HER MIND, THEN HE CAN. I NEED TO PULL THE STOPLIGHT FOOTAGE OF THAT FIGHT AND ANALYZE KARMA'S GEAR--STARTING WITH THAT MASK.
BRUCE SAYS THINGS, BUT HE'S JUST TESTING YOU. HE WANTS YOU TO IGNORE HIS RULE. THAT'S HOW YOU PASS, SPARKY.
GORDON, YOU JUST MADE THAT UP. DIDN'T YOU?
HE'S DONE IT. ONCE. WITH NIGHTWING. BUT IT DID HAPPEN.
JEFFERSON, YOU SAW WHAT THAT MAN CAN DO. WE WON'T JUST SIT HERE AND LET HIM DO IT AGAIN.
HERE'S A WILD GUESS--
--THIS IS ONE OF THOSE SITUATIONS WHERE BATMAN SAYS HE HAS IT UNDER CONTROL, BUT HE REALLY DOESN'T, WON'T ADMIT IT, AND HE'S GOING TO NEED HELP.
YUP.
HMM-MM.
BINGO.
IF KARMA CAN READ MINDS, THAT'S A PROBLEM.
DAMMIT.
OKAY. I'M NOT SAYING YES, BUT...
TEACH ME WHAT YOU ALL CAN DO.

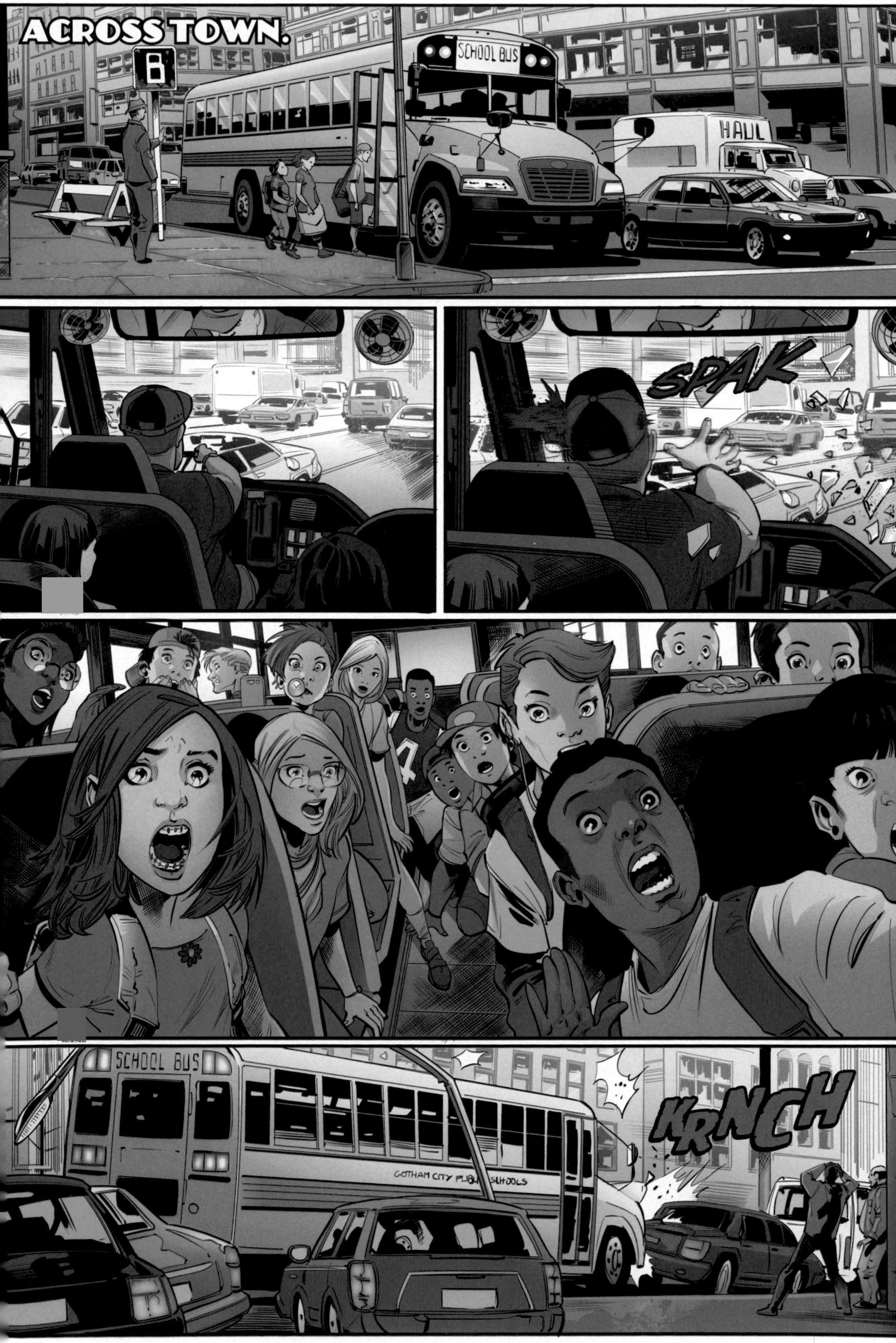
ACROSS TOWN.
B
SCHOOL BUS
HAUL
SPAK
SCHOOL BUS
KRNCH

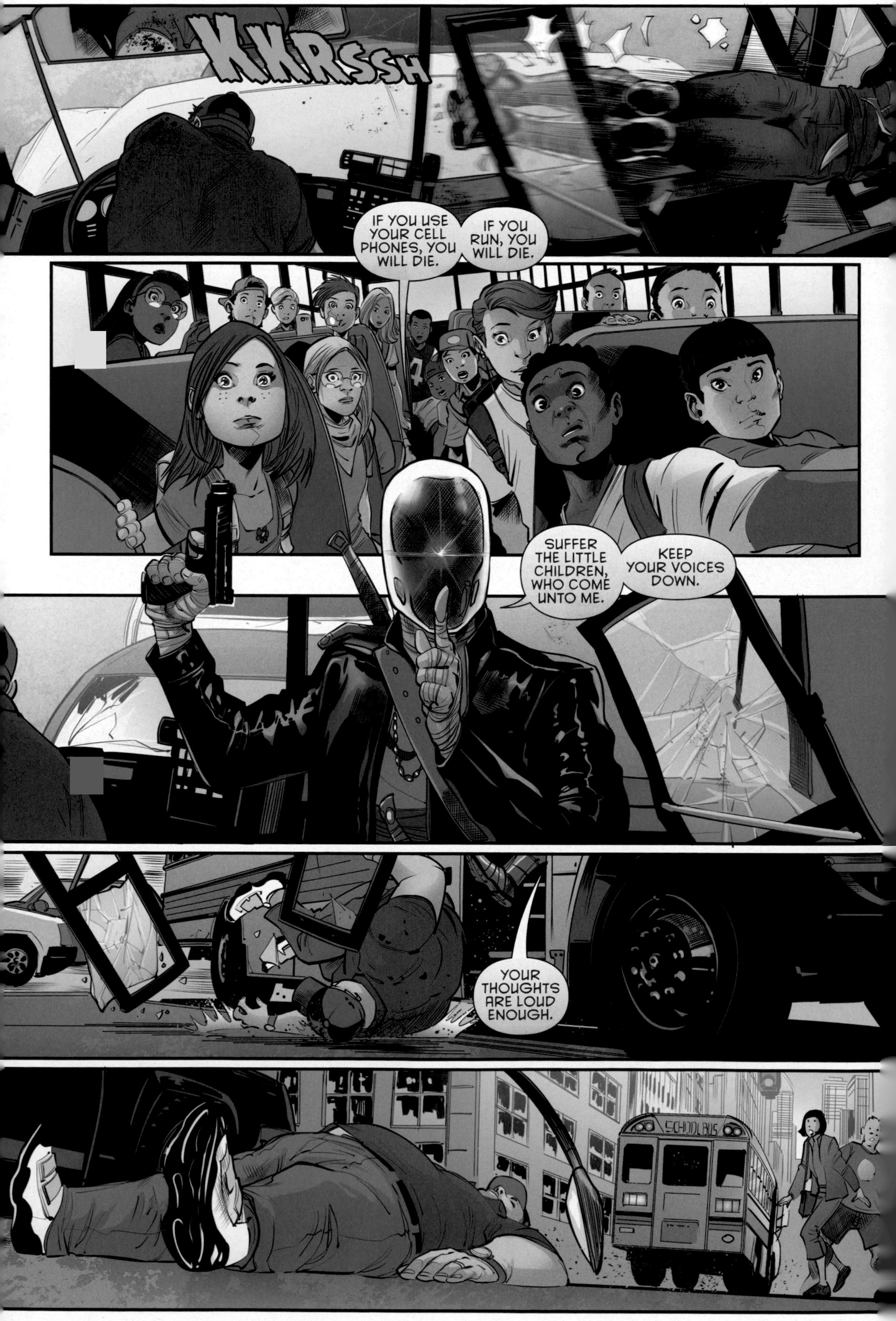
KKRSSH
IF YOU USE YOUR CELL PHONES, YOU WILL DIE.
IF YOU RUN, YOU WILL DIE.
SUFFER THE LITTLE CHILDREN, WHO COME UNTO ME.
KEEP YOUR VOICES DOWN.
YOUR THOUGHTS ARE LOUD ENOUGH.
SCHOOLBUS

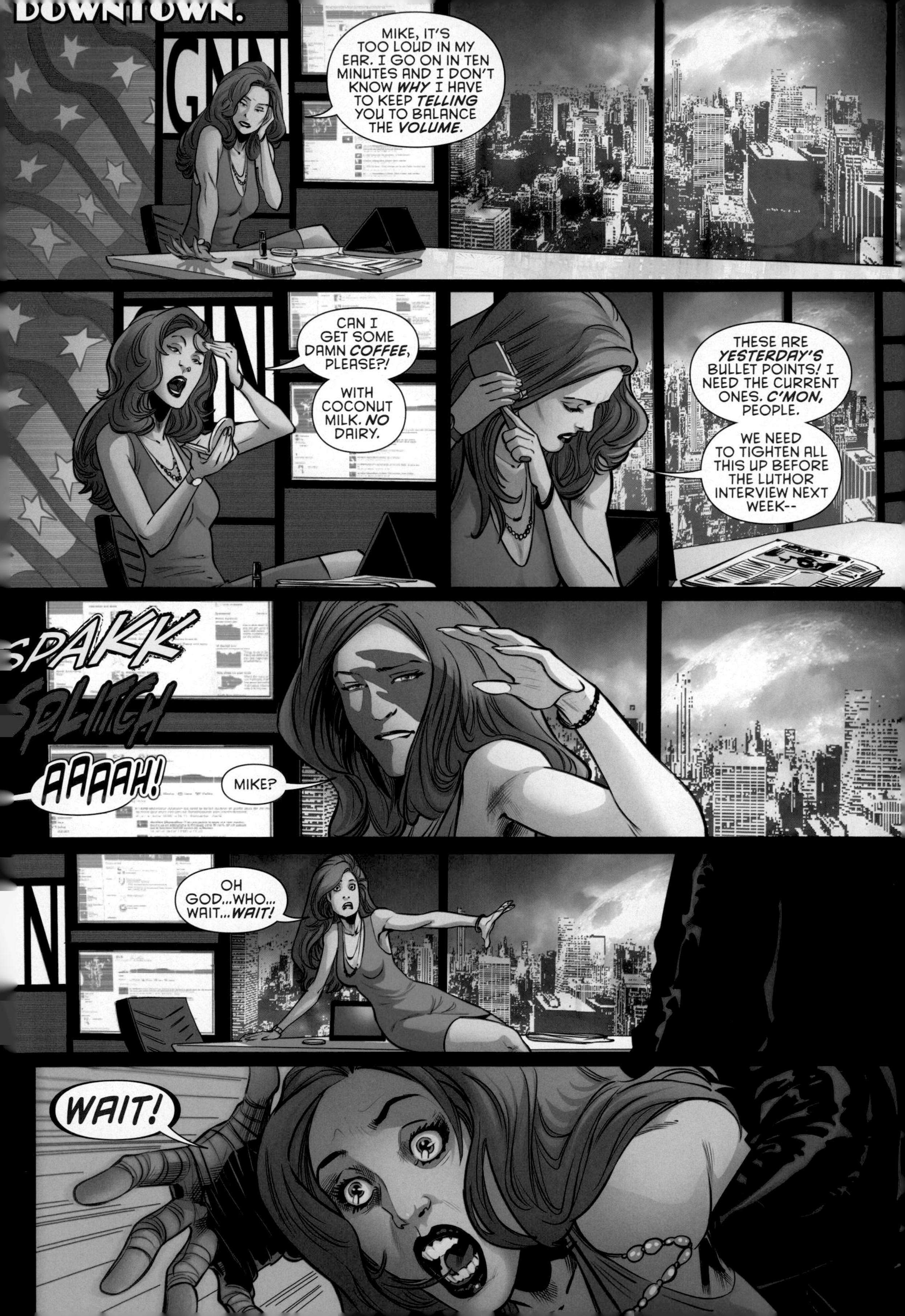
DOWNTOWN.
MIKE, IT'S TOO LOUD IN MY EAR. I GO ON IN TEN MINUTES AND I DON'T KNOW *WHY* I HAVE TO KEEP *TELLING* YOU TO BALANCE THE *VOLUME.*
CAN I GET SOME DAMN *COFFEE,* PLEASE?!
WITH COCONUT MILK. *NO* DAIRY.
THESE ARE *YESTERDAY'S* BULLET POINTS! I NEED THE CURRENT ONES. *C'MON,* PEOPLE.
WE NEED TO TIGHTEN ALL THIS UP BEFORE THE LUTHOR INTERVIEW NEXT WEEK--
SPAKK
SPLITCH
AAAAH!
MIKE?
OH GOD...WHO... WAIT...*WAIT!*
WAIT!

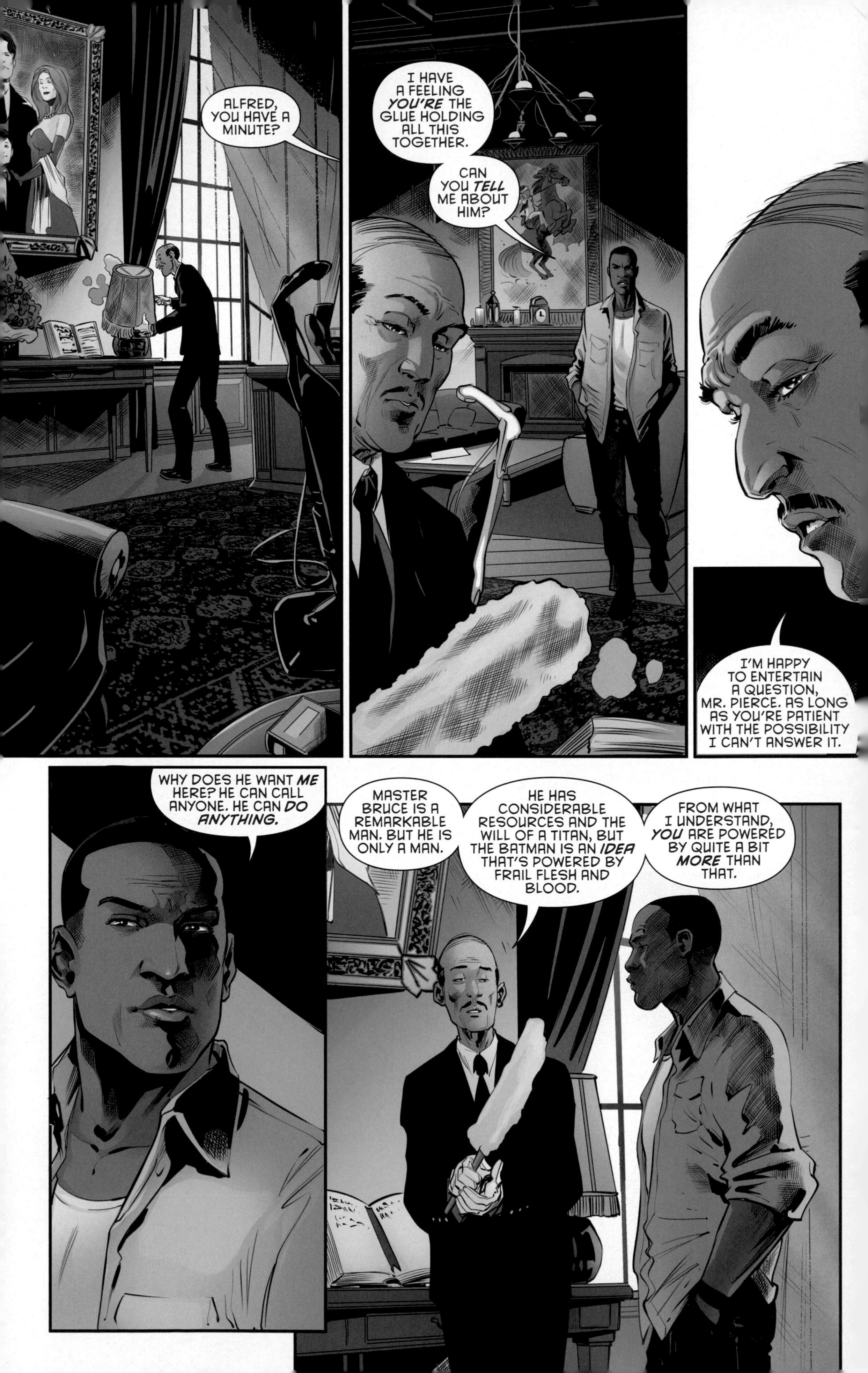
ALFRED, YOU HAVE A MINUTE?
I HAVE A FEELING *YOU'RE* THE GLUE HOLDING ALL THIS TOGETHER.
CAN YOU *TELL* ME ABOUT HIM?
I'M HAPPY TO ENTERTAIN A QUESTION, MR. PIERCE. AS LONG AS YOU'RE PATIENT WITH THE POSSIBILITY I CAN'T ANSWER IT.
WHY DOES HE WANT *ME* HERE? HE CAN CALL ANYONE. HE CAN *DO ANYTHING.*
MASTER BRUCE IS A REMARKABLE MAN. BUT HE IS ONLY A MAN.
HE HAS CONSIDERABLE RESOURCES AND THE WILL OF A TITAN, BUT THE BATMAN IS AN *IDEA* THAT'S POWERED BY FRAIL FLESH AND BLOOD.
FROM WHAT I UNDERSTAND, *YOU* ARE POWERED BY QUITE A BIT *MORE* THAN THAT.

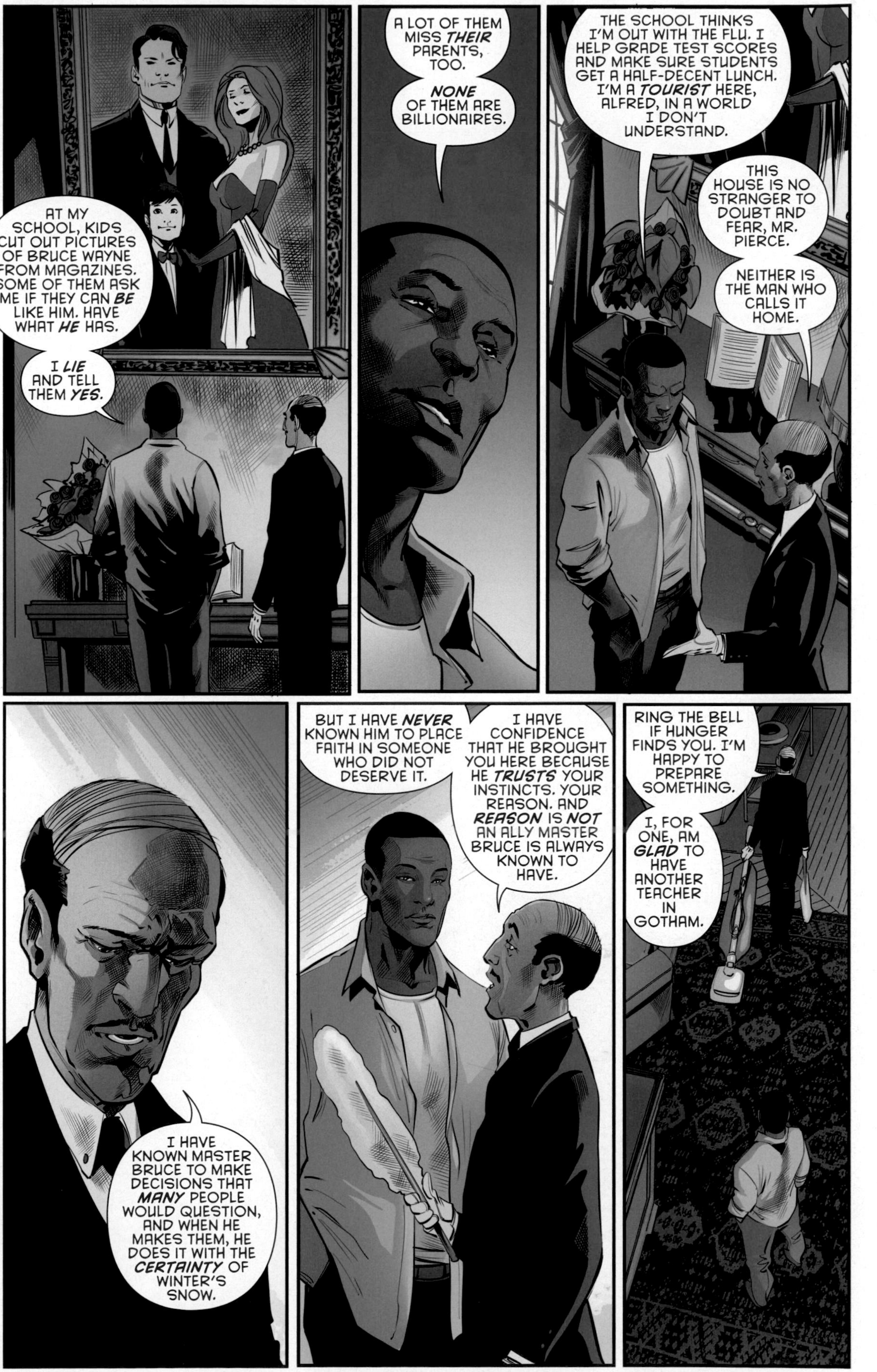
AT MY SCHOOL, KIDS CUT OUT PICTURES OF BRUCE WAYNE FROM MAGAZINES. SOME OF THEM ASK ME IF THEY CAN *BE* LIKE HIM. HAVE WHAT *HE* HAS.
I *LIE* AND TELL THEM *YES.*
A LOT OF THEM MISS *THEIR* PARENTS, TOO.
NONE OF THEM ARE BILLIONAIRES.
THE SCHOOL THINKS I'M OUT WITH THE FLU. I HELP GRADE TEST SCORES AND MAKE SURE STUDENTS GET A HALF-DECENT LUNCH. I'M A *TOURIST* HERE, ALFRED, IN A WORLD I DON'T UNDERSTAND.
THIS HOUSE IS NO STRANGER TO DOUBT AND FEAR, MR. PIERCE.
NEITHER IS THE MAN WHO CALLS IT HOME.
I HAVE KNOWN MASTER BRUCE TO MAKE DECISIONS THAT *MANY* PEOPLE WOULD QUESTION, AND WHEN HE MAKES THEM, HE DOES IT WITH THE *CERTAINTY* OF WINTER'S SNOW.
BUT I HAVE *NEVER* KNOWN HIM TO PLACE FAITH IN SOMEONE WHO DID NOT DESERVE IT.
I HAVE CONFIDENCE THAT HE BROUGHT YOU HERE BECAUSE HE *TRUSTS* YOUR INSTINCTS. YOUR REASON. AND *REASON* IS *NOT* AN ALLY MASTER BRUCE IS ALWAYS KNOWN TO HAVE.
RING THE BELL IF HUNGER FINDS YOU. I'M HAPPY TO PREPARE SOMETHING.
I, FOR ONE, AM *GLAD* TO HAVE ANOTHER TEACHER IN GOTHAM.

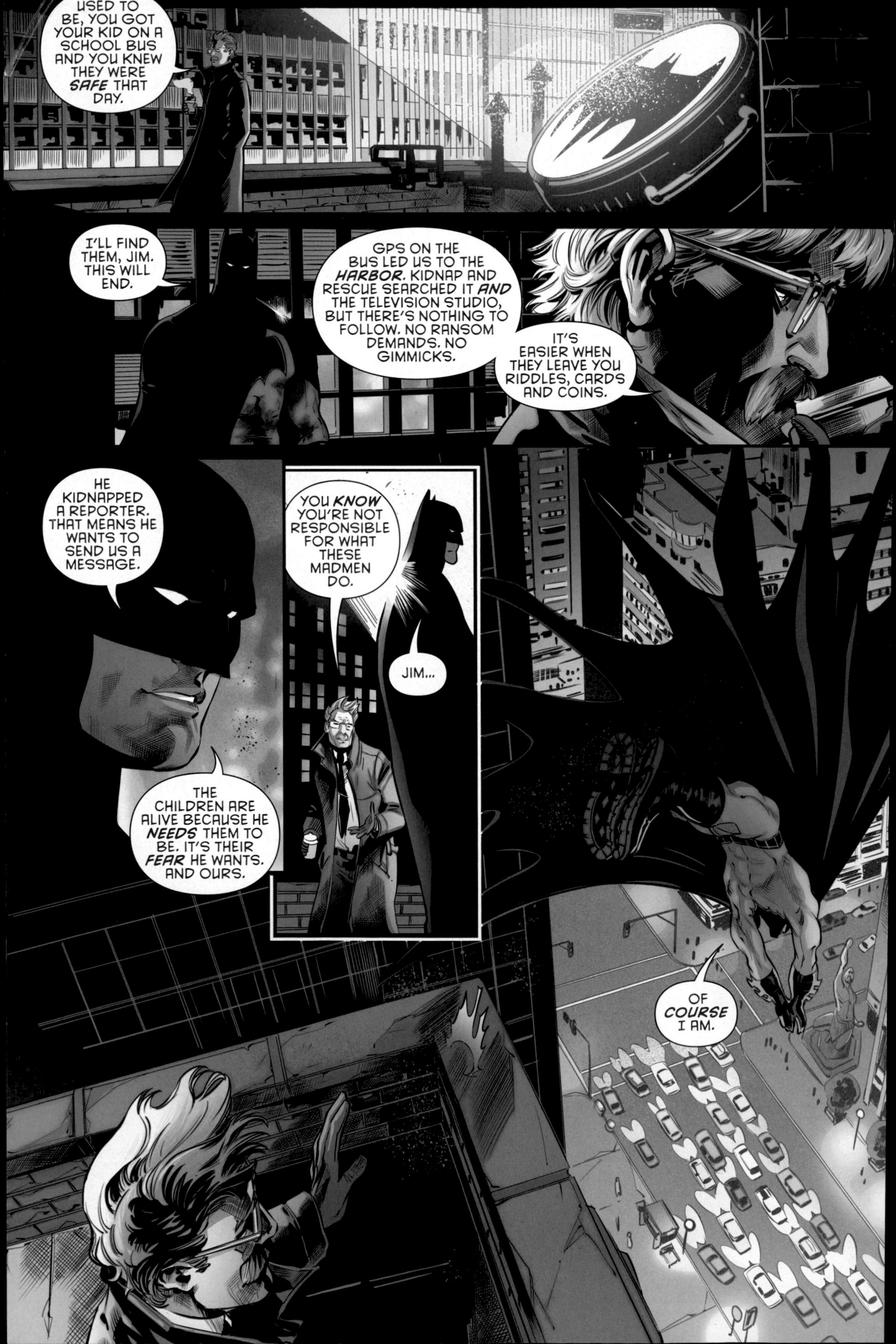
USED TO BE, YOU GOT YOUR KID ON A SCHOOL BUS AND YOU KNEW THEY WERE *SAFE* THAT DAY.
I'LL FIND THEM, JIM. THIS WILL END.
GPS ON THE BUS LED US TO THE *HARBOR*. KIDNAP AND RESCUE SEARCHED IT *AND* THE TELEVISION STUDIO, BUT THERE'S NOTHING TO FOLLOW. NO RANSOM DEMANDS. NO GIMMICKS.
IT'S EASIER WHEN THEY LEAVE YOU RIDDLES, CARDS AND COINS.
HE KIDNAPPED A REPORTER. THAT MEANS HE WANTS TO SEND US A MESSAGE.
THE CHILDREN ARE ALIVE BECAUSE HE *NEEDS* THEM TO BE. IT'S THEIR *FEAR* HE WANTS. AND OURS.
YOU *KNOW* YOU'RE NOT RESPONSIBLE FOR WHAT THESE MADMEN DO.
JIM...
OF *COURSE* I AM.

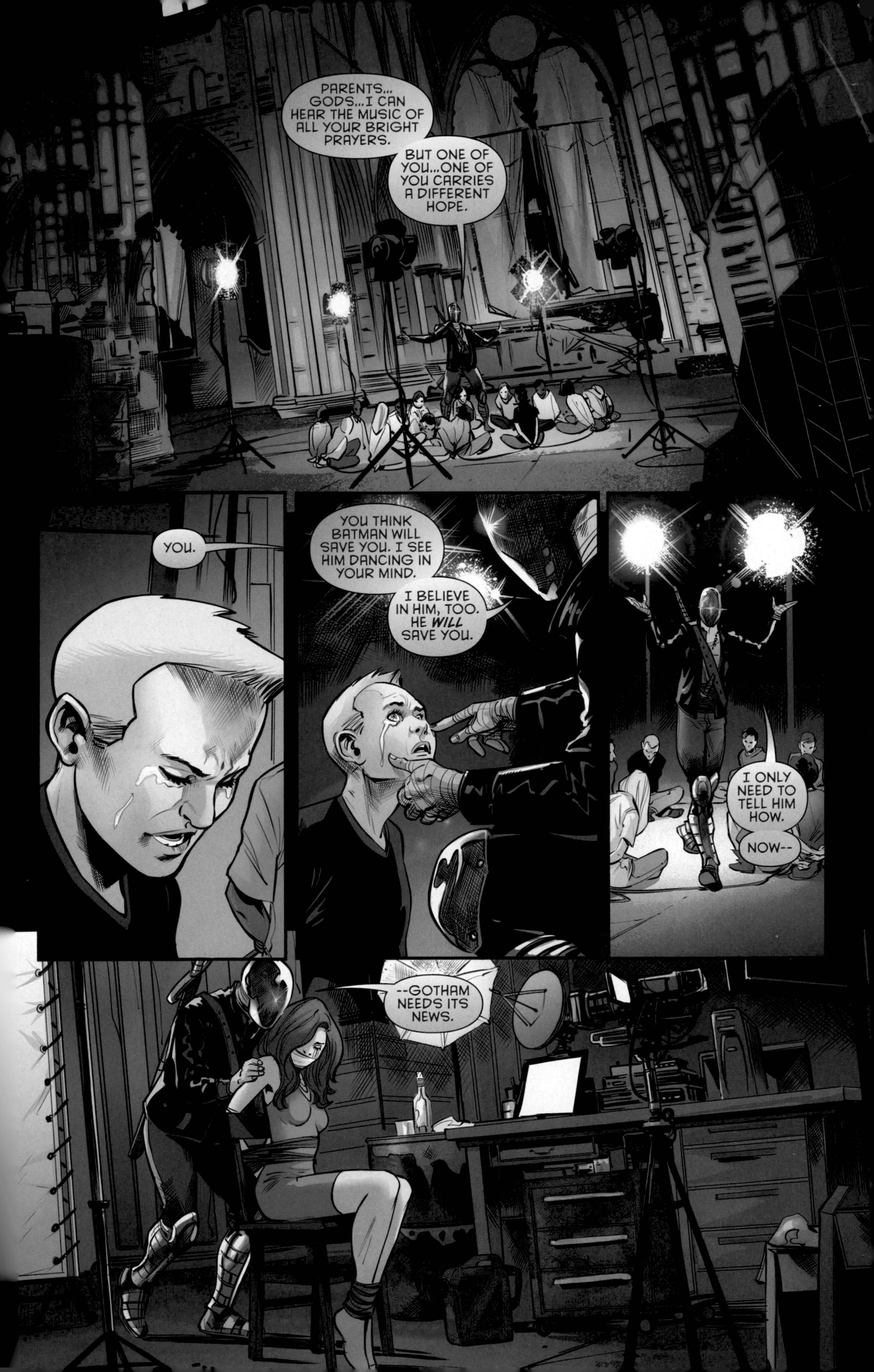
PARENTS... GODS...I CAN HEAR THE MUSIC OF ALL YOUR BRIGHT PRAYERS.
BUT ONE OF YOU...ONE OF YOU CARRIES A DIFFERENT HOPE.
YOU.
YOU THINK BATMAN WILL SAVE YOU. I SEE HIM DANCING IN YOUR MIND.
I BELIEVE IN HIM, TOO. HE *WILL* SAVE YOU.
I ONLY NEED TO TELL HIM HOW.
NOW--
--GOTHAM NEEDS ITS NEWS.

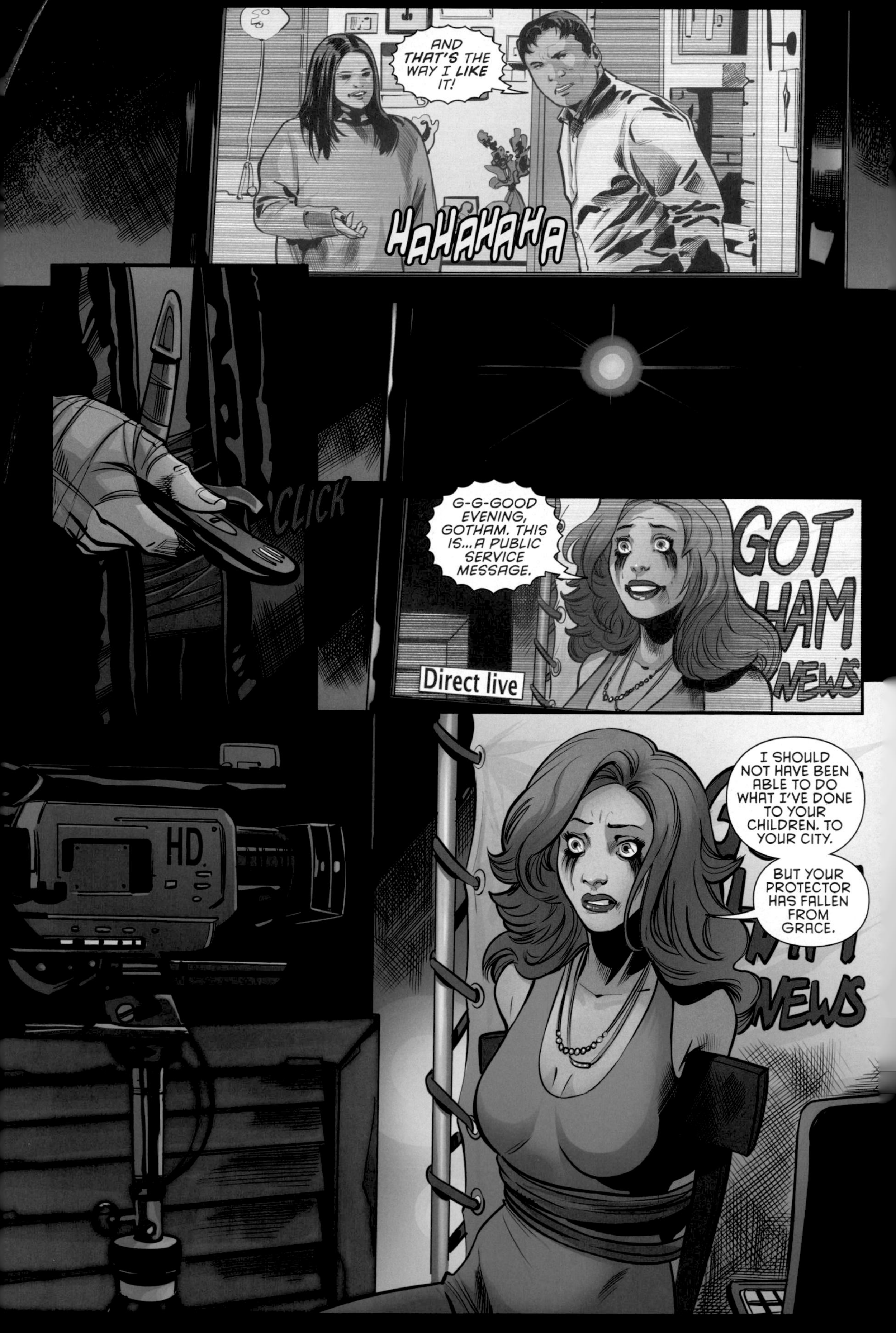
AND THAT'S THE WAY I LIKE IT!
HAHAHAHAHA
CLICK
G-G-GOOD EVENING, GOTHAM. THIS IS...A PUBLIC SERVICE MESSAGE.
GOTHAM NEWS
Direct live
I SHOULD NOT HAVE BEEN ABLE TO DO WHAT I'VE DONE TO YOUR CHILDREN. TO YOUR CITY.
BUT YOUR PROTECTOR HAS FALLEN FROM GRACE.
NEWS

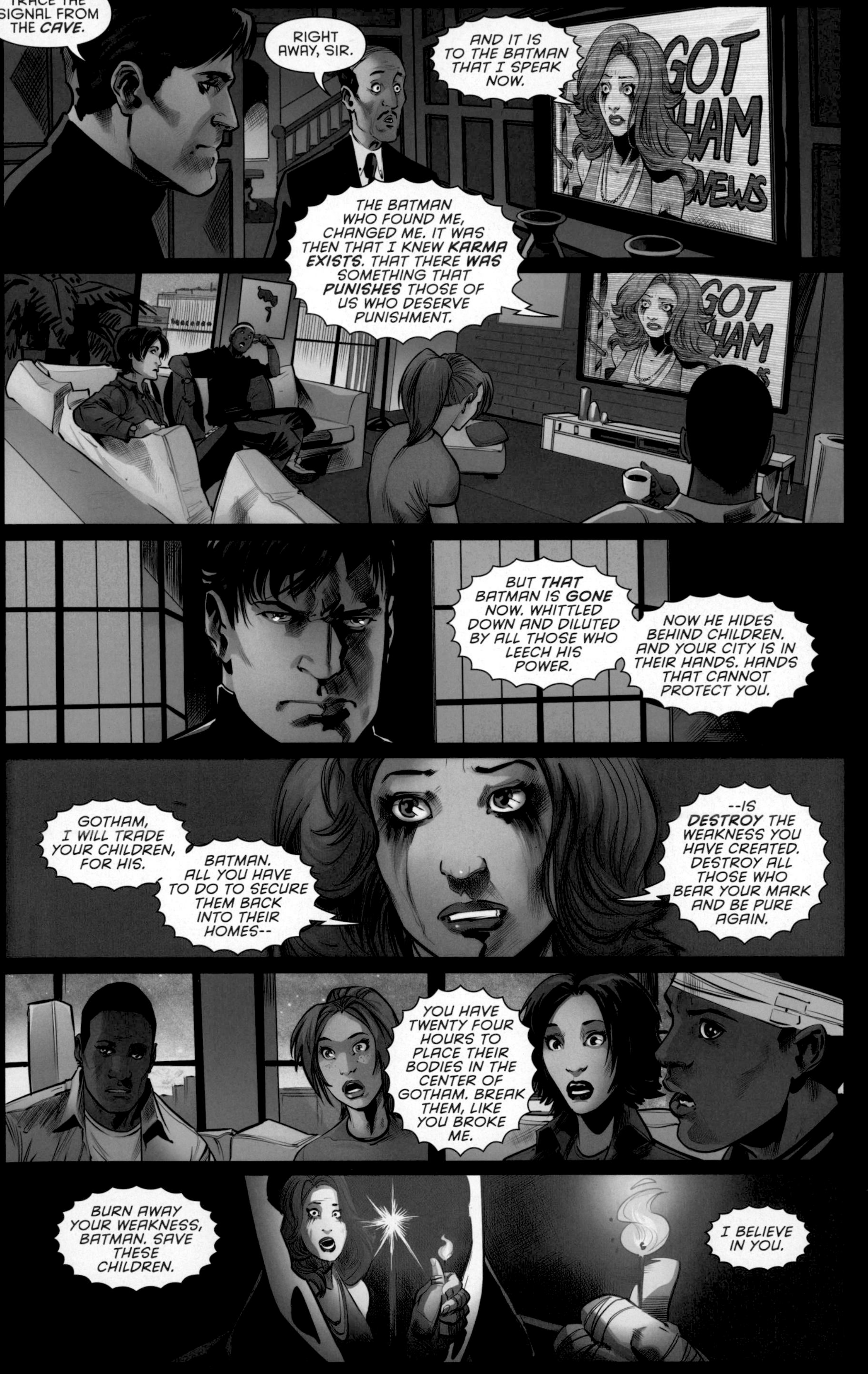
TRACE THE SIGNAL FROM THE *CAVE*.
RIGHT AWAY, SIR.
AND IT IS TO THE BATMAN THAT I SPEAK NOW.
GOT HAM NEWS
THE BATMAN WHO FOUND ME, CHANGED ME. IT WAS THEN THAT I KNEW **KARMA EXISTS**. THAT THERE **WAS** SOMETHING THAT **PUNISHES** THOSE OF US WHO DESERVE PUNISHMENT.
GOT HAM
BUT **THAT** BATMAN IS **GONE** NOW. WHITTLED DOWN AND DILUTED BY ALL THOSE WHO LEECH HIS POWER.
NOW HE HIDES BEHIND CHILDREN. AND YOUR CITY IS IN THEIR HANDS. HANDS THAT CANNOT PROTECT YOU.
GOTHAM, I WILL TRADE YOUR CHILDREN, FOR HIS.
BATMAN. ALL YOU HAVE TO DO TO SECURE THEM BACK INTO THEIR HOMES--
--IS **DESTROY** THE WEAKNESS YOU HAVE CREATED. DESTROY ALL THOSE WHO BEAR YOUR MARK AND BE PURE AGAIN.
YOU HAVE TWENTY FOUR HOURS TO PLACE THEIR BODIES IN THE CENTER OF GOTHAM. BREAK THEM, LIKE YOU BROKE ME.
BURN AWAY YOUR WEAKNESS, BATMAN. SAVE THESE CHILDREN.
I BELIEVE IN YOU.

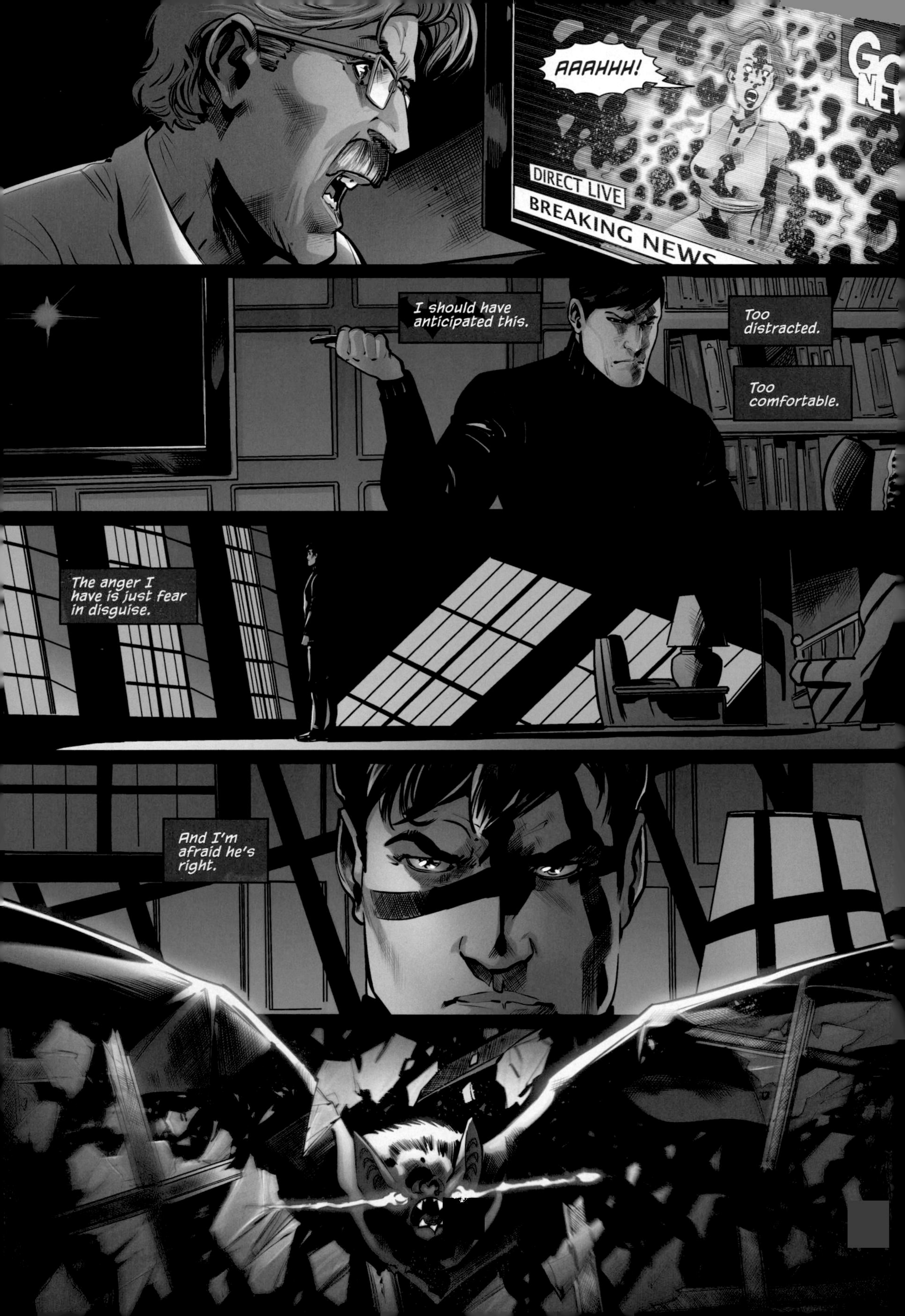
AAAHHH!
DIRECT LIVE
BREAKING NEWS
I should have anticipated this.
Too distracted.
Too comfortable.
The anger I have is just fear in disguise.
And I'm afraid he's right.

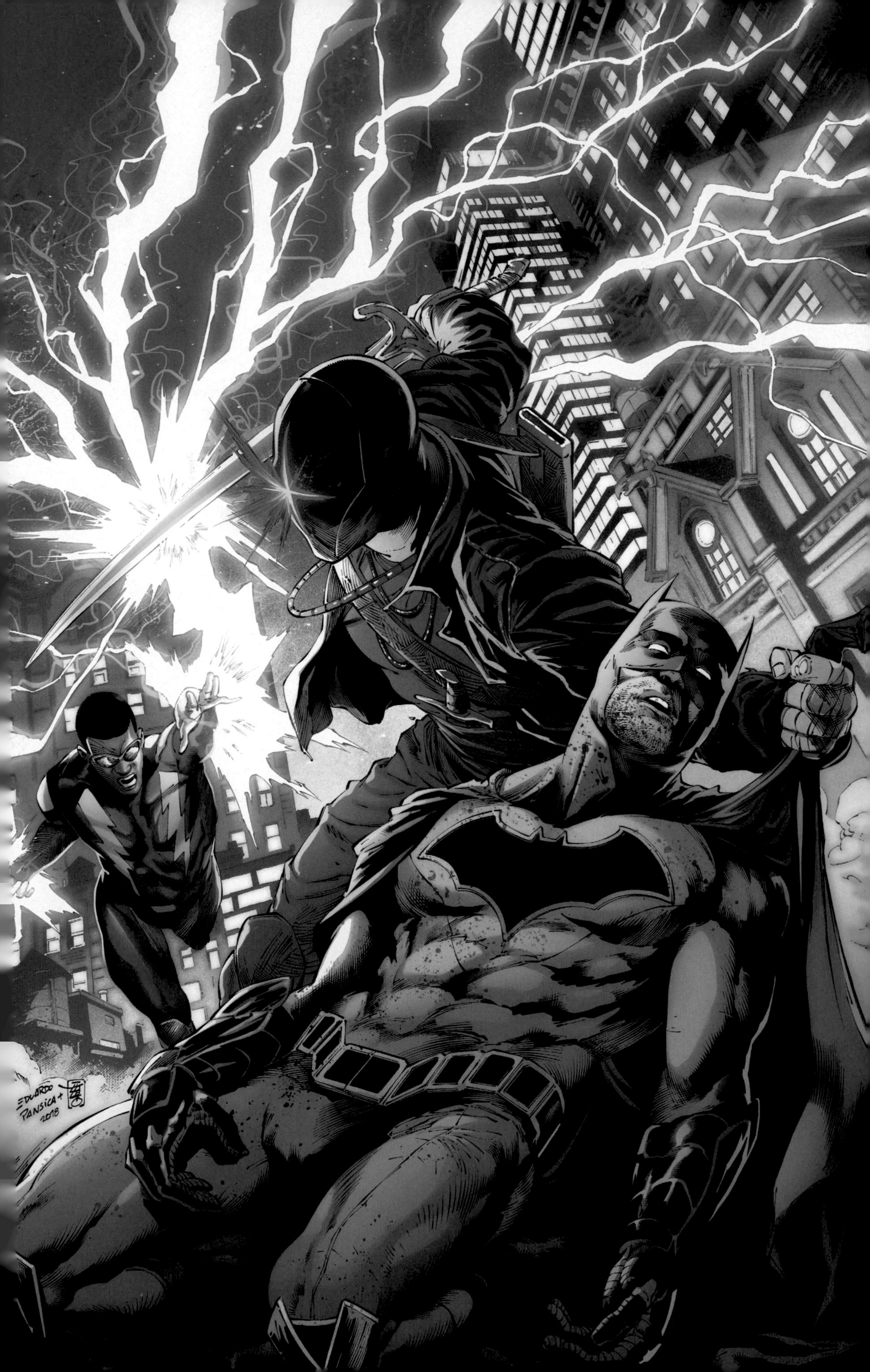
EDUARDO PANSICA +
2018

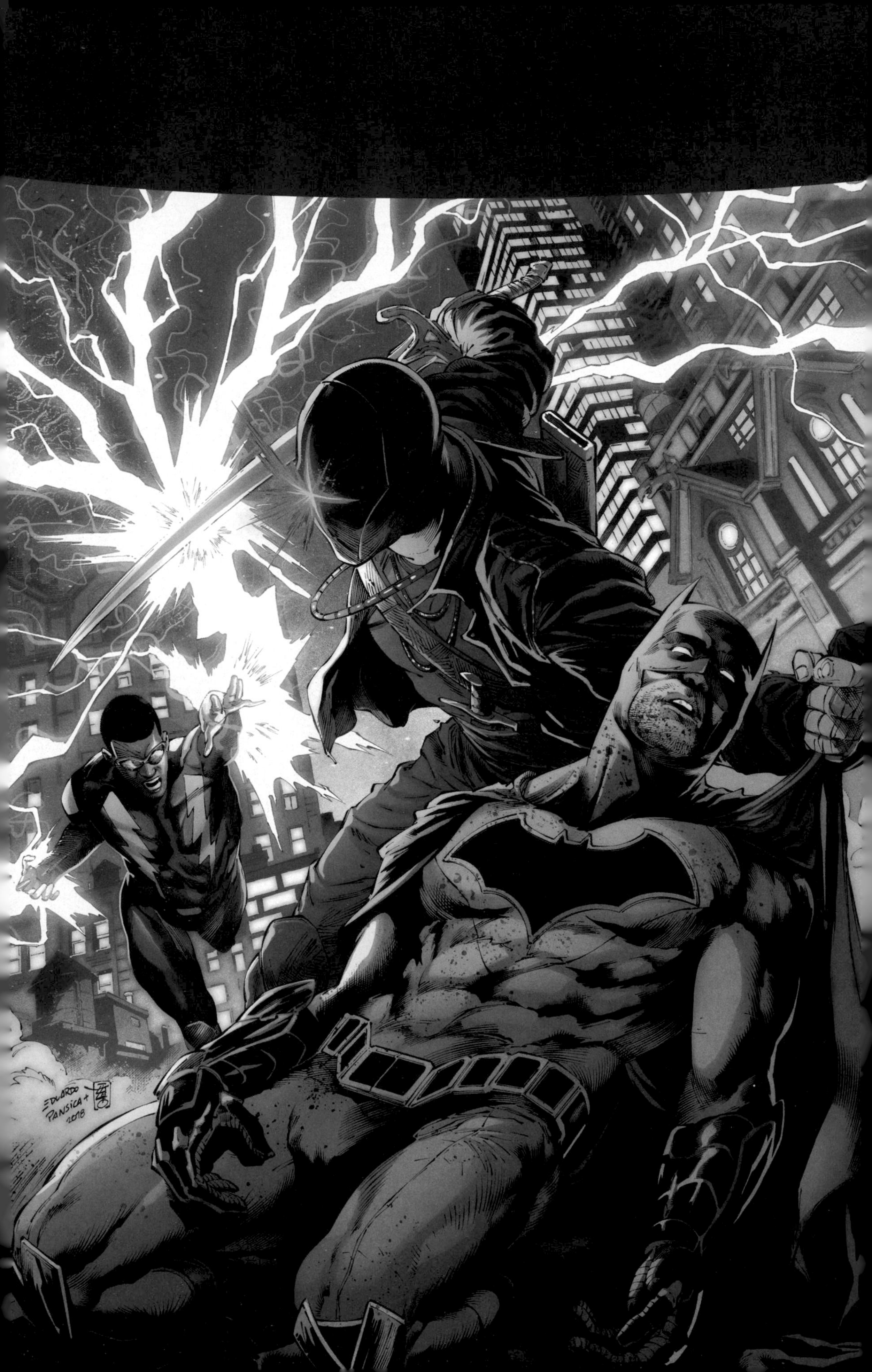
EDUARDO PANSICA+ 2018

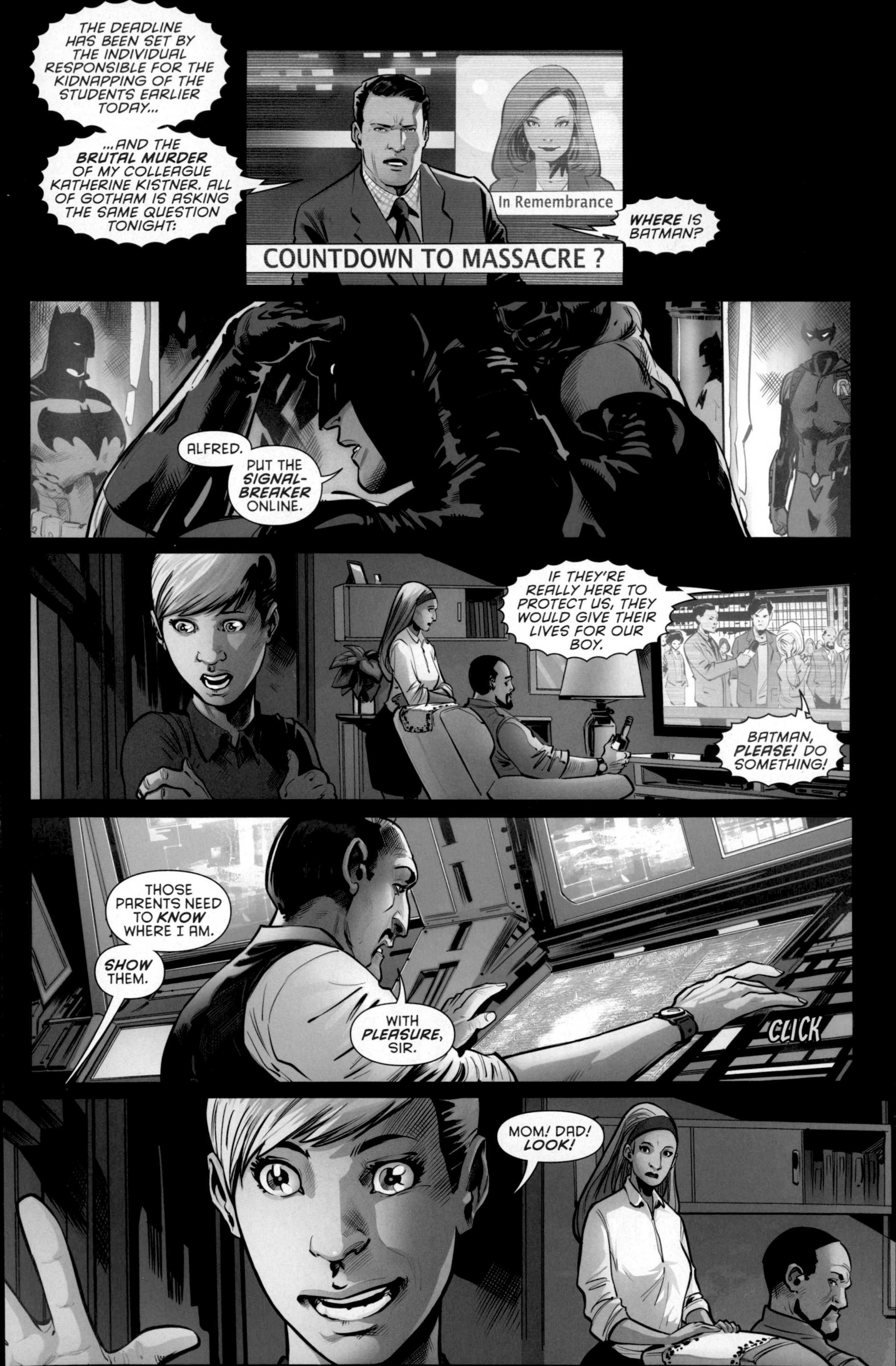
THE DEADLINE HAS BEEN SET BY THE INDIVIDUAL RESPONSIBLE FOR THE KIDNAPPING OF THE STUDENTS EARLIER TODAY...
...AND THE BRUTAL MURDER OF MY COLLEAGUE KATHERINE KISTNER. ALL OF GOTHAM IS ASKING THE SAME QUESTION TONIGHT:
In Remembrance
WHERE IS BATMAN?
COUNTDOWN TO MASSACRE ?
ALFRED.
PUT THE SIGNAL-BREAKER ONLINE.
IF THEY'RE REALLY HERE TO PROTECT US, THEY WOULD GIVE THEIR LIVES FOR OUR BOY.
BATMAN, PLEASE! DO SOMETHING!
THOSE PARENTS NEED TO KNOW WHERE I AM.
SHOW THEM.
WITH PLEASURE, SIR.
CLICK
MOM! DAD! LOOK!

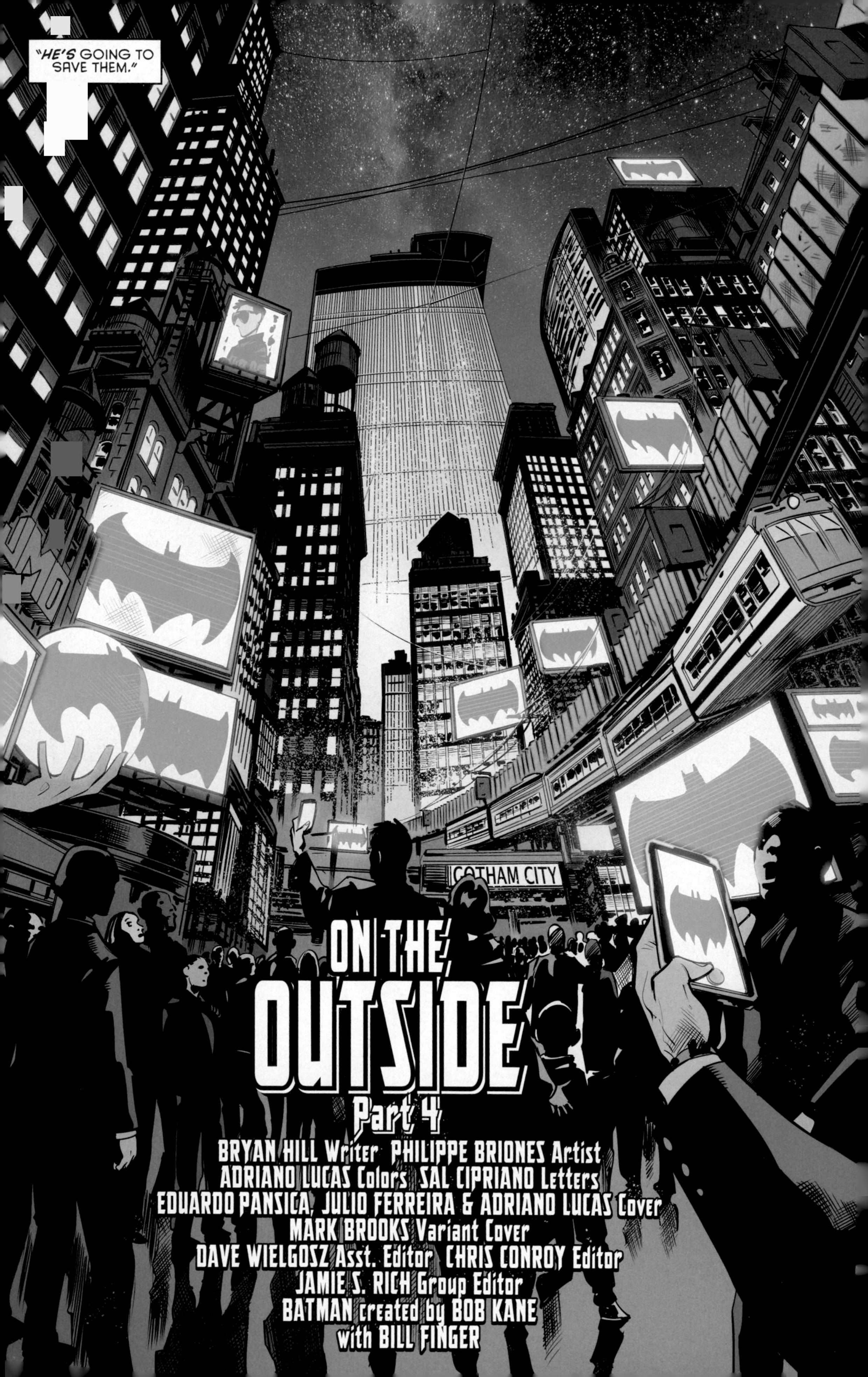
"HE'S GOING TO SAVE THEM."
GOTHAM CITY
ON THE
OUTSIDE
Part 4
BRYAN HILL Writer PHILIPPE BRIONES Artist
ADRIANO LUCAS Colors SAL CIPRIANO Letters
EDUARDO PANSICA, JULIO FERREIRA & ADRIANO LUCAS Cover
MARK BROOKS Variant Cover
DAVE WIELGOSZ Asst. Editor CHRIS CONROY Editor
JAMIE S. RICH Group Editor
BATMAN created by BOB KANE
with BILL FINGER

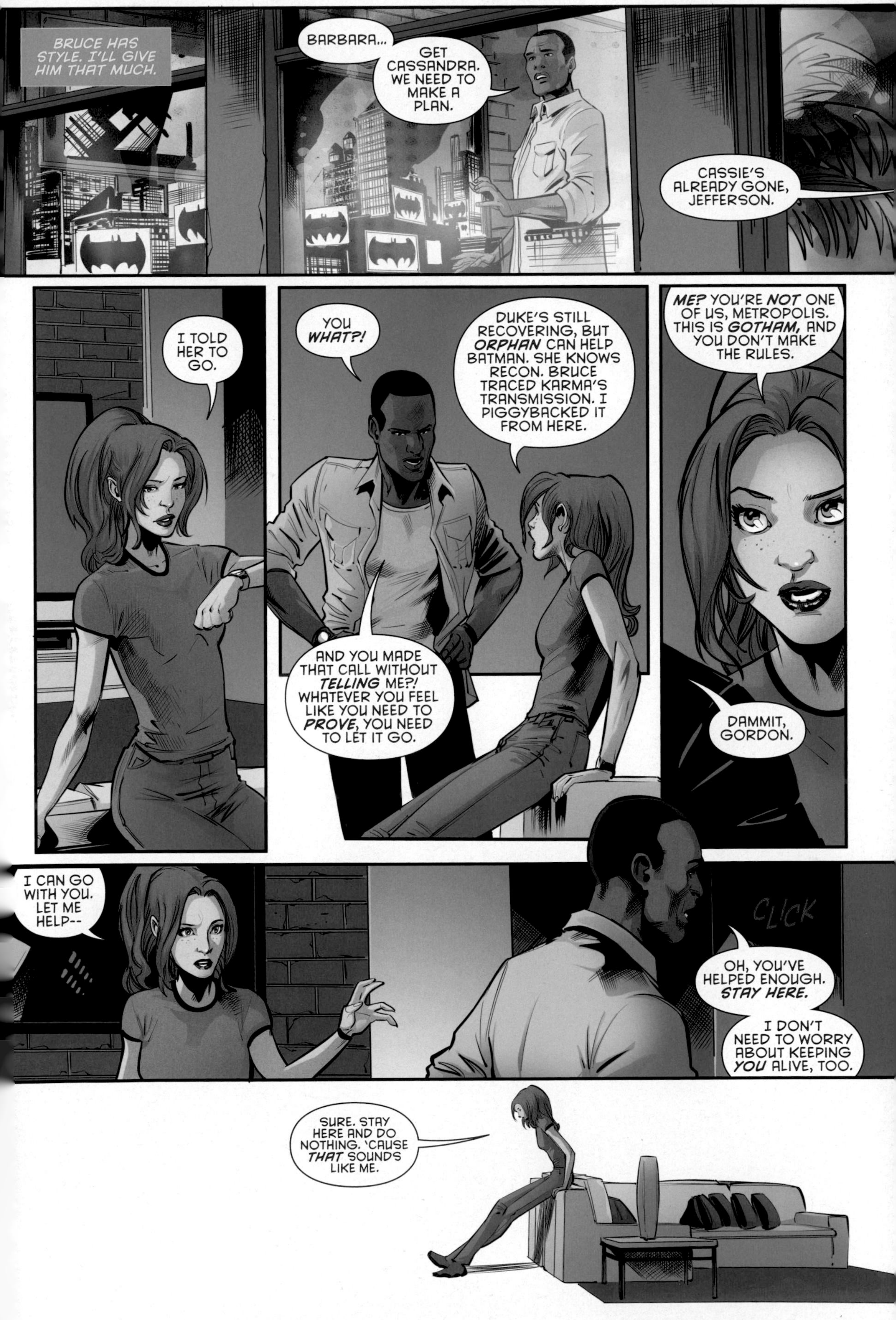
BRUCE HAS STYLE. I'LL GIVE HIM THAT MUCH.
BARBARA...
GET CASSANDRA. WE NEED TO MAKE A PLAN.
CASSIE'S ALREADY GONE, JEFFERSON.
I TOLD HER TO GO.
YOU *WHAT?!*
DUKE'S STILL RECOVERING, BUT *ORPHAN* CAN HELP BATMAN. SHE KNOWS RECON. BRUCE TRACED KARMA'S TRANSMISSION. I PIGGYBACKED IT FROM HERE.
AND YOU MADE THAT CALL WITHOUT *TELLING* ME?! WHATEVER YOU FEEL LIKE YOU NEED TO *PROVE*, YOU NEED TO LET IT GO.
ME? YOU'RE *NOT* ONE OF US, METROPOLIS. THIS IS *GOTHAM,* AND YOU DON'T MAKE THE RULES.
DAMMIT, GORDON.
I CAN GO WITH YOU. LET ME HELP--
CLICK
OH, YOU'VE HELPED ENOUGH. *STAY HERE.*
I DON'T NEED TO WORRY ABOUT KEEPING *YOU* ALIVE, TOO.
SURE. STAY HERE AND DO NOTHING. 'CAUSE *THAT* SOUNDS LIKE ME.

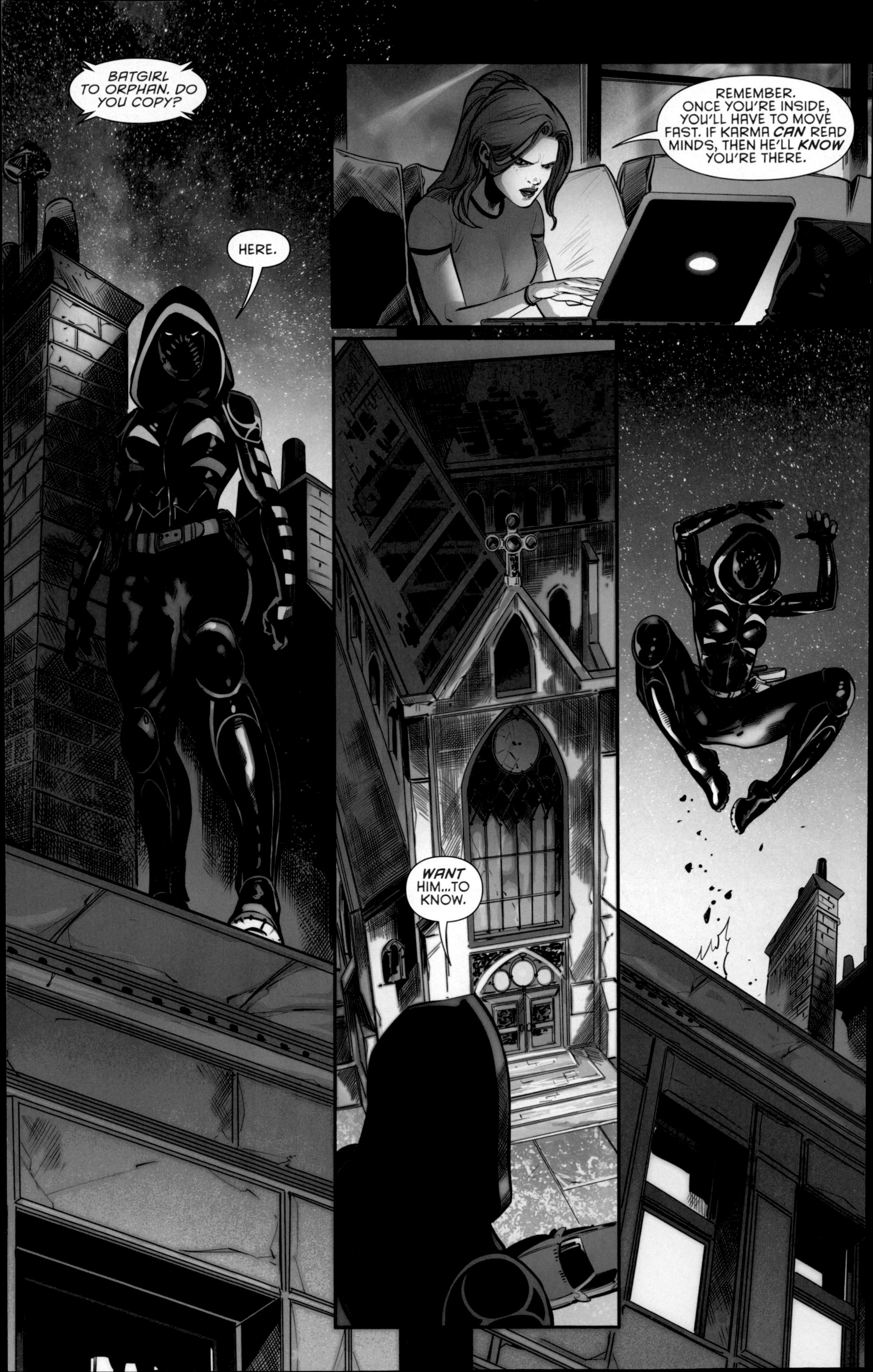
BATGIRL TO ORPHAN. DO YOU COPY?
HERE.
REMEMBER. ONCE YOU'RE INSIDE, YOU'LL HAVE TO MOVE FAST. IF KARMA ***CAN*** READ MINDS, THEN HE'LL ***KNOW*** YOU'RE THERE.
WANT HIM...TO KNOW.

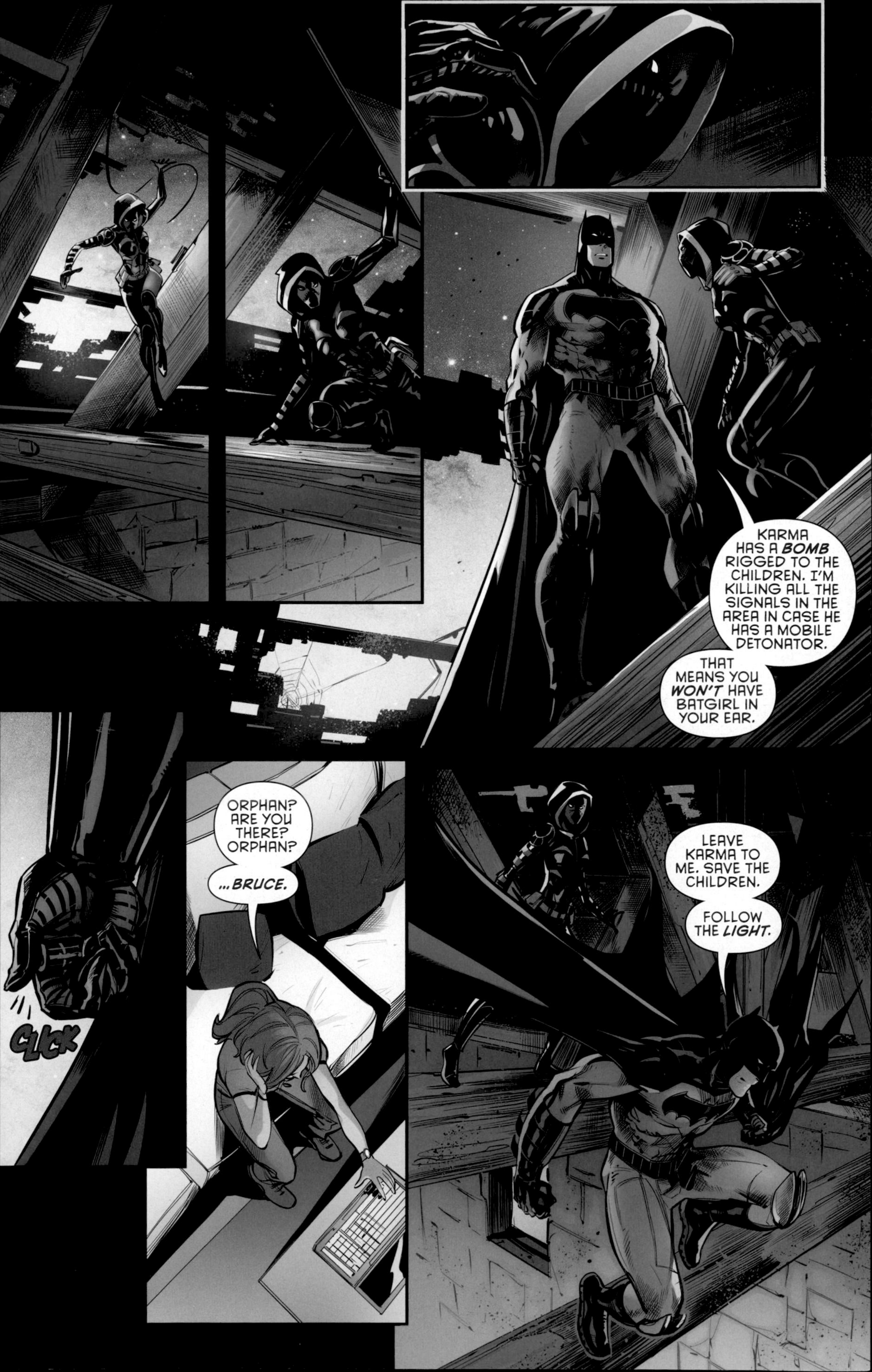

KARMA HAS A *BOMB* RIGGED TO THE CHILDREN. I'M KILLING ALL THE SIGNALS IN THE AREA IN CASE HE HAS A MOBILE DETONATOR.
THAT MEANS YOU *WON'T* HAVE BATGIRL IN YOUR EAR.
CLICK
ORPHAN? ARE YOU THERE? ORPHAN?
...BRUCE.
LEAVE KARMA TO ME. SAVE THE CHILDREN.
FOLLOW THE *LIGHT.*

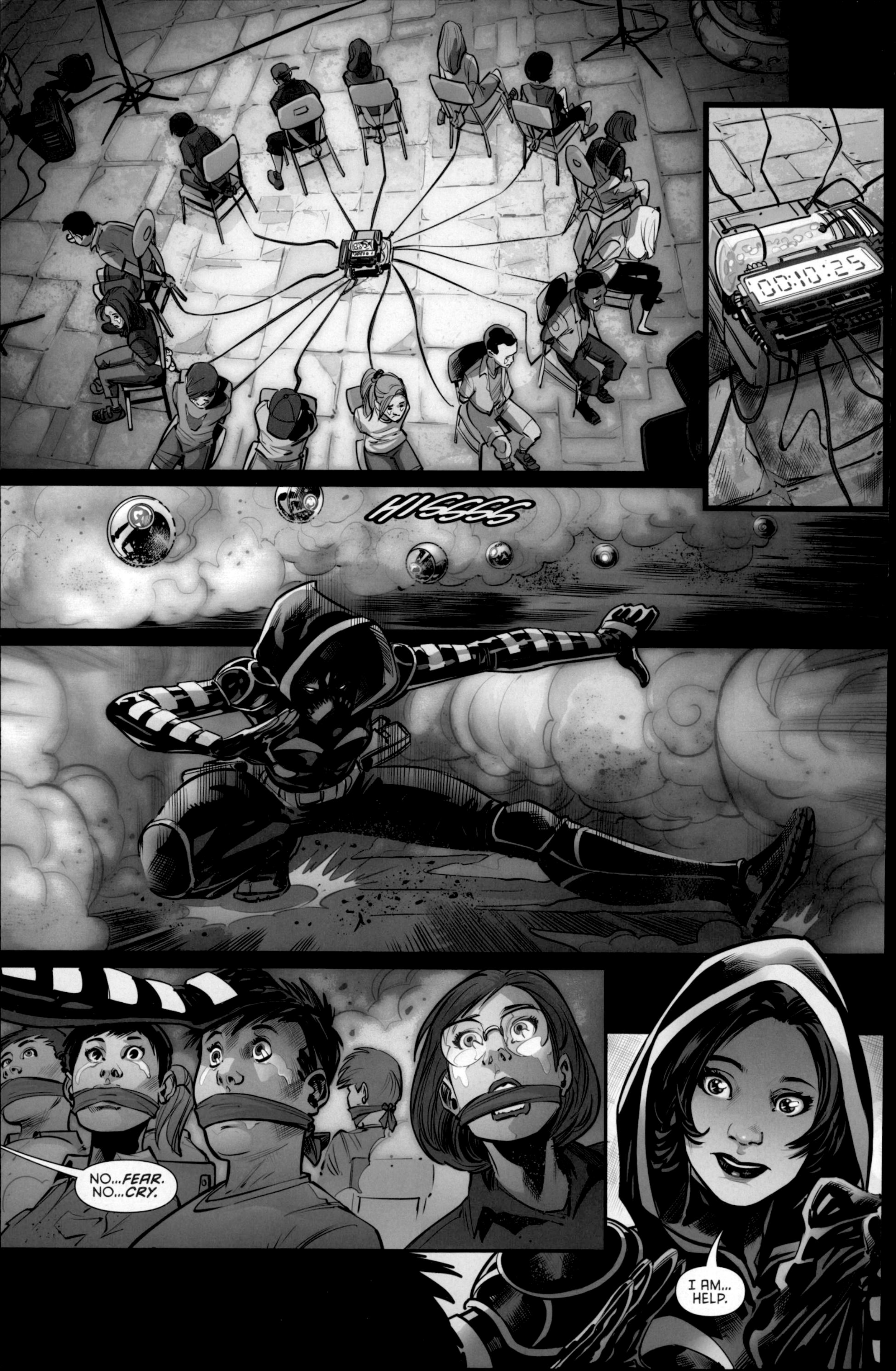
00:10:25
HISSSS
NO...FEAR.
NO...CRY.
I AM...
HELP.

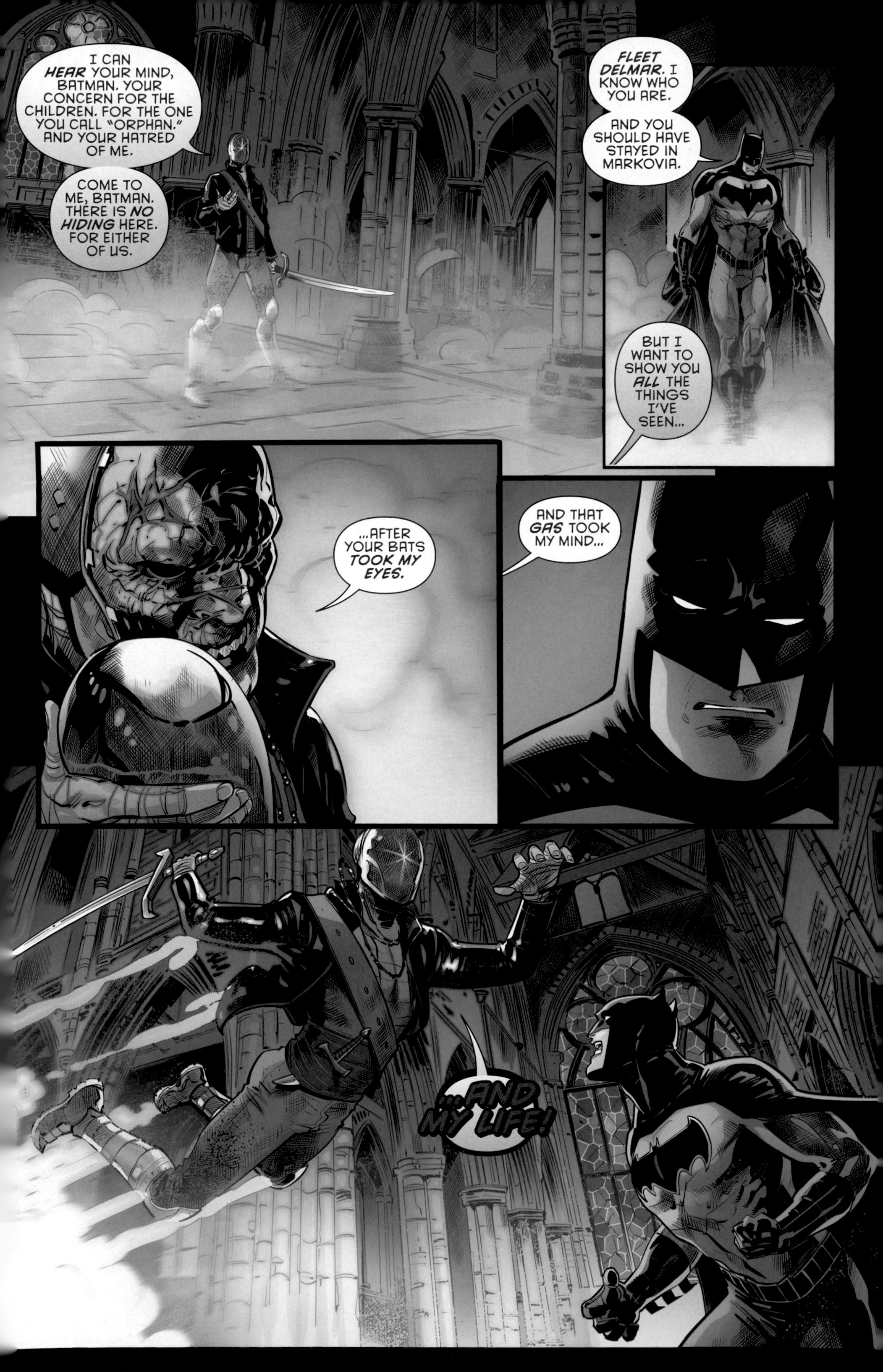
I CAN *HEAR* YOUR MIND, BATMAN. YOUR CONCERN FOR THE CHILDREN. FOR THE ONE YOU CALL "ORPHAN." AND YOUR HATRED OF ME.
COME TO ME, BATMAN. THERE IS *NO HIDING* HERE. FOR EITHER OF US.
FLEET DELMAR. I KNOW WHO YOU ARE.
AND YOU SHOULD HAVE STAYED IN MARKOVIA.
BUT I WANT TO SHOW YOU *ALL* THE THINGS I'VE SEEN...
...AFTER YOUR BATS *TOOK MY EYES.*
AND THAT *GAS* TOOK MY MIND...
...AND MY LIFE!

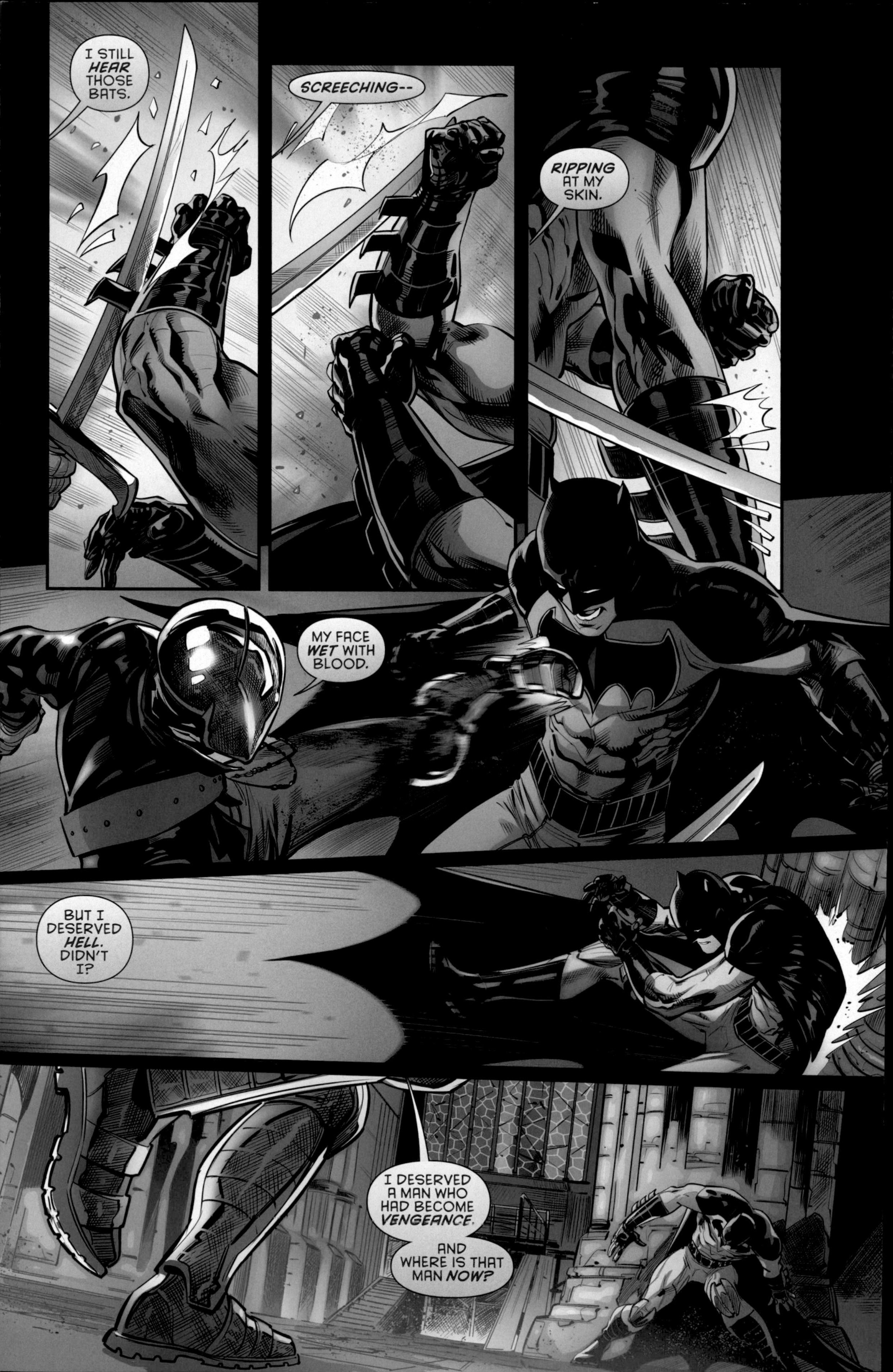
I STILL *HEAR* THOSE BATS.
SCREECHING--
RIPPING AT MY SKIN.
MY FACE *WET* WITH BLOOD.
BUT I DESERVED *HELL*. DIDN'T I?
I DESERVED A MAN WHO HAD BECOME *VENGEANCE*.
AND WHERE IS THAT MAN *NOW?*

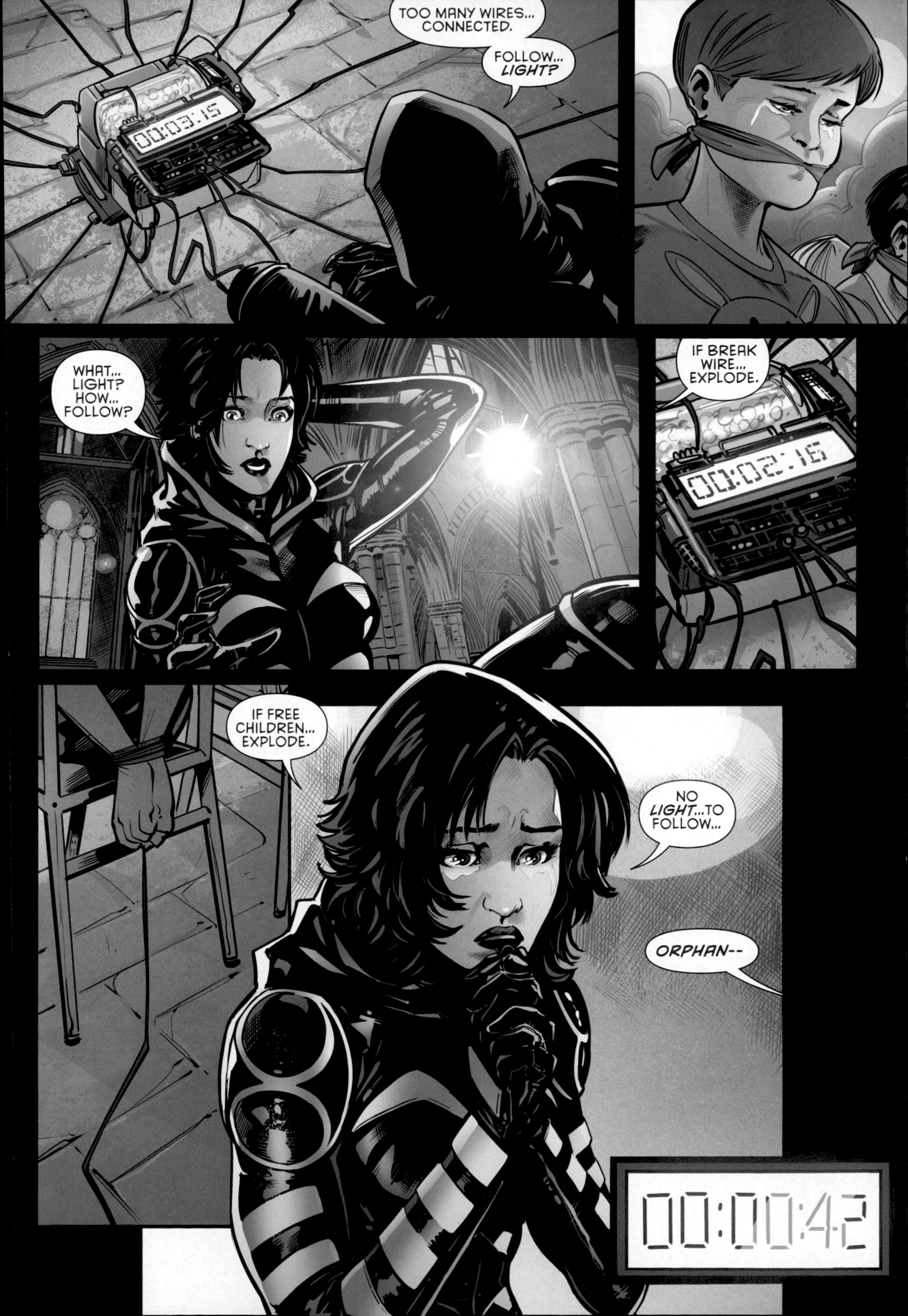
TOO MANY WIRES... CONNECTED.
FOLLOW... *LIGHT?*
00:03:15
WHAT... LIGHT? HOW... FOLLOW?
IF BREAK WIRE... EXPLODE.
00:02:16
IF FREE CHILDREN... EXPLODE.
NO *LIGHT*...TO FOLLOW...
ORPHAN--
00:00:42

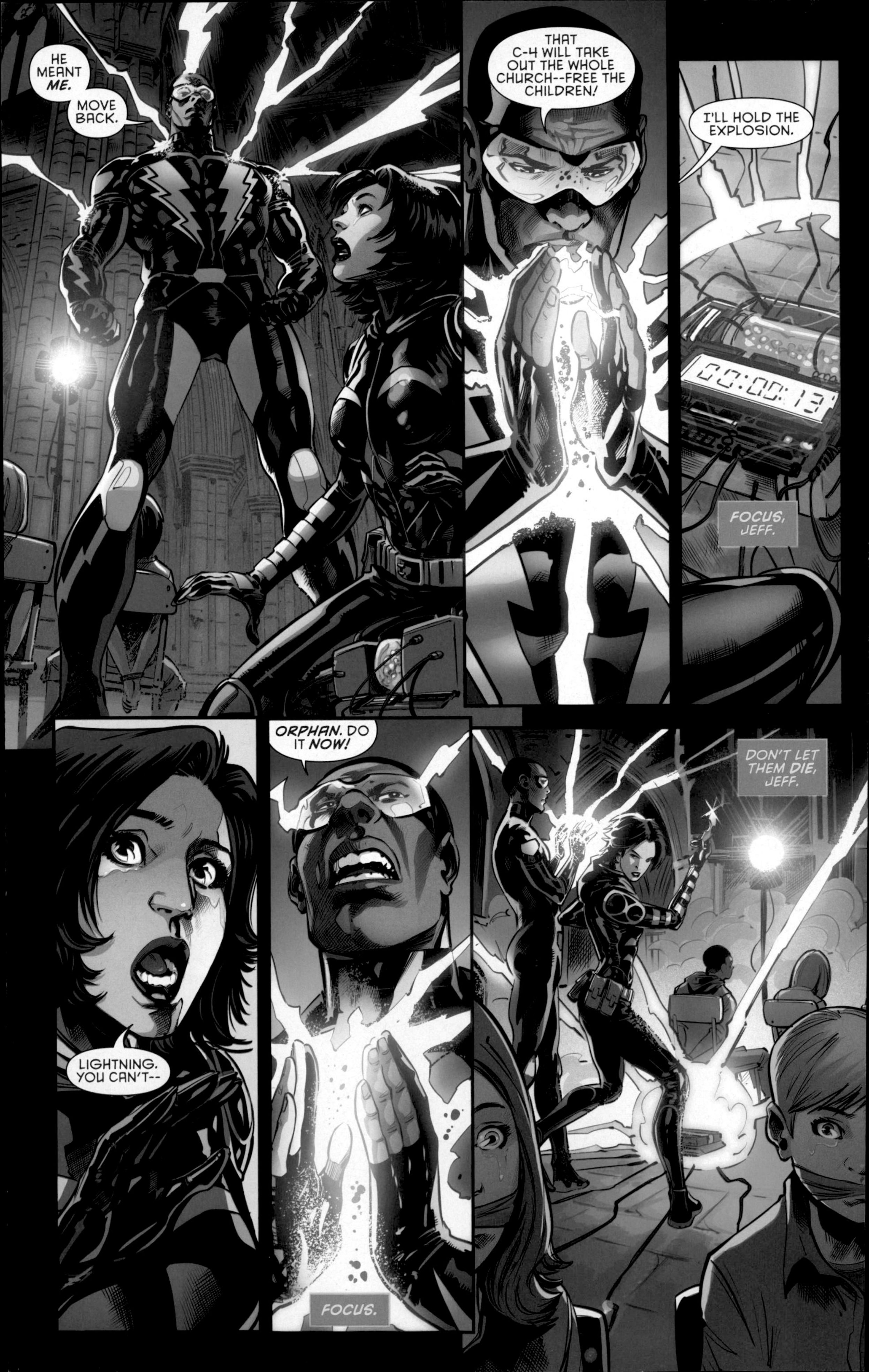
HE MEANT *ME.*
MOVE BACK.
THAT C-4 WILL TAKE OUT THE WHOLE CHURCH--FREE THE CHILDREN!
I'LL HOLD THE EXPLOSION.
FOCUS, JEFF.
LIGHTNING. YOU CAN'T--
ORPHAN. DO IT *NOW!*
FOCUS.
DON'T LET THEM *DIE,* JEFF.

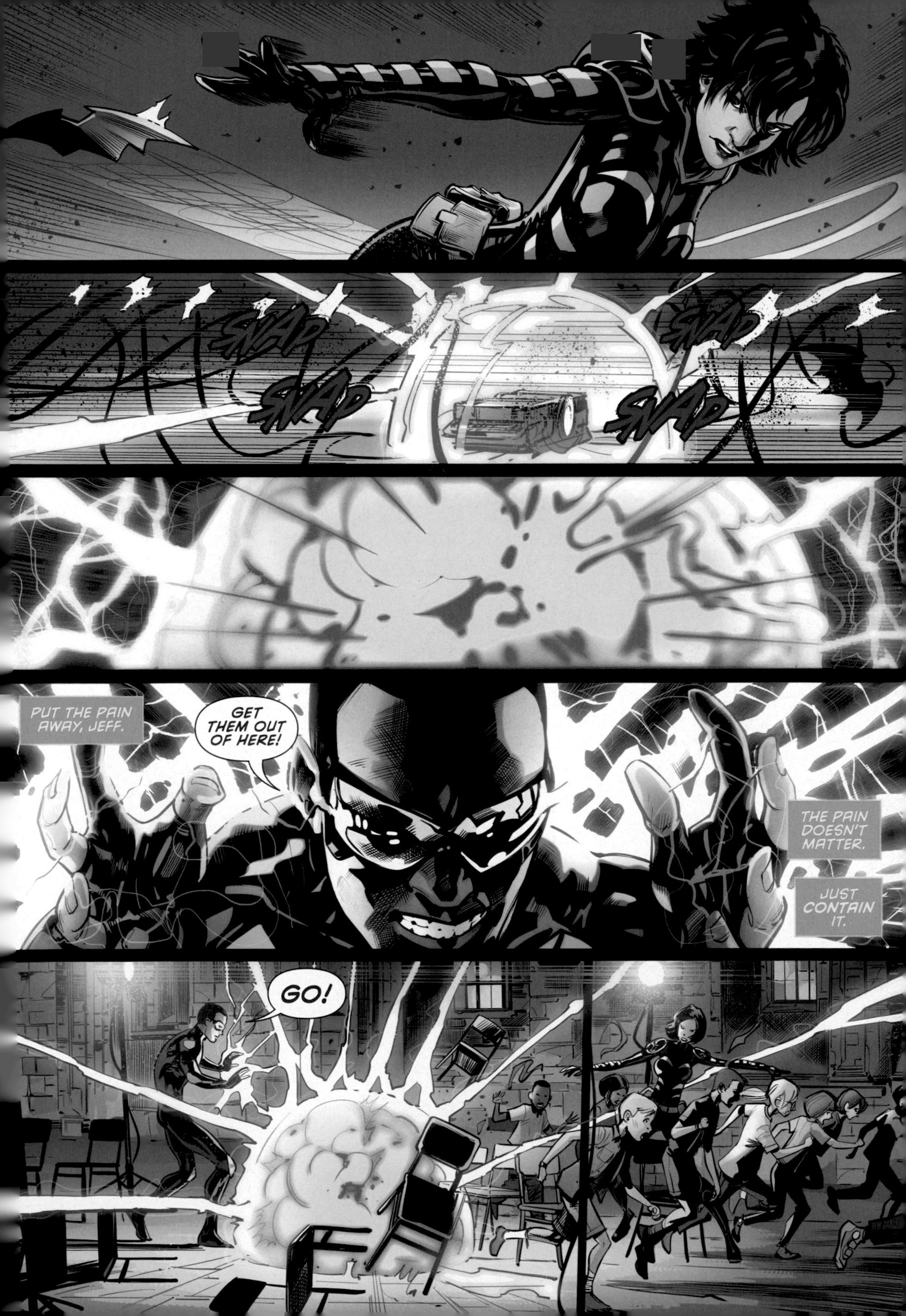
SNAP
SNAP
SNAP
SNAP
PUT THE PAIN AWAY, JEFF.
GET THEM OUT OF HERE!
THE PAIN DOESN'T MATTER.
JUST CONTAIN IT.
GO!

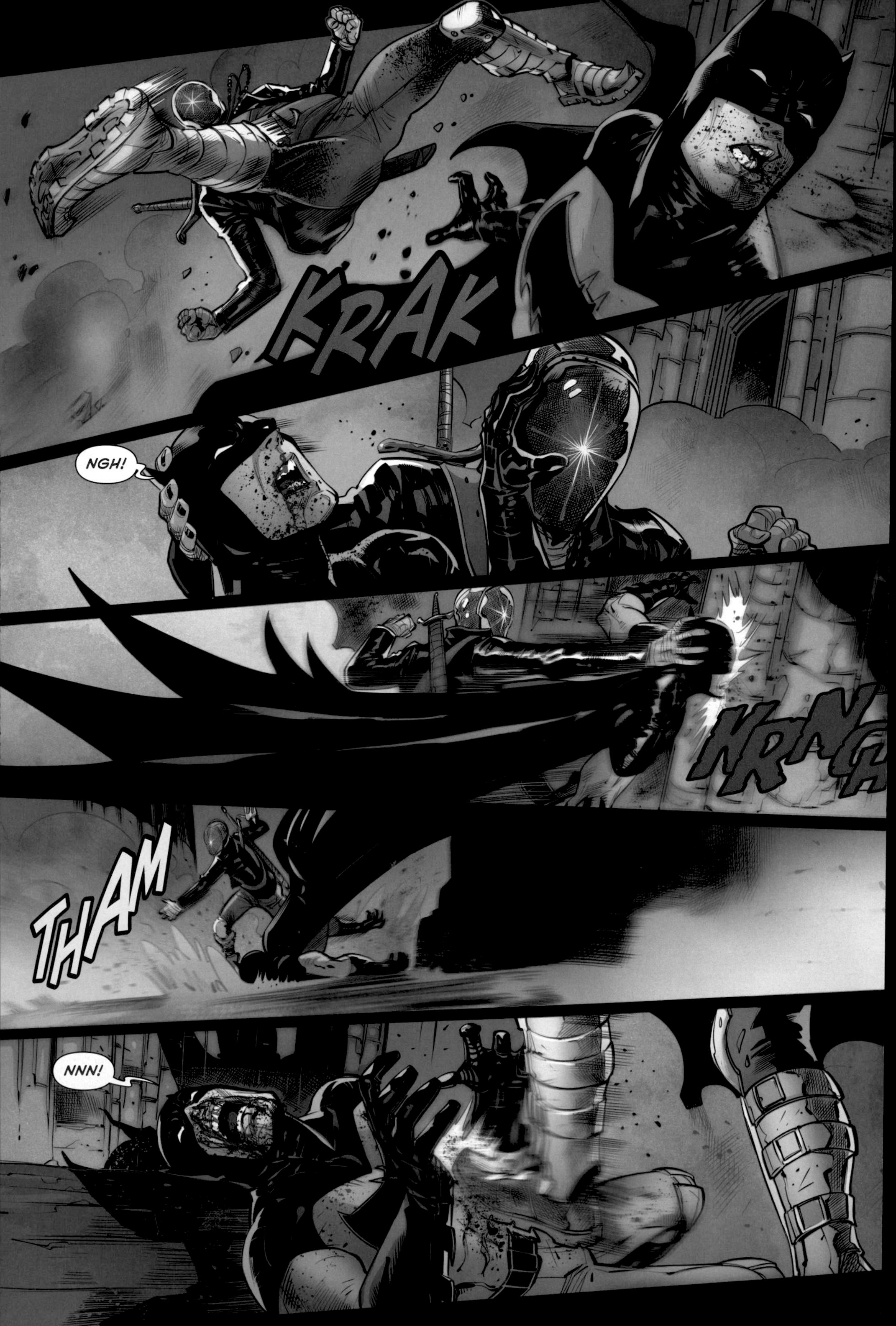
KRAK
NGH!
HRNGH
THAM
NNN!

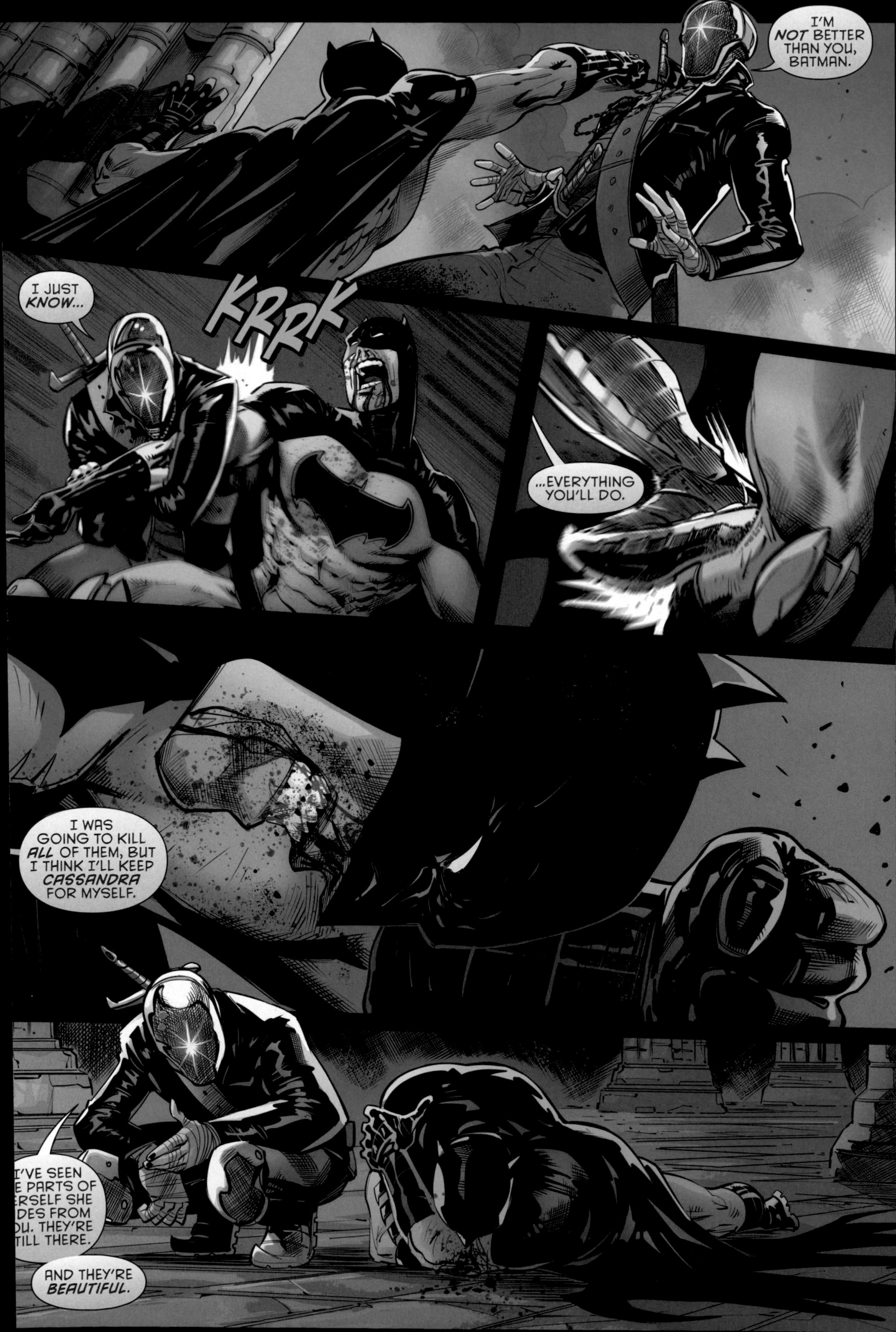
I'M *NOT* BETTER THAN YOU, BATMAN.
I JUST *KNOW*...
KRRK
...EVERYTHING YOU'LL DO.
I WAS GOING TO KILL *ALL* OF THEM, BUT I THINK I'LL KEEP *CASSANDRA* FOR MYSELF.
I'VE SEEN E PARTS OF ERSELF SHE DES FROM OU. THEY'RE TILL THERE.
AND THEY'RE *BEAUTIFUL*.

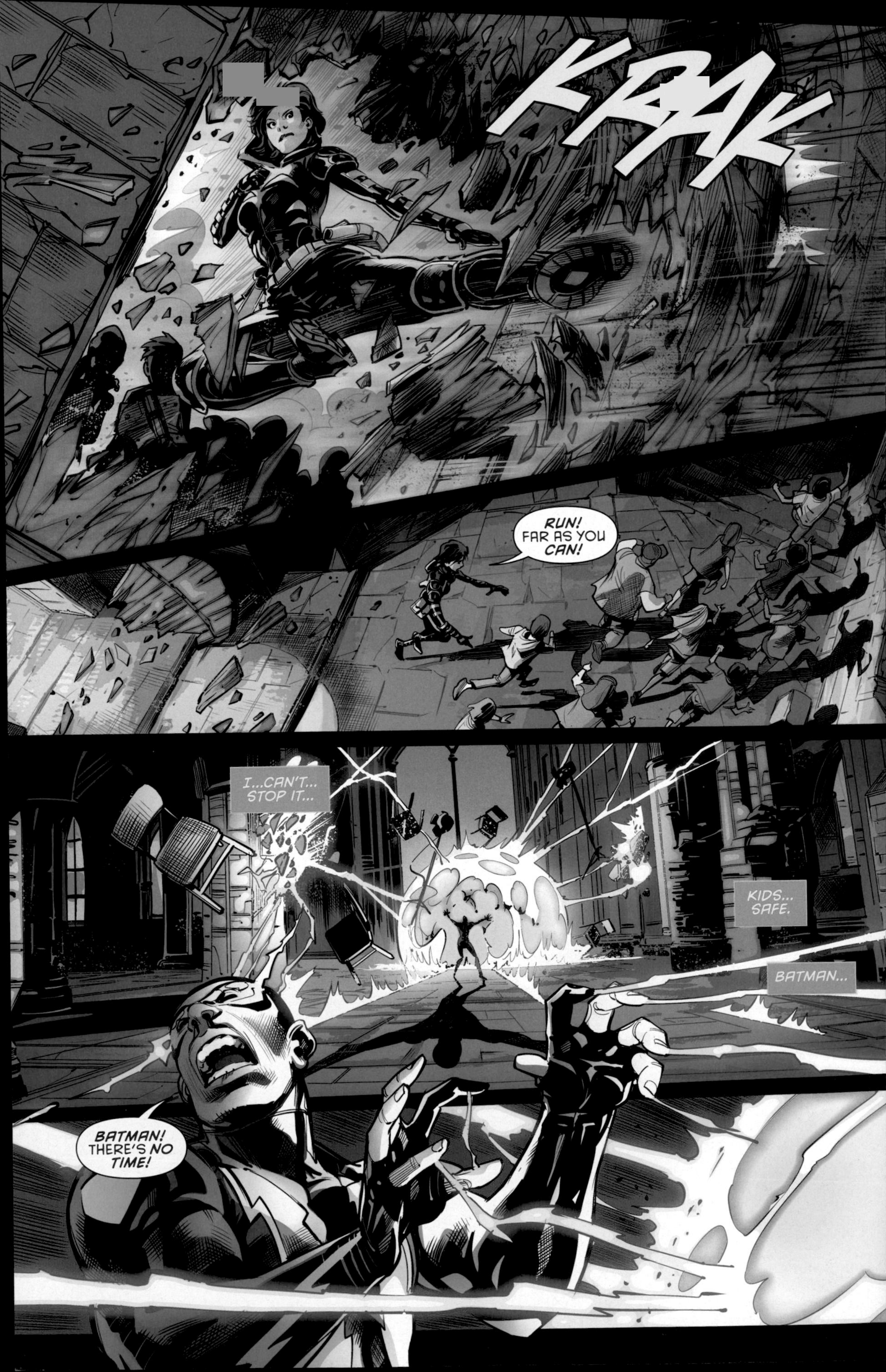
KRAK
RUN! FAR AS YOU CAN!
I...CAN'T... STOP IT...
KIDS... SAFE.
BATMAN...
BATMAN! THERE'S NO TIME!

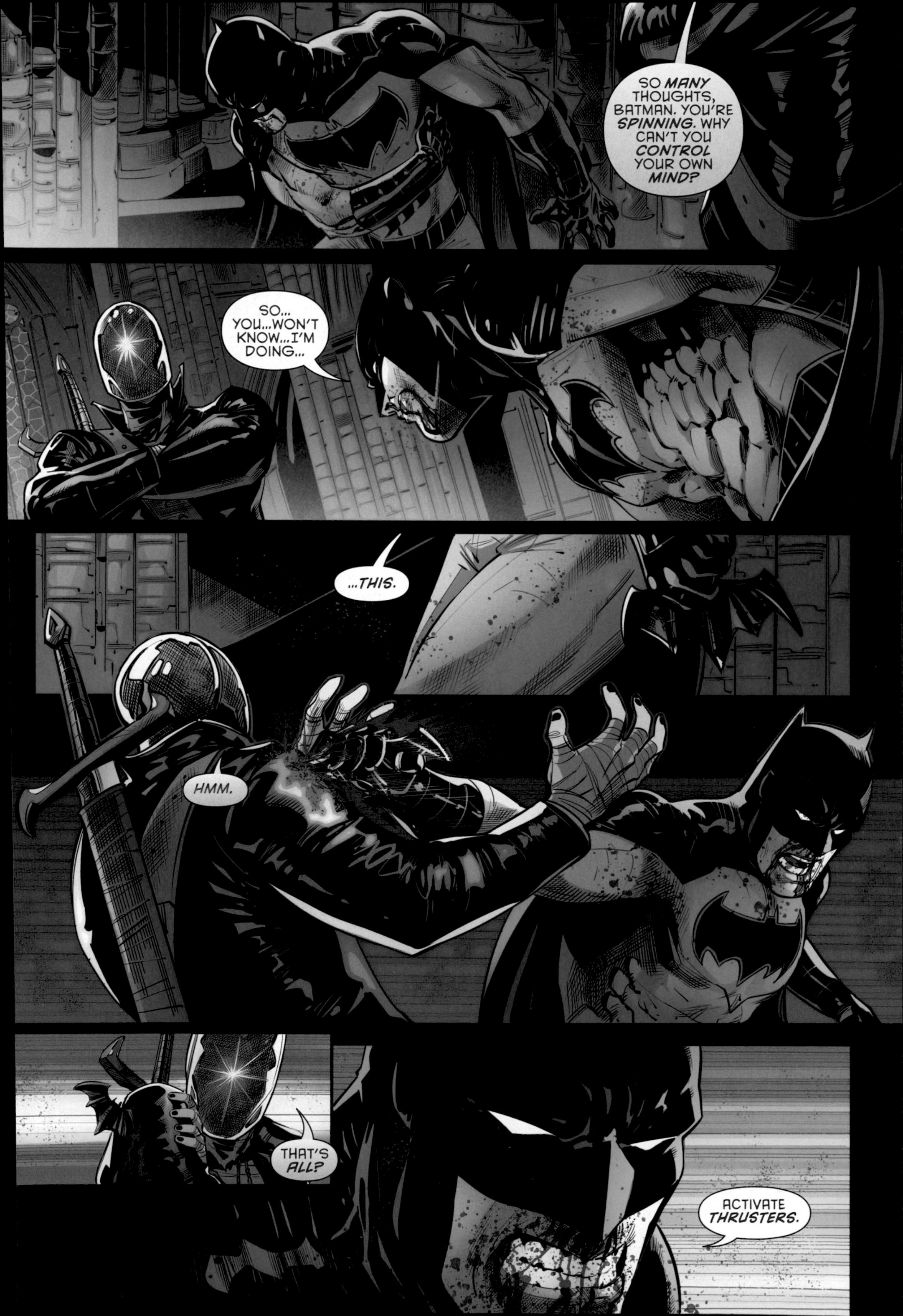
SO *MANY* THOUGHTS, BATMAN. YOU'RE *SPINNING*. WHY CAN'T YOU *CONTROL* YOUR OWN *MIND?*
SO... YOU...WON'T KNOW...I'M DOING...
...*THIS.*
HMM.
THAT'S *ALL?*
ACTIVATE *THRUSTERS.*

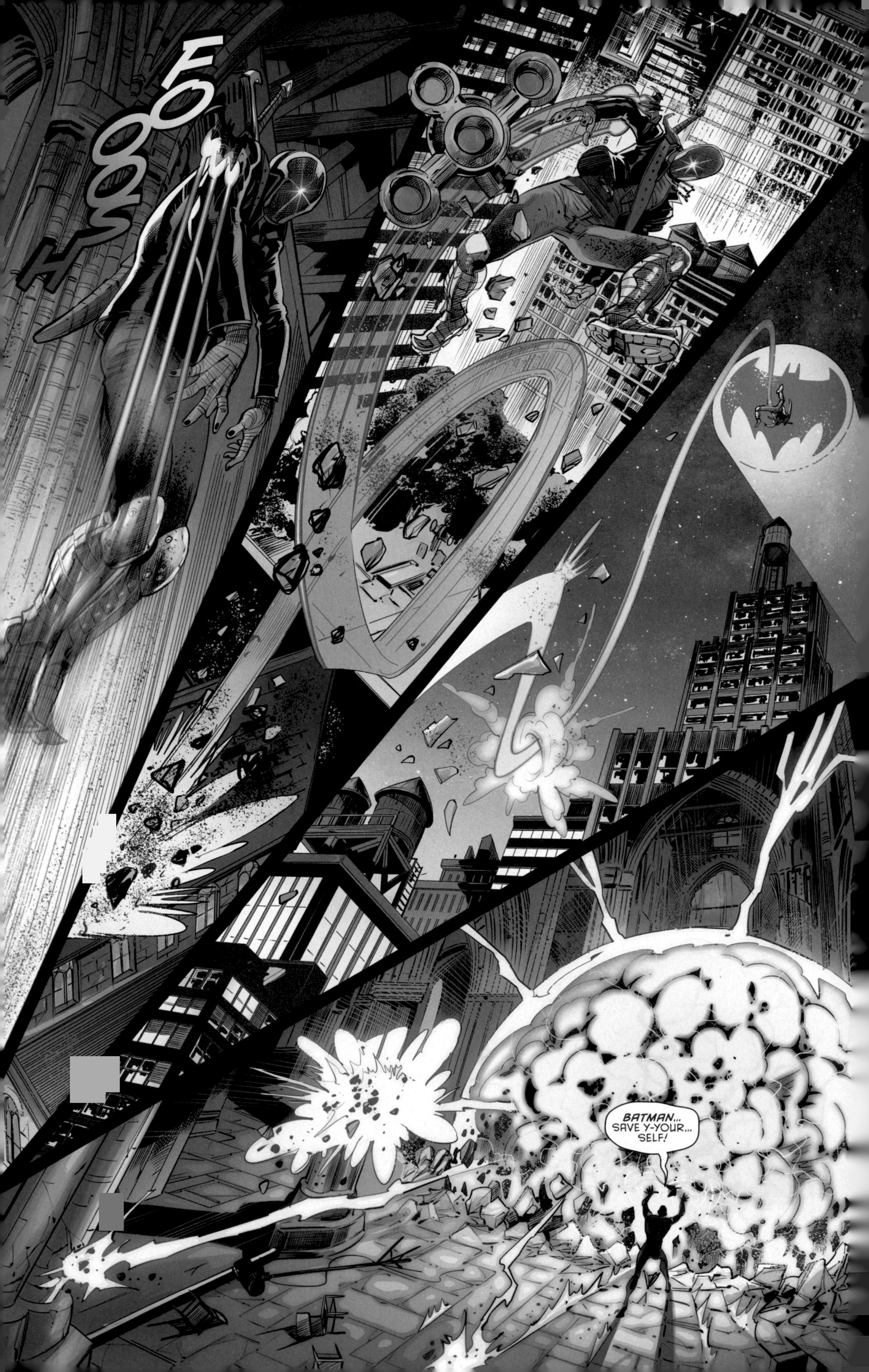
FOOOSH
BATMAN... SAVE Y-YOUR... SELF!

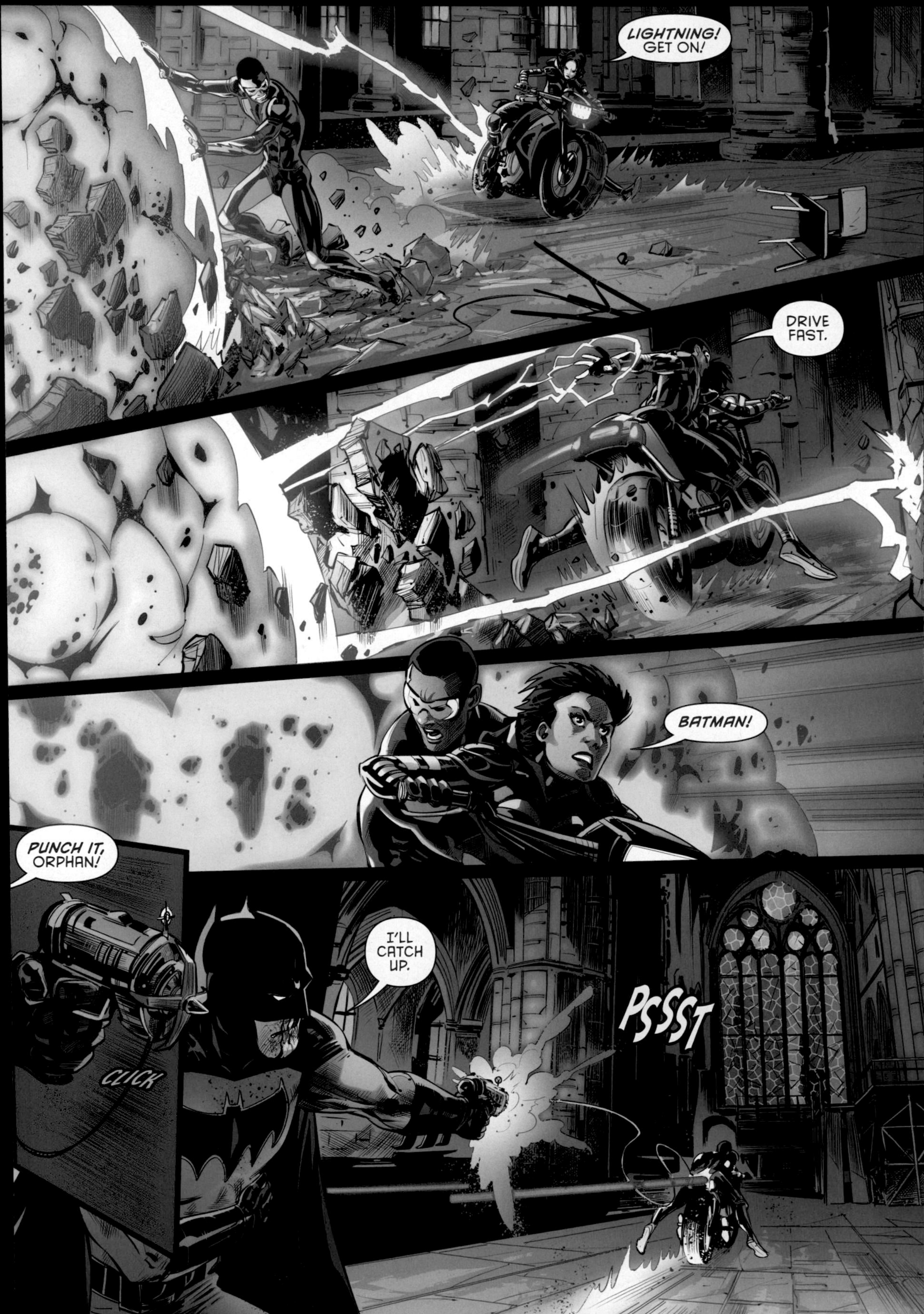
LIGHTNING! GET ON!
DRIVE FAST.
BATMAN!
PUNCH IT, ORPHAN!
I'LL CATCH UP.
PSSST
CLICK

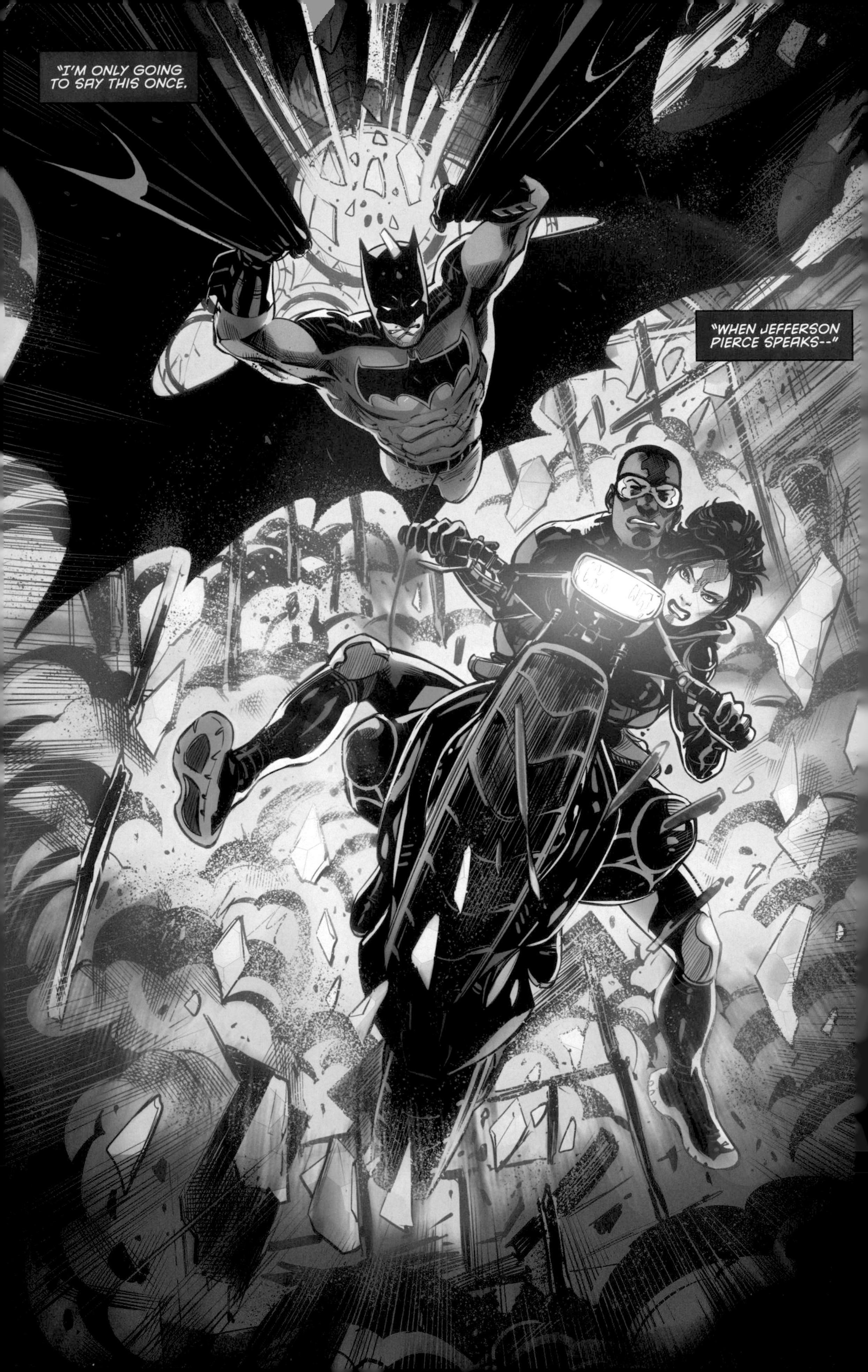
"I'M ONLY GOING TO SAY THIS ONCE.
"WHEN JEFFERSON PIERCE SPEAKS--"

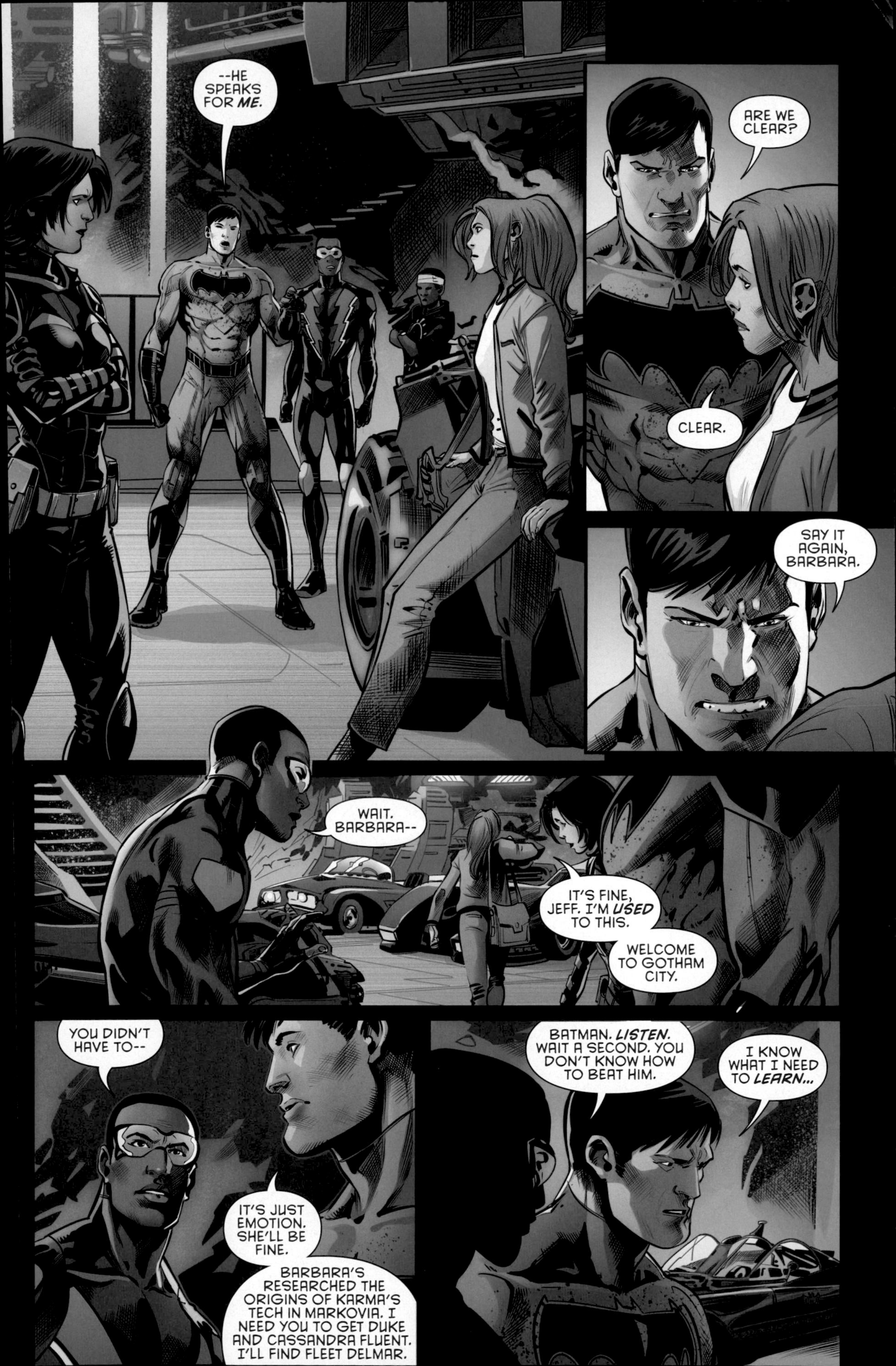
--HE SPEAKS FOR *ME.*
ARE WE CLEAR?
CLEAR.
SAY IT AGAIN, BARBARA.
WAIT. BARBARA--
IT'S FINE, JEFF. I'M *USED* TO THIS.
WELCOME TO GOTHAM CITY.
YOU DIDN'T HAVE TO--
IT'S JUST EMOTION. SHE'LL BE FINE.
BARBARA'S RESEARCHED THE ORIGINS OF KARMA'S TECH IN MARKOVIA. I NEED YOU TO GET DUKE AND CASSANDRA FLUENT. I'LL FIND FLEET DELMAR.
BATMAN. *LISTEN.* WAIT A SECOND. YOU DON'T KNOW HOW TO BEAT HIM.
I KNOW WHAT I NEED TO *LEARN...*

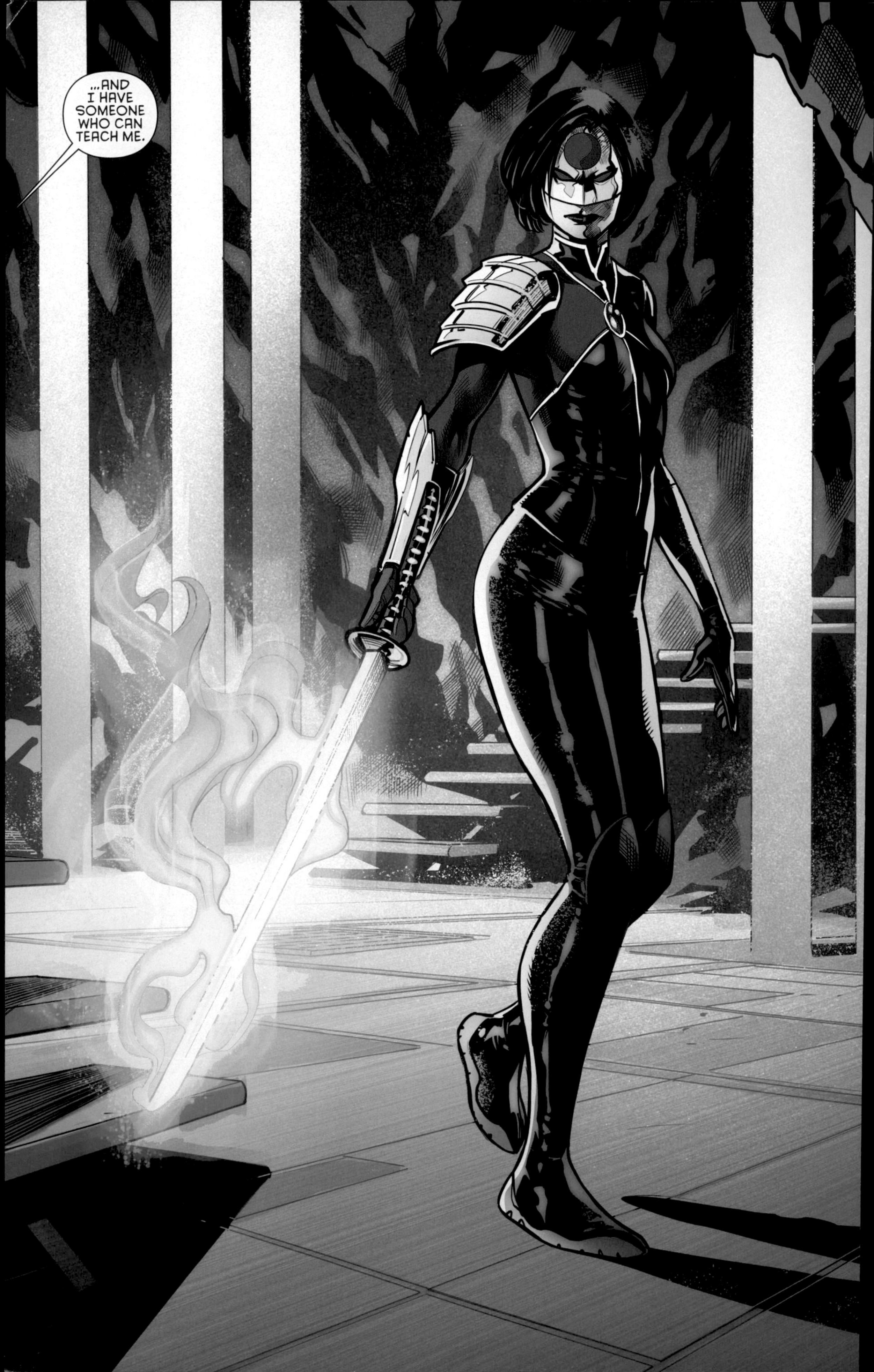
...AND I HAVE SOMEONE WHO CAN TEACH ME.

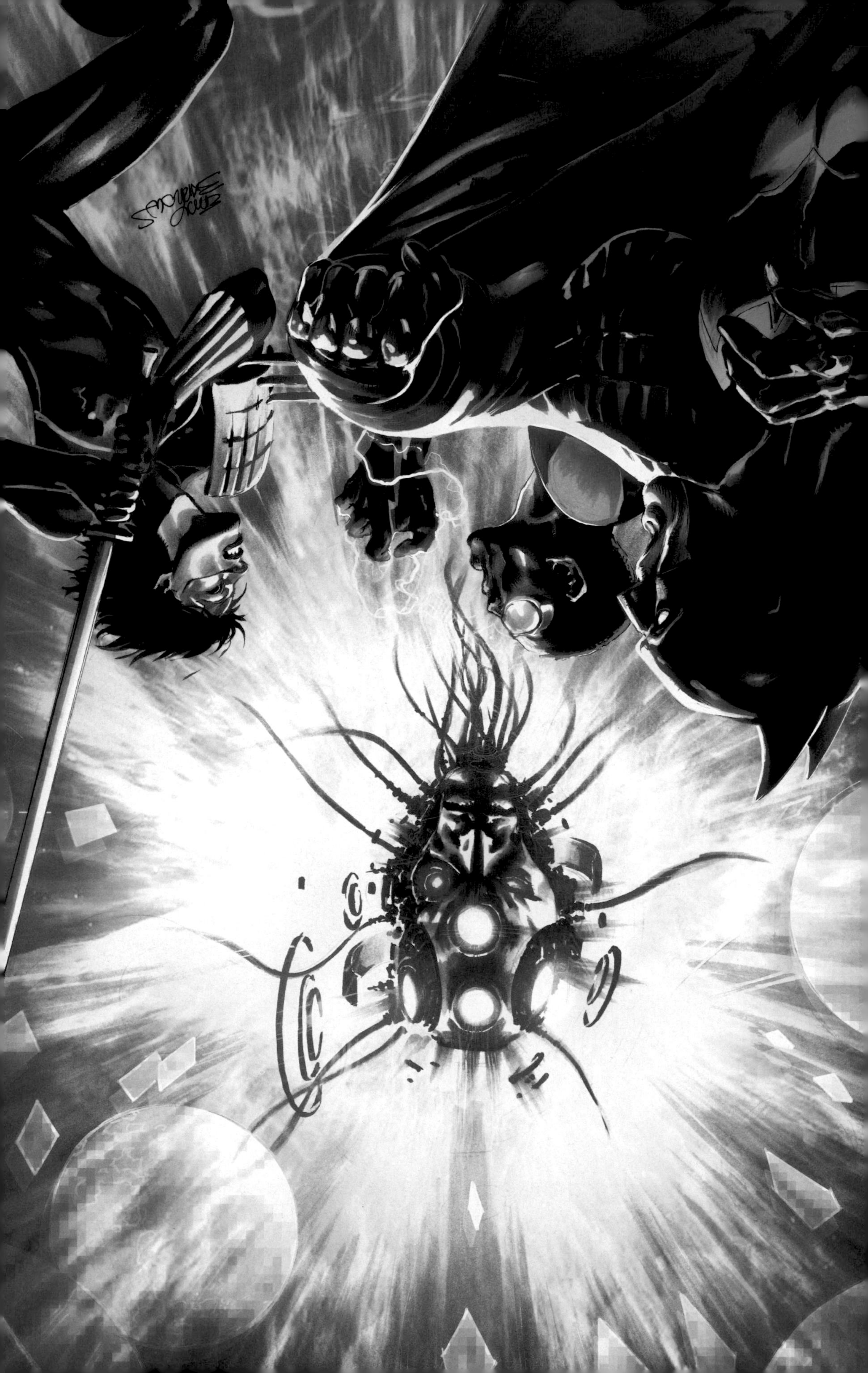

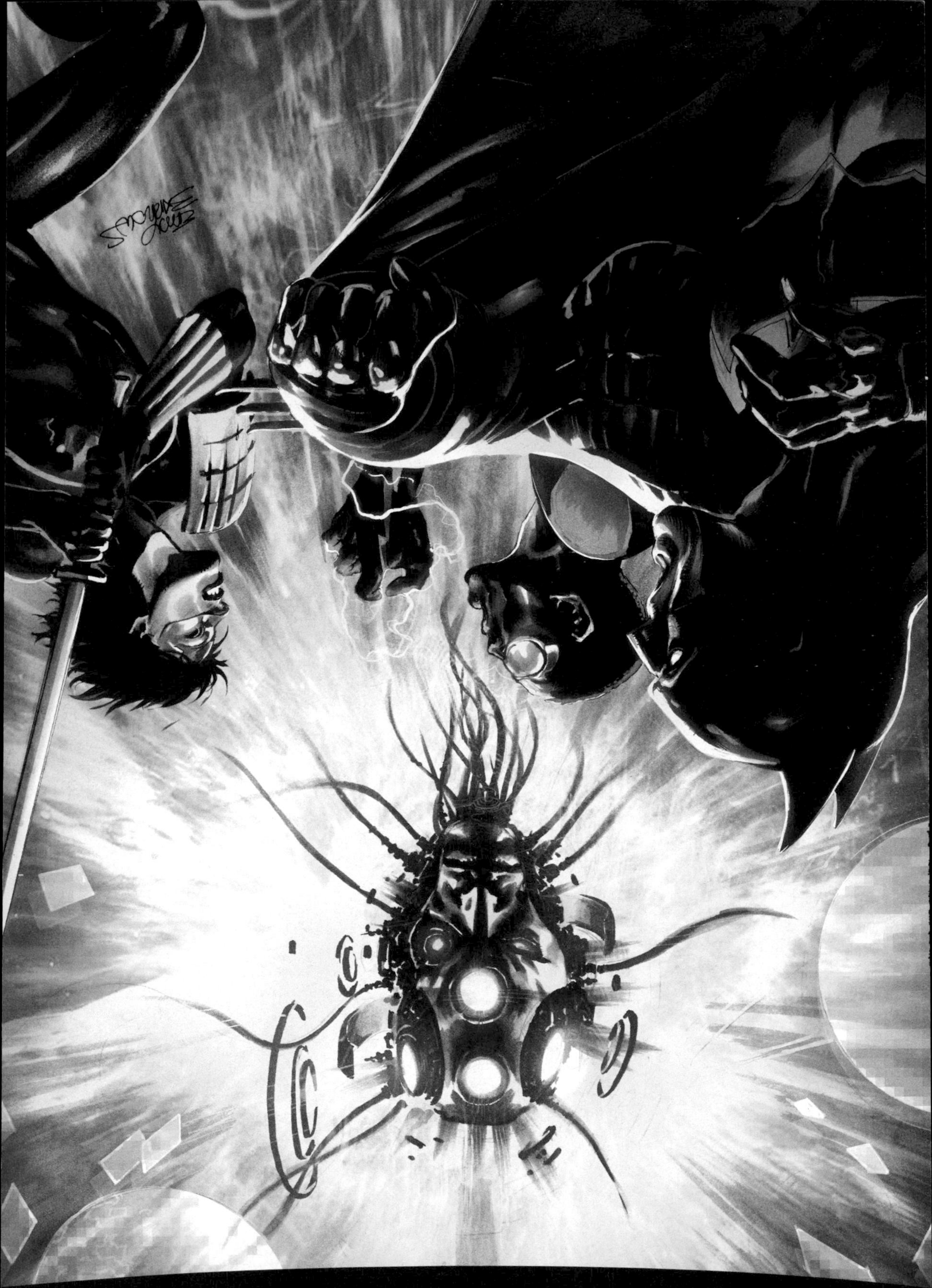

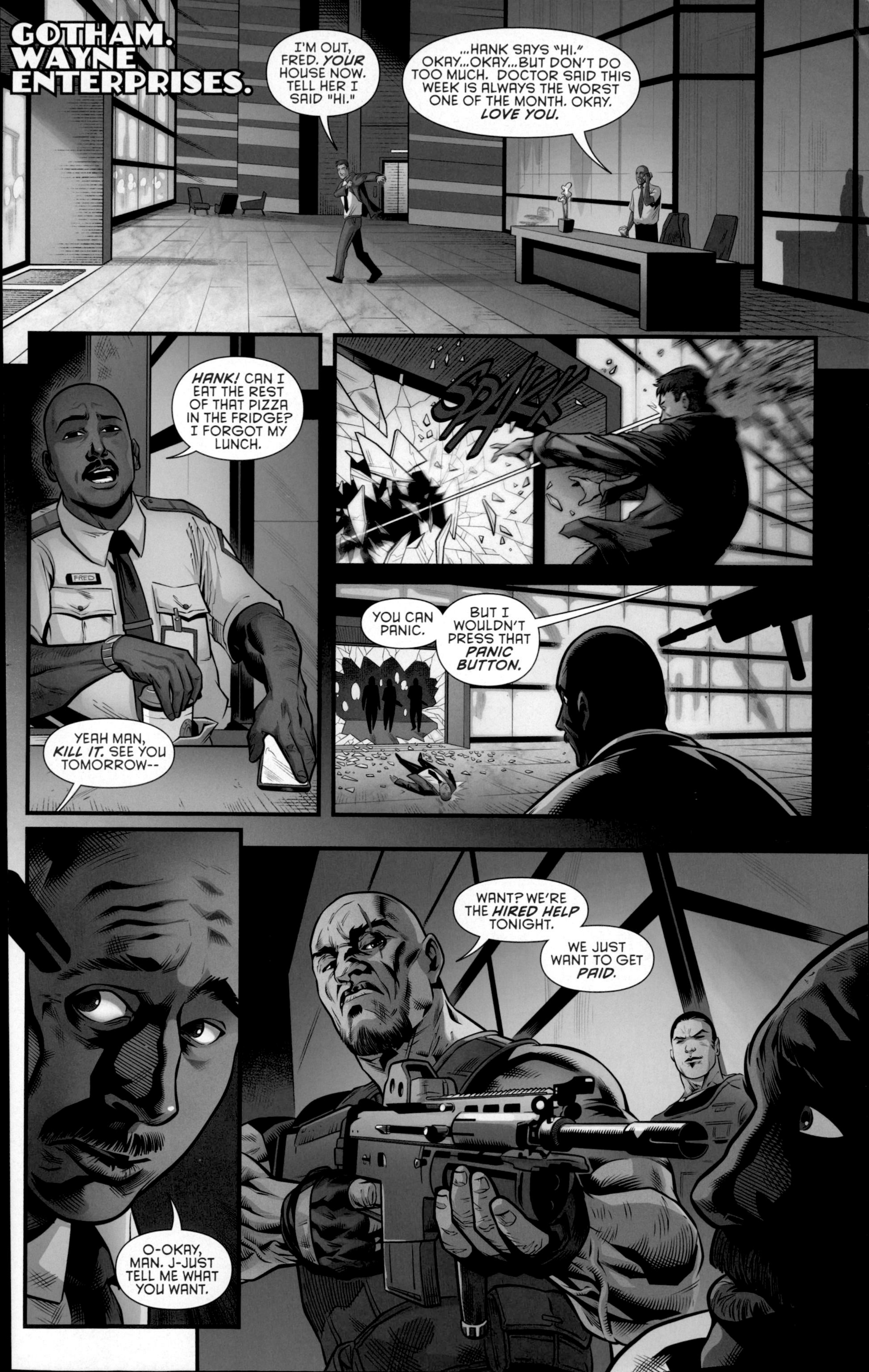
GOTHAM. WAYNE ENTERPRISES.
I'M OUT, FRED. YOUR HOUSE NOW. TELL HER I SAID "HI."
...HANK SAYS "HI." OKAY...OKAY...BUT DON'T DO TOO MUCH. DOCTOR SAID THIS WEEK IS ALWAYS THE WORST ONE OF THE MONTH. OKAY. LOVE YOU.
HANK! CAN I EAT THE REST OF THAT PIZZA IN THE FRIDGE? I FORGOT MY LUNCH.
YEAH MAN, KILL IT. SEE YOU TOMORROW--
FRED
SPAKK
YOU CAN PANIC.
BUT I WOULDN'T PRESS THAT PANIC BUTTON.
O-OKAY, MAN. J-JUST TELL ME WHAT YOU WANT.
WANT? WE'RE THE HIRED HELP TONIGHT.
WE JUST WANT TO GET PAID.

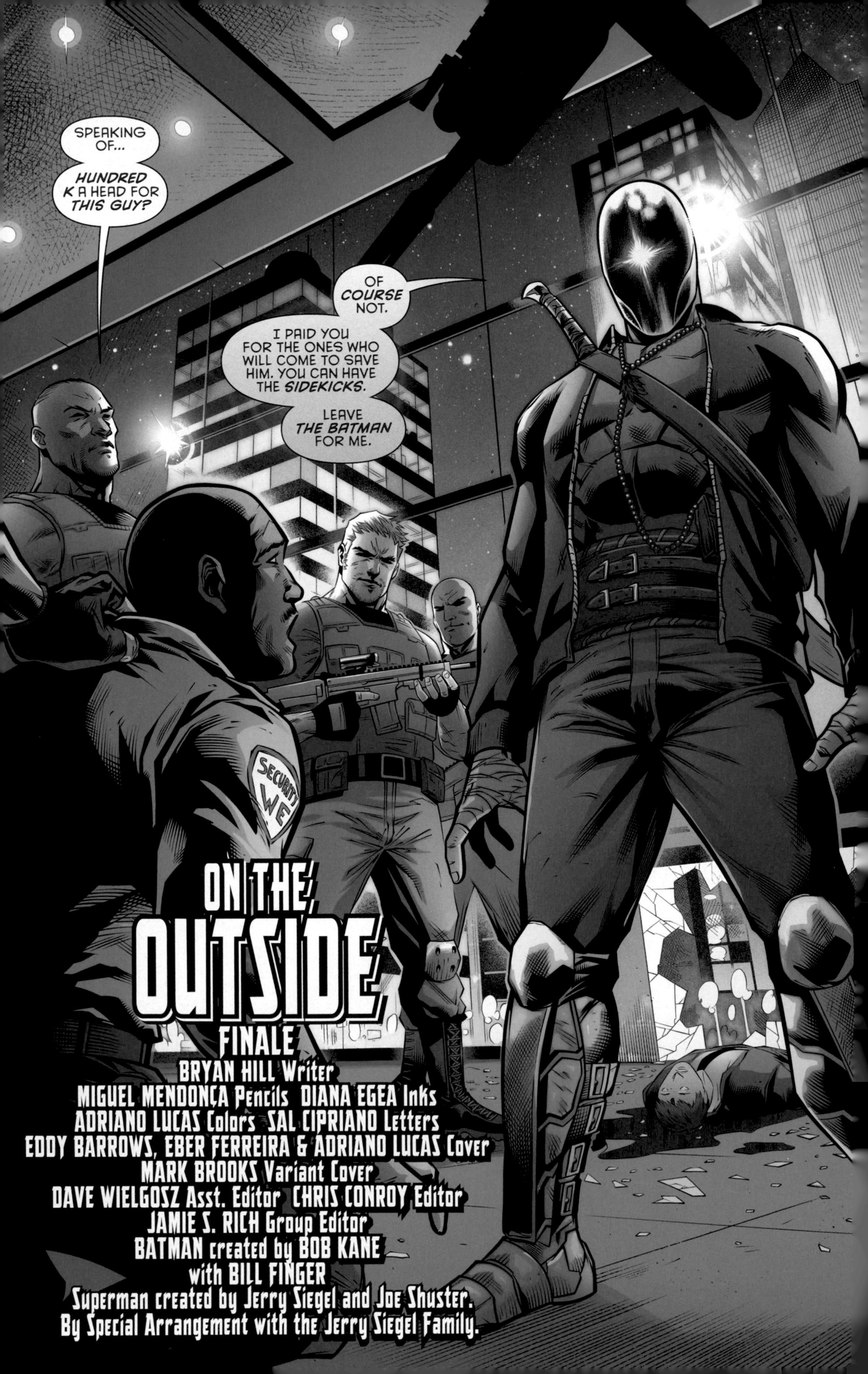
SPEAKING OF...
HUNDRED K A HEAD FOR THIS GUY?
OF COURSE NOT.
I PAID YOU FOR THE ONES WHO WILL COME TO SAVE HIM. YOU CAN HAVE THE SIDEKICKS.
LEAVE THE BATMAN FOR ME.
SECURITY WE
ON THE OUTSIDE
FINALE
BRYAN HILL Writer
MIGUEL MENDONÇA Pencils DIANA EGEA Inks
ADRIANO LUCAS Colors SAL CIPRIANO Letters
EDDY BARROWS, EBER FERREIRA & ADRIANO LUCAS Cover
MARK BROOKS Variant Cover
DAVE WIELGOSZ Asst. Editor CHRIS CONROY Editor
JAMIE S. RICH Group Editor
BATMAN created by BOB KANE
with BILL FINGER
Superman created by Jerry Siegel and Joe Shuster.
By Special Arrangement with the Jerry Siegel Family.

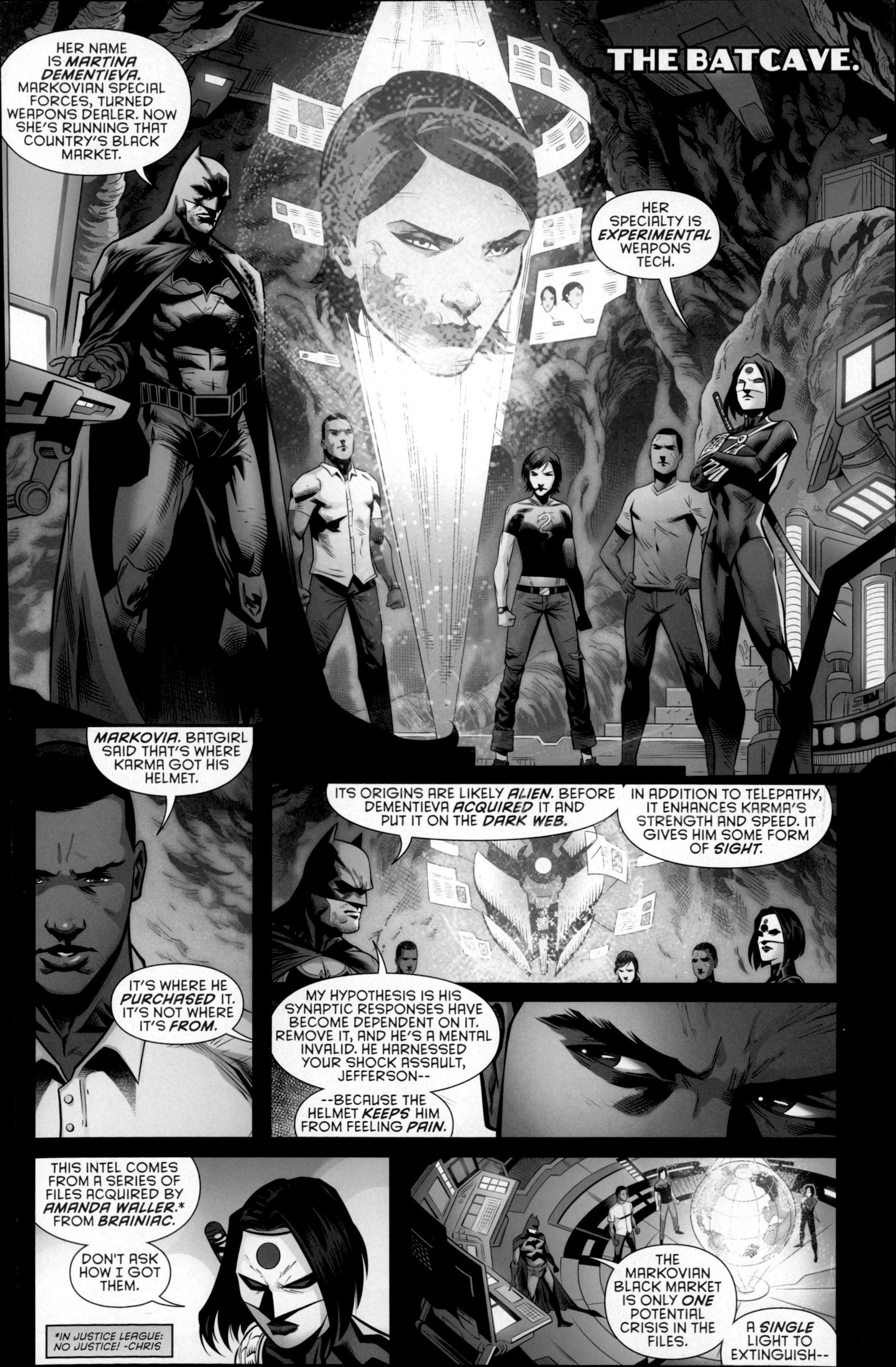
THE BATCAVE.
HER NAME IS *MARTINA DEMENTIEVA.* MARKOVIAN SPECIAL FORCES, TURNED WEAPONS DEALER. NOW SHE'S RUNNING THAT COUNTRY'S BLACK MARKET.
HER SPECIALTY IS *EXPERIMENTAL* WEAPONS TECH.
MARKOVIA. BATGIRL SAID THAT'S WHERE KARMA GOT HIS HELMET.
IT'S WHERE HE *PURCHASED* IT. IT'S NOT WHERE IT'S *FROM.*
ITS ORIGINS ARE LIKELY *ALIEN.* BEFORE DEMENTIEVA *ACQUIRED* IT AND PUT IT ON THE *DARK WEB.*
IN ADDITION TO TELEPATHY, IT ENHANCES KARMA'S STRENGTH AND SPEED. IT GIVES HIM SOME FORM OF *SIGHT.*
MY HYPOTHESIS IS HIS SYNAPTIC RESPONSES HAVE BECOME DEPENDENT ON IT. REMOVE IT, AND HE'S A MENTAL INVALID. HE HARNESSED YOUR SHOCK ASSAULT, JEFFERSON--
--BECAUSE THE HELMET *KEEPS* HIM FROM FEELING *PAIN.*
THIS INTEL COMES FROM A SERIES OF FILES ACQUIRED BY *AMANDA WALLER.** FROM *BRAINIAC.*
DON'T ASK HOW I GOT THEM.
*IN *JUSTICE LEAGUE: NO JUSTICE!* -CHRIS
THE MARKOVIAN BLACK MARKET IS ONLY *ONE* POTENTIAL CRISIS IN THE FILES.
A *SINGLE* LIGHT TO EXTINGUISH--

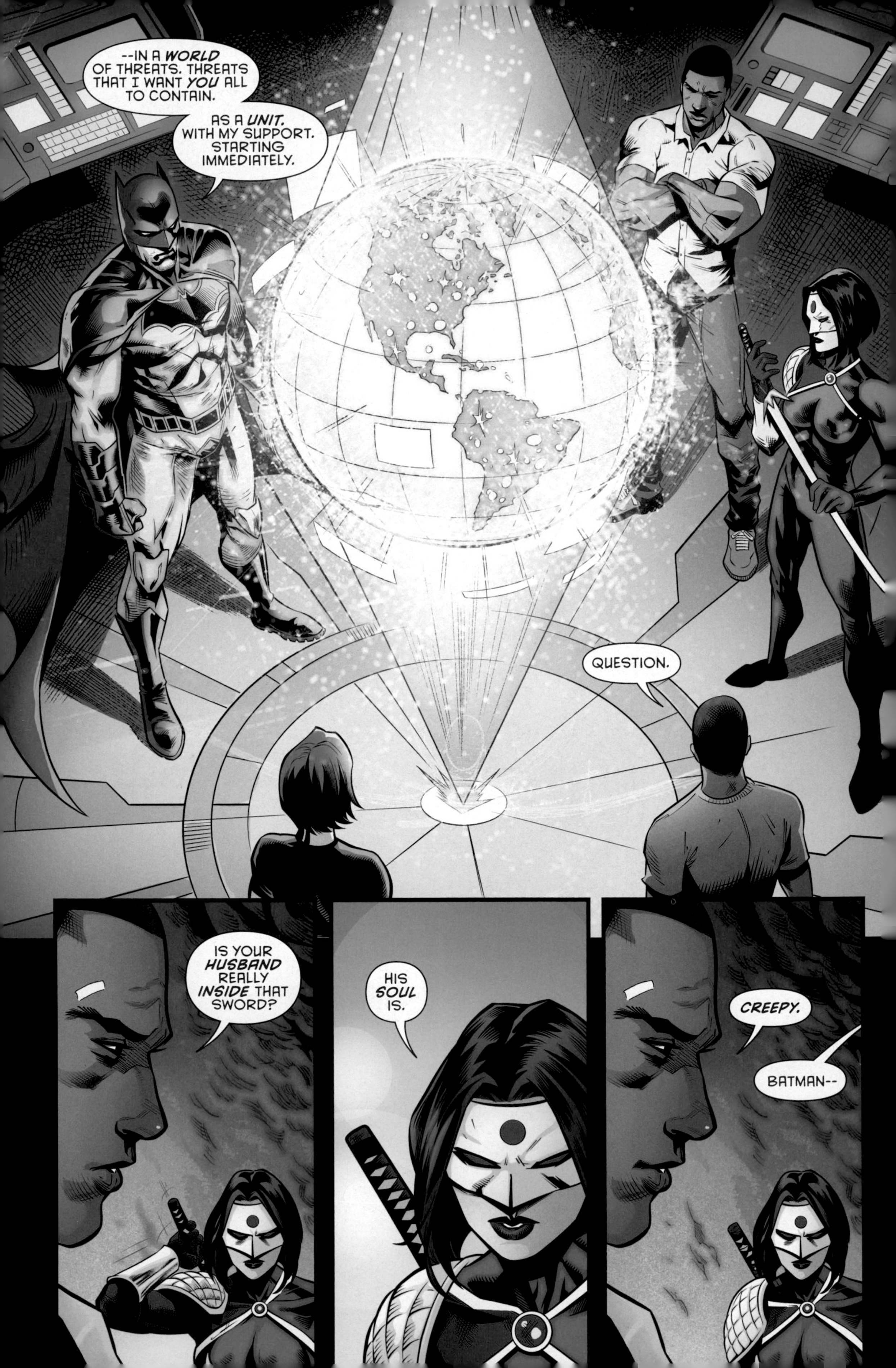
--IN A *WORLD* OF THREATS. THREATS THAT I WANT *YOU* ALL TO CONTAIN.
AS A *UNIT.* WITH MY SUPPORT. STARTING IMMEDIATELY.
QUESTION.
IS YOUR *HUSBAND* REALLY *INSIDE* THAT SWORD?
HIS *SOUL* IS.
CREEPY.
BATMAN--

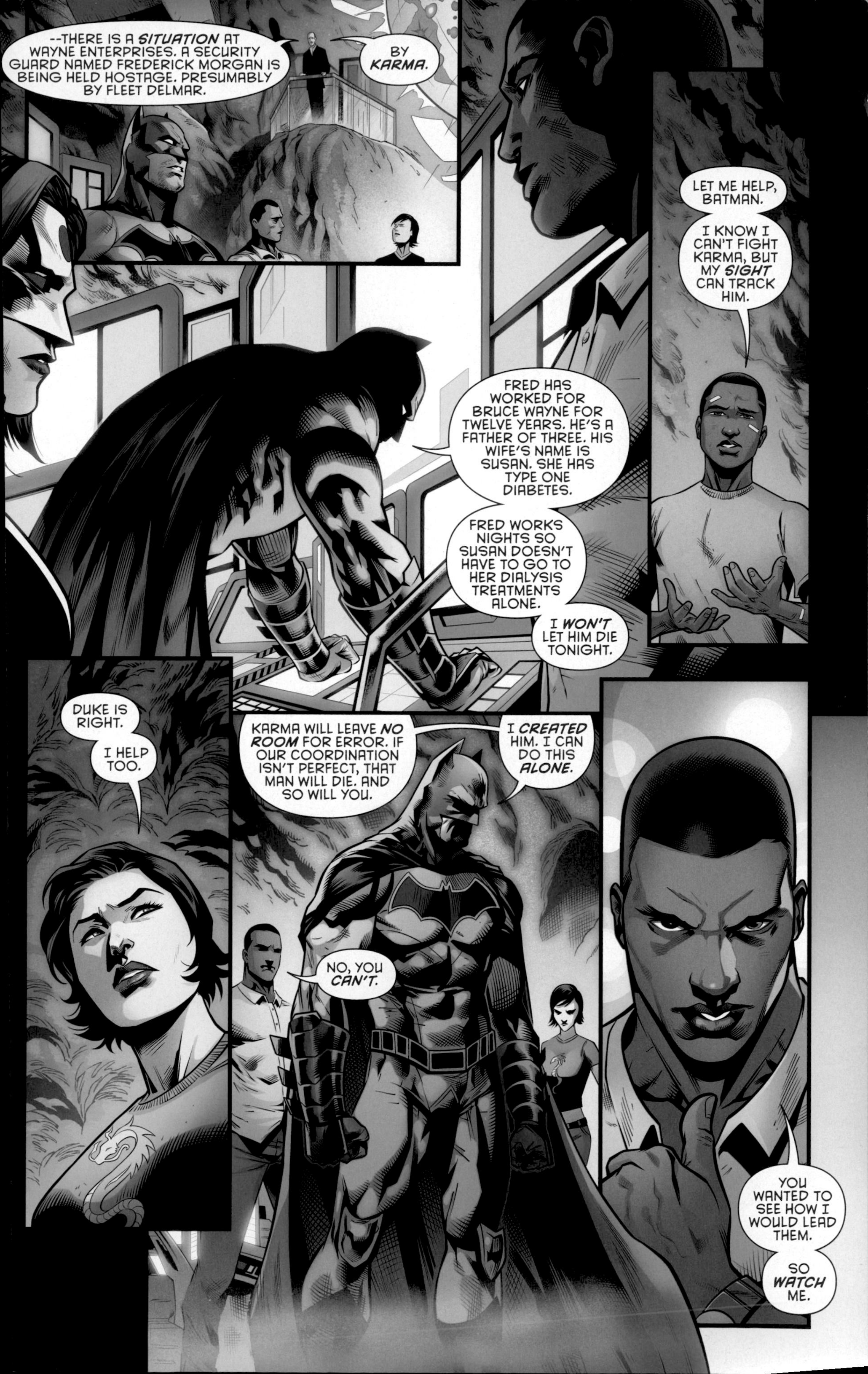
--THERE IS A *SITUATION* AT WAYNE ENTERPRISES. A SECURITY GUARD NAMED FREDERICK MORGAN IS BEING HELD HOSTAGE. PRESUMABLY BY FLEET DELMAR.
BY *KARMA*.
FRED HAS WORKED FOR BRUCE WAYNE FOR TWELVE YEARS. HE'S A FATHER OF THREE. HIS WIFE'S NAME IS SUSAN. SHE HAS TYPE ONE DIABETES.
FRED WORKS NIGHTS SO SUSAN DOESN'T HAVE TO GO TO HER DIALYSIS TREATMENTS ALONE.
I *WON'T* LET HIM DIE TONIGHT.
LET ME HELP, BATMAN.
I KNOW I CAN'T FIGHT KARMA, BUT MY *SIGHT* CAN TRACK HIM.
DUKE IS RIGHT.
I HELP TOO.
KARMA WILL LEAVE *NO ROOM* FOR ERROR. IF OUR COORDINATION ISN'T PERFECT, THAT MAN WILL DIE. AND SO WILL YOU.
I *CREATED* HIM. I CAN DO THIS *ALONE*.
NO, YOU *CAN'T*.
YOU WANTED TO SEE HOW I WOULD LEAD THEM.
SO *WATCH* ME.

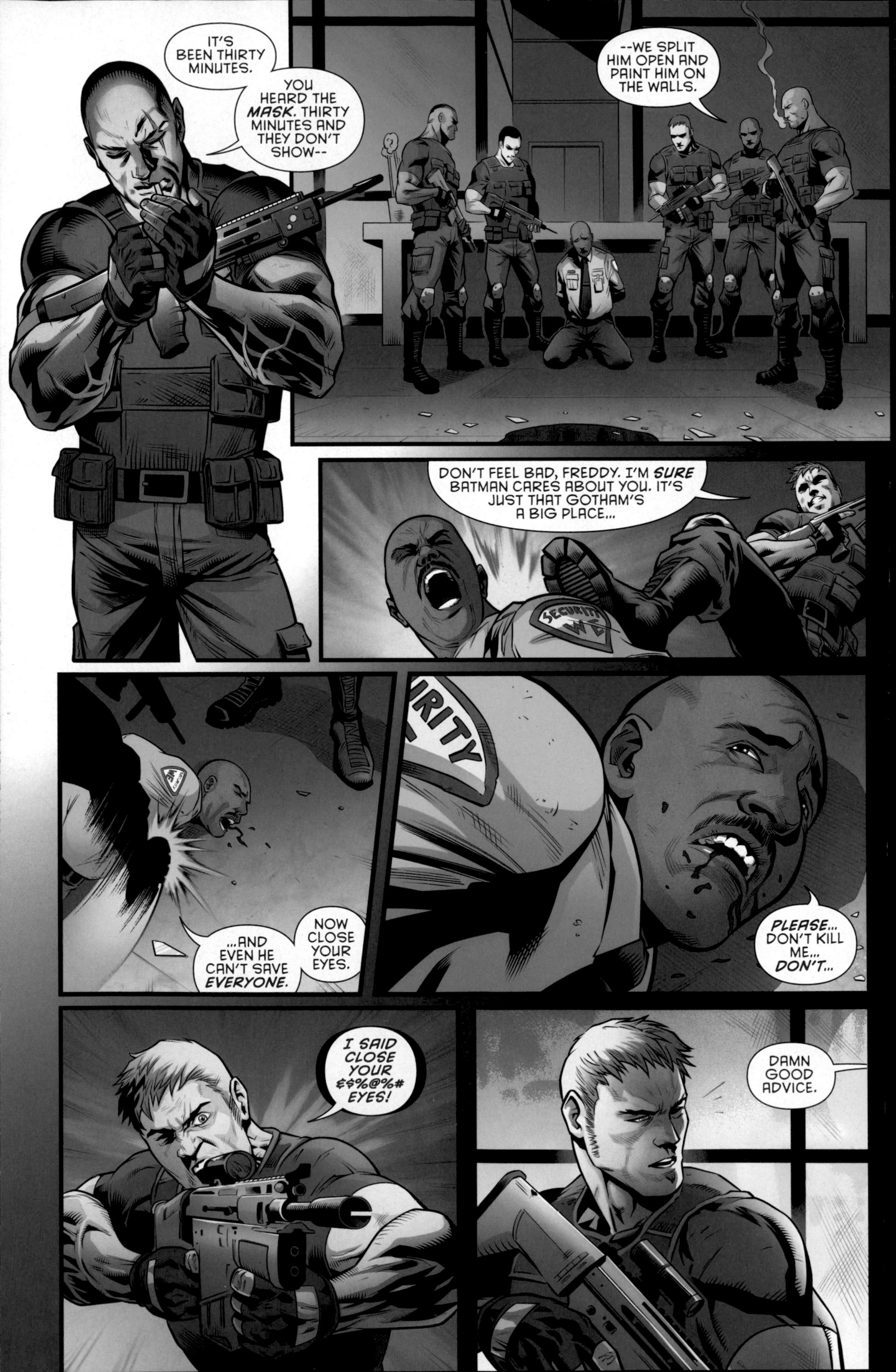
IT'S BEEN THIRTY MINUTES.
YOU HEARD THE *MASK*. THIRTY MINUTES AND THEY DON'T SHOW--
--WE SPLIT HIM OPEN AND PAINT HIM ON THE WALLS.
DON'T FEEL BAD, FREDDY. I'M *SURE* BATMAN CARES ABOUT YOU. IT'S JUST THAT GOTHAM'S A BIG PLACE...
SECURITY
WE
NOW CLOSE YOUR EYES.
...AND EVEN HE CAN'T SAVE *EVERYONE*.
PLEASE... DON'T KILL ME... *DON'T*...
I SAID CLOSE YOUR $%@%# EYES!
DAMN GOOD ADVICE.

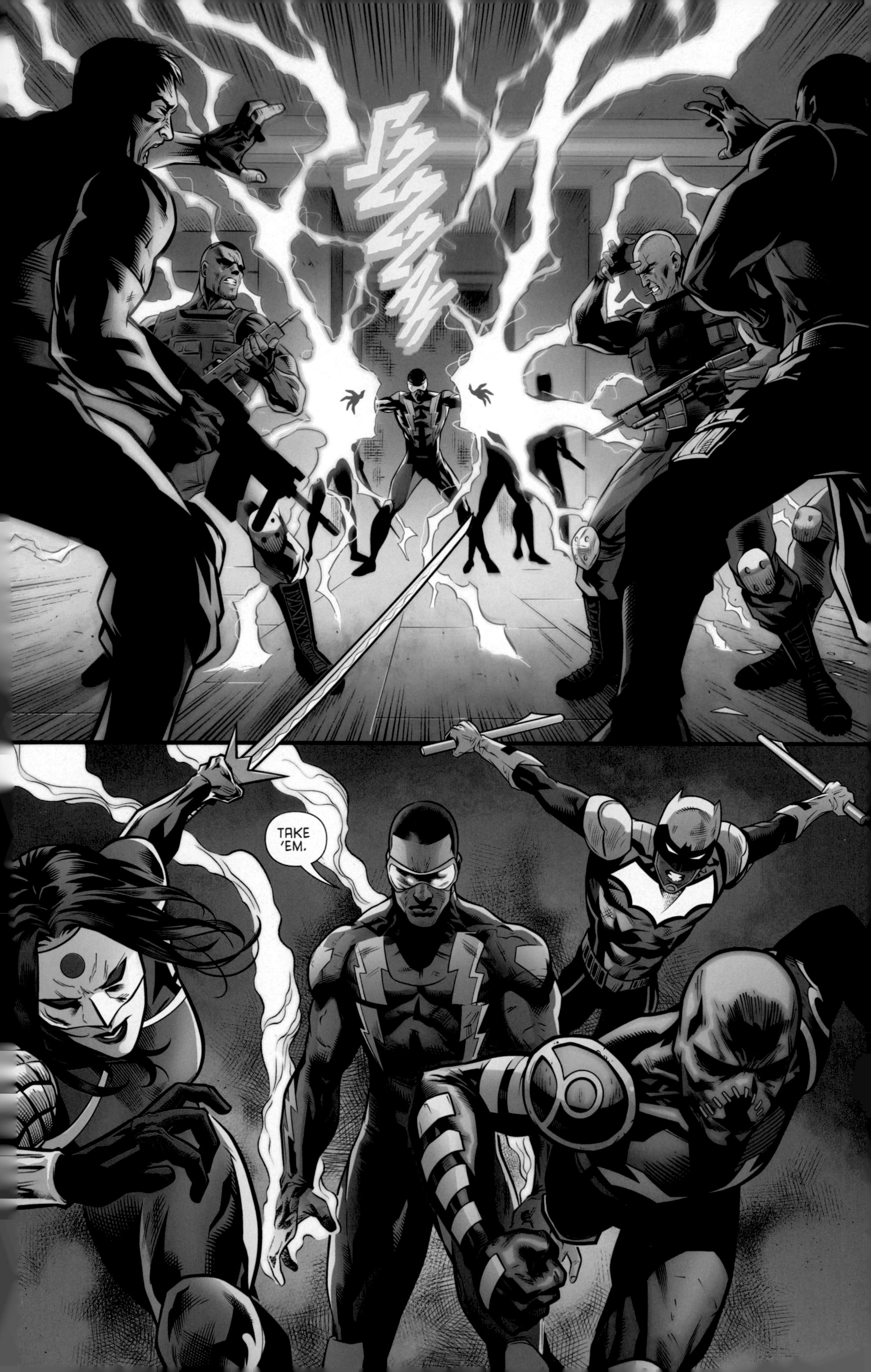
TAKE 'EM.

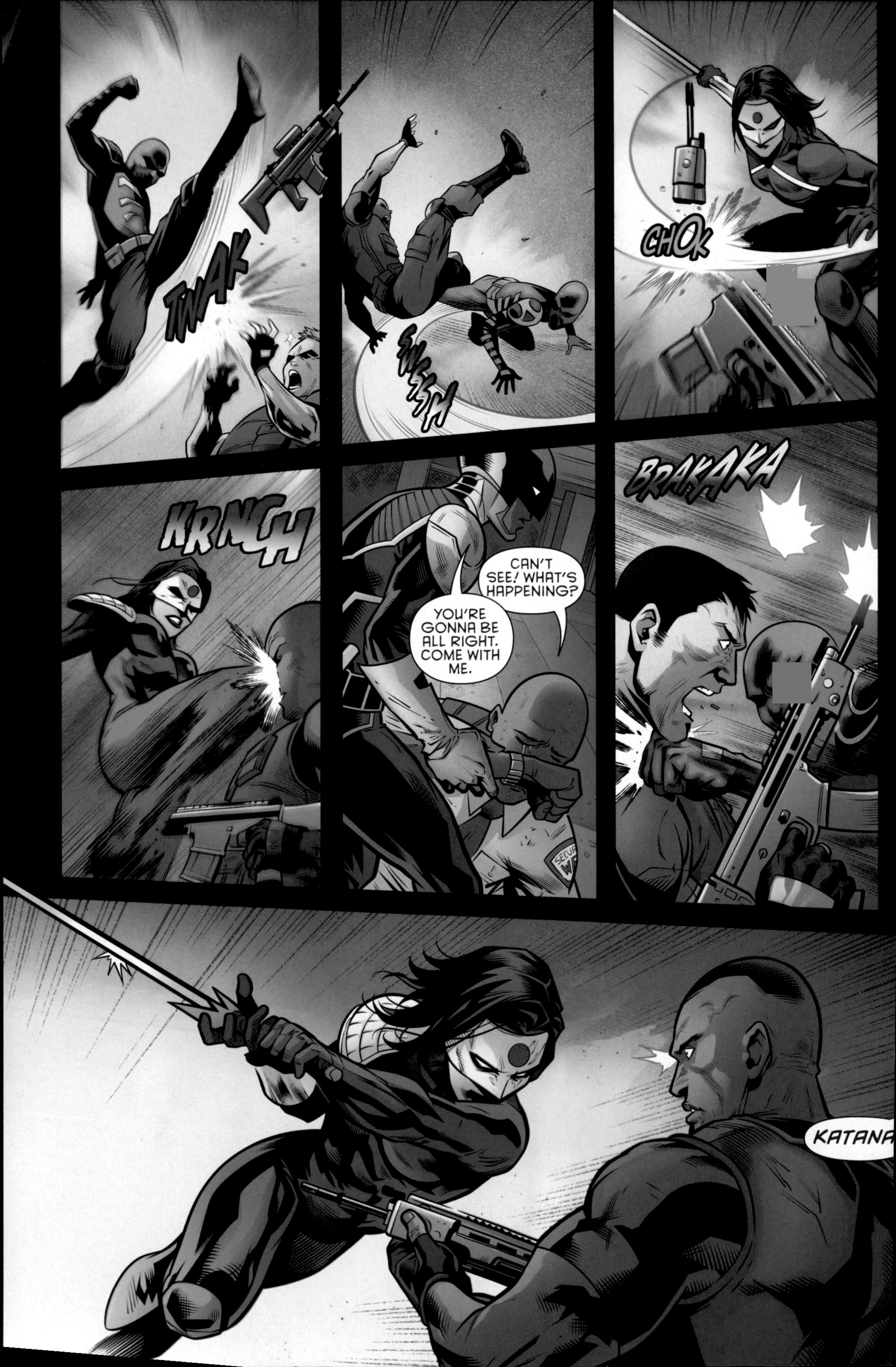
TWAK
SWSSH
CHOK
KRNCH
CAN'T SEE! WHAT'S HAPPENING?
YOU'RE GONNA BE ALL RIGHT. COME WITH ME.
BRAKAKA
KATANA

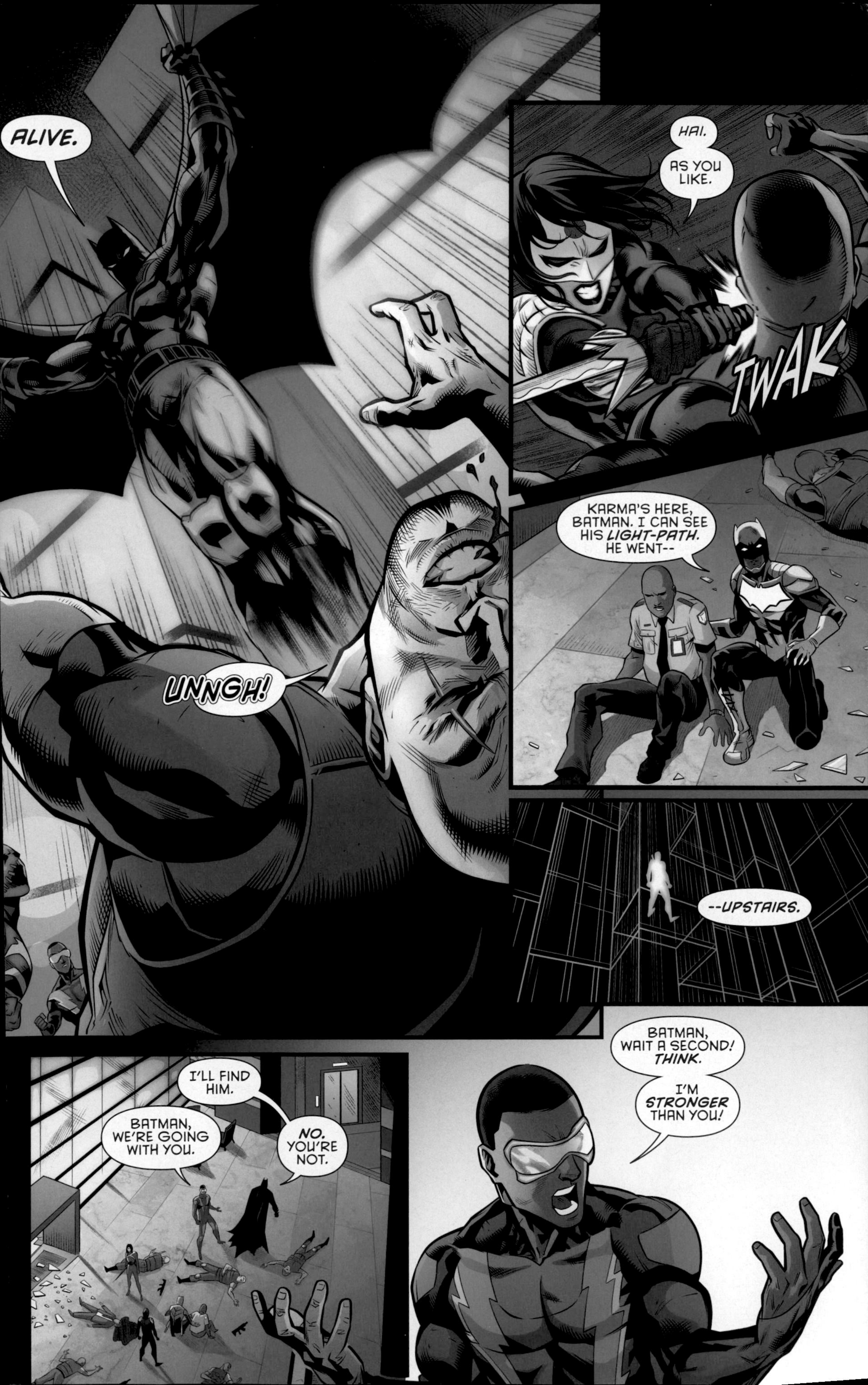
ALIVE.
HAI.
AS YOU LIKE.
TWAK
UNNGH!
KARMA'S HERE, BATMAN. I CAN SEE HIS LIGHT-PATH. HE WENT--
--UPSTAIRS.
I'LL FIND HIM.
BATMAN, WE'RE GOING WITH YOU.
NO. YOU'RE NOT.
BATMAN, WAIT A SECOND! THINK.
I'M STRONGER THAN YOU!

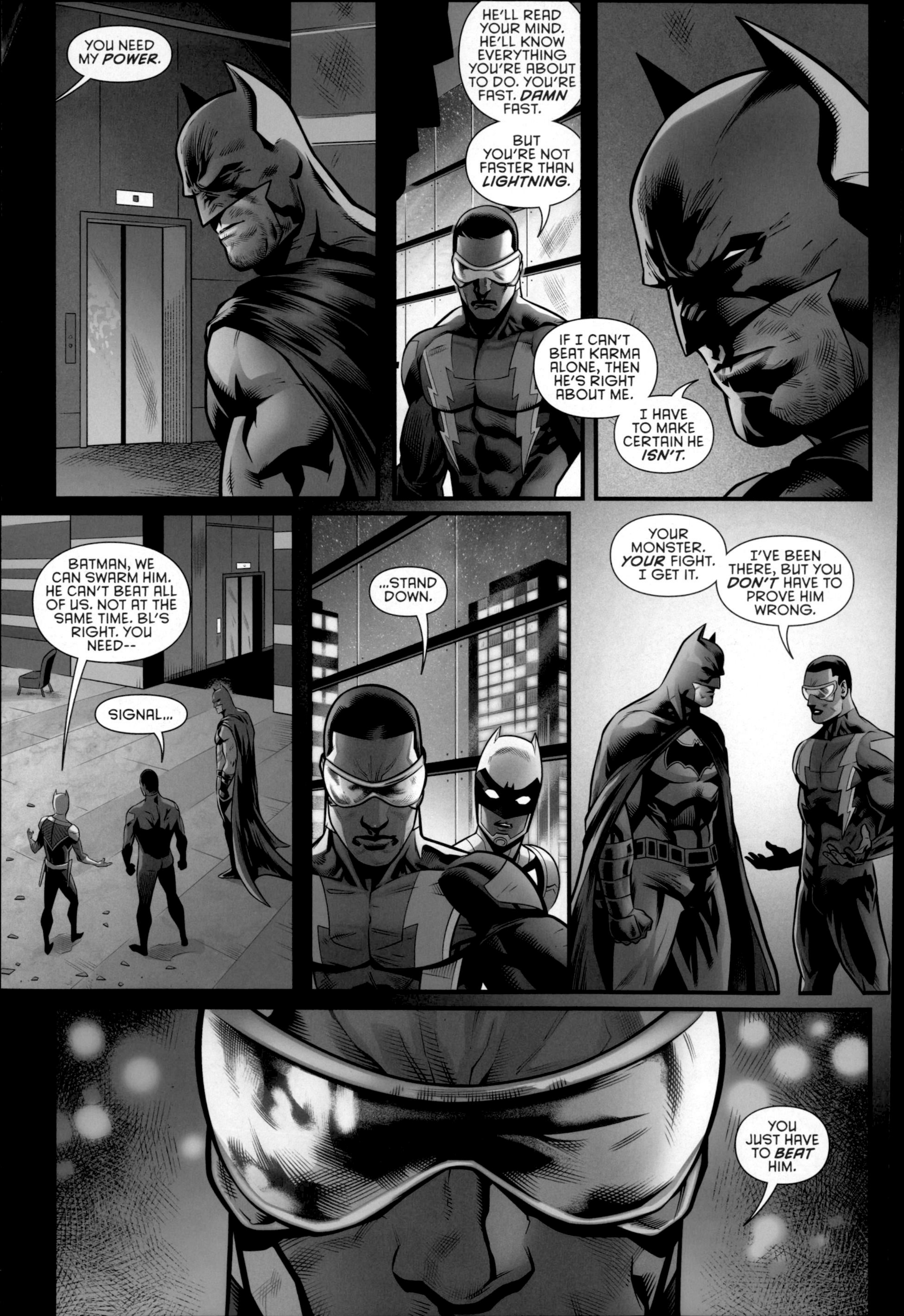
YOU NEED MY *POWER*.
HE'LL READ YOUR MIND. HE'LL KNOW EVERYTHING YOU'RE ABOUT TO DO. YOU'RE FAST. *DAMN* FAST.
BUT YOU'RE NOT FASTER THAN *LIGHTNING*.
IF I CAN'T BEAT KARMA ALONE, THEN HE'S RIGHT ABOUT ME.
I HAVE TO MAKE CERTAIN HE *ISN'T*.
BATMAN, WE CAN SWARM HIM. HE CAN'T BEAT ALL OF US. NOT AT THE SAME TIME. BL'S RIGHT. YOU NEED--
SIGNAL...
...STAND DOWN.
YOUR MONSTER. *YOUR* FIGHT. I GET IT.
I'VE BEEN THERE, BUT YOU *DON'T* HAVE TO PROVE HIM WRONG.
YOU JUST HAVE TO *BEAT* HIM.

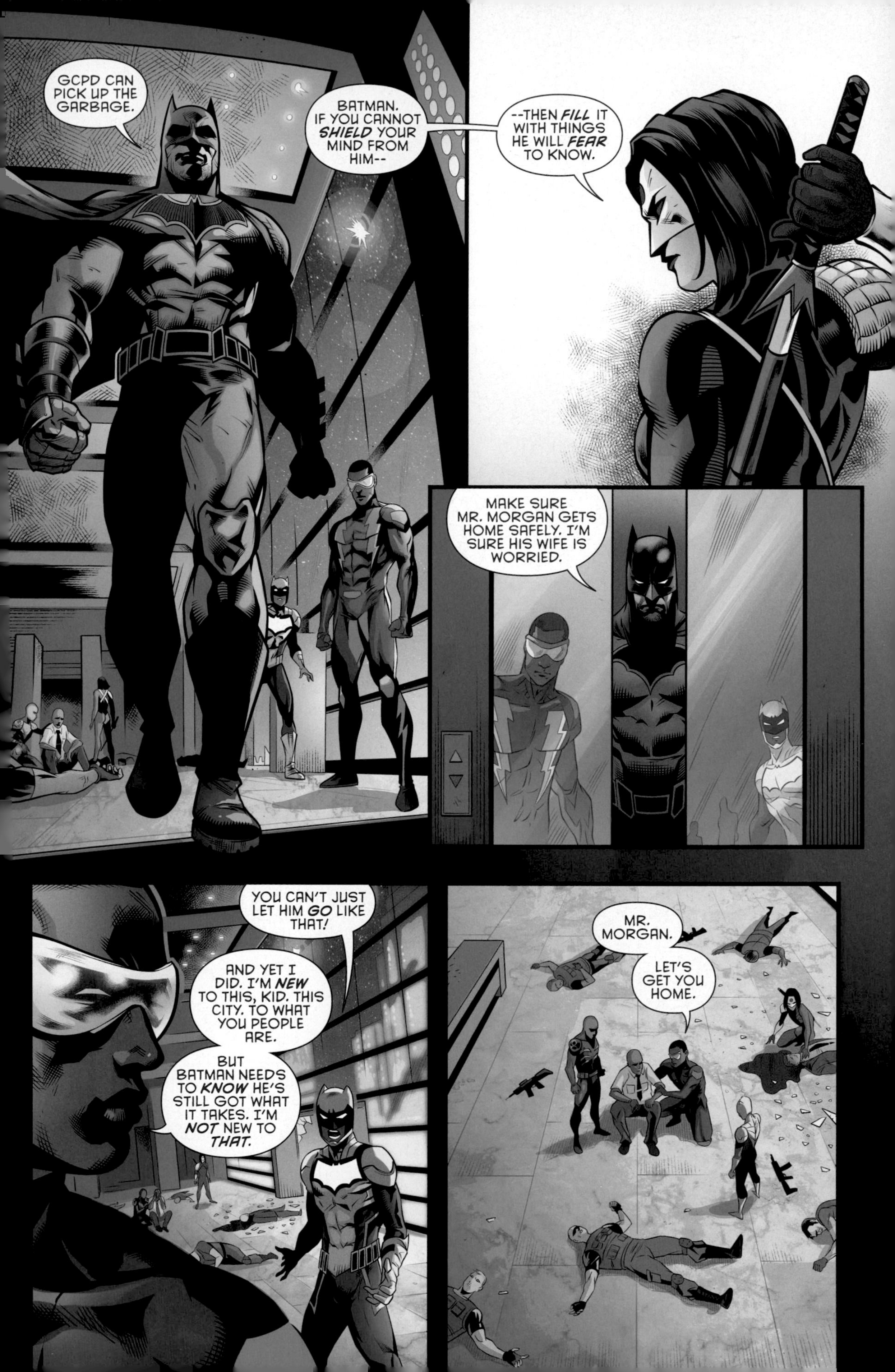
GCPD CAN PICK UP THE GARBAGE.
BATMAN. IF YOU CANNOT SHIELD YOUR MIND FROM HIM--
--THEN FILL IT WITH THINGS HE WILL FEAR TO KNOW.
MAKE SURE MR. MORGAN GETS HOME SAFELY. I'M SURE HIS WIFE IS WORRIED.
YOU CAN'T JUST LET HIM GO LIKE THAT!
AND YET I DID. I'M NEW TO THIS, KID. THIS CITY. TO WHAT YOU PEOPLE ARE.
BUT BATMAN NEEDS TO KNOW HE'S STILL GOT WHAT IT TAKES. I'M NOT NEW TO THAT.
MR. MORGAN.
LET'S GET YOU HOME.

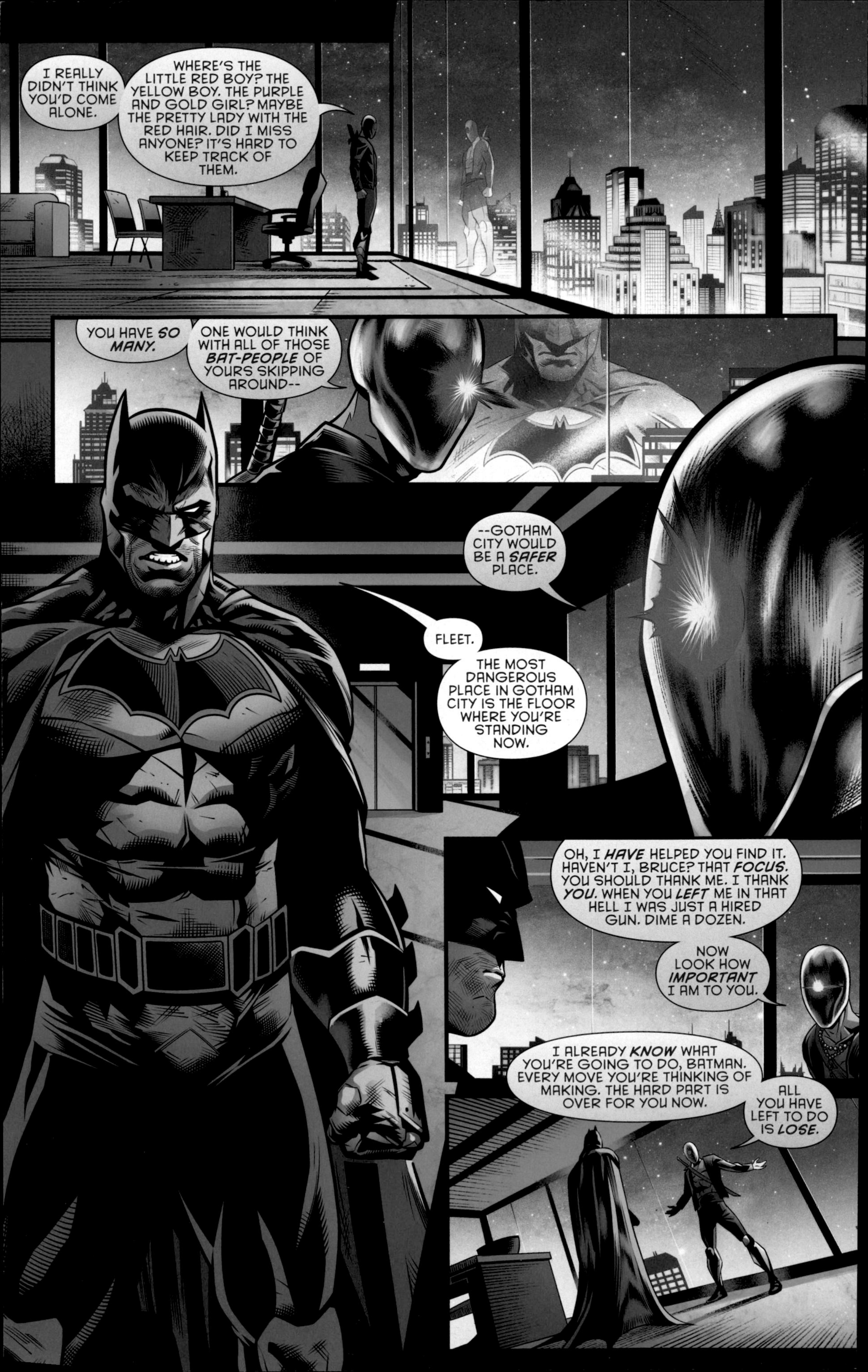
I REALLY DIDN'T THINK YOU'D COME ALONE.
WHERE'S THE LITTLE RED BOY? THE YELLOW BOY. THE PURPLE AND GOLD GIRL? MAYBE THE PRETTY LADY WITH THE RED HAIR. DID I MISS ANYONE? IT'S HARD TO KEEP TRACK OF THEM.
YOU HAVE *SO MANY.*
ONE WOULD THINK WITH ALL OF THOSE *BAT-PEOPLE* OF YOURS SKIPPING AROUND--
--GOTHAM CITY WOULD BE A *SAFER* PLACE.
FLEET.
THE MOST DANGEROUS PLACE IN GOTHAM CITY IS THE FLOOR WHERE YOU'RE STANDING NOW.
OH, I *HAVE* HELPED YOU FIND IT. HAVEN'T I, BRUCE? THAT *FOCUS.* YOU SHOULD THANK ME. I THANK *YOU.* WHEN YOU *LEFT* ME IN THAT HELL I WAS JUST A HIRED GUN. DIME A DOZEN.
NOW LOOK HOW *IMPORTANT* I AM TO YOU.
I ALREADY *KNOW* WHAT YOU'RE GOING TO DO, BATMAN. EVERY MOVE YOU'RE THINKING OF MAKING. THE HARD PART IS OVER FOR YOU NOW.
ALL YOU HAVE LEFT TO DO IS *LOSE.*

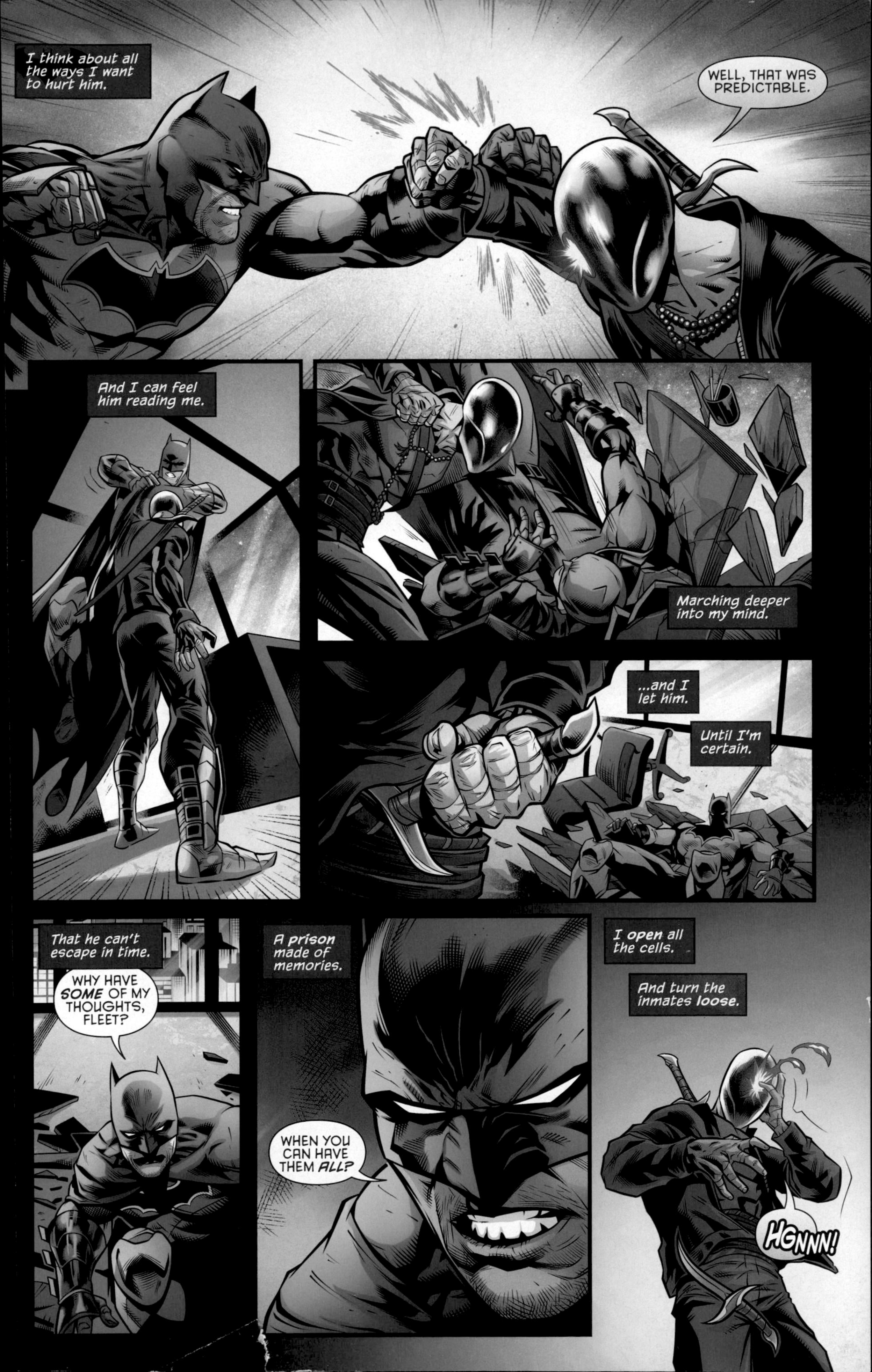
I think about all the ways I want to hurt him.
WELL, THAT WAS PREDICTABLE.
And I can feel him reading me.
Marching deeper into my mind.
...and I let him.
Until I'm certain.
That he can't escape in time.
WHY HAVE SOME OF MY THOUGHTS, FLEET?
A prison made of memories.
WHEN YOU CAN HAVE THEM ALL?
I open all the cells.
And turn the inmates loose.
HGNNN!

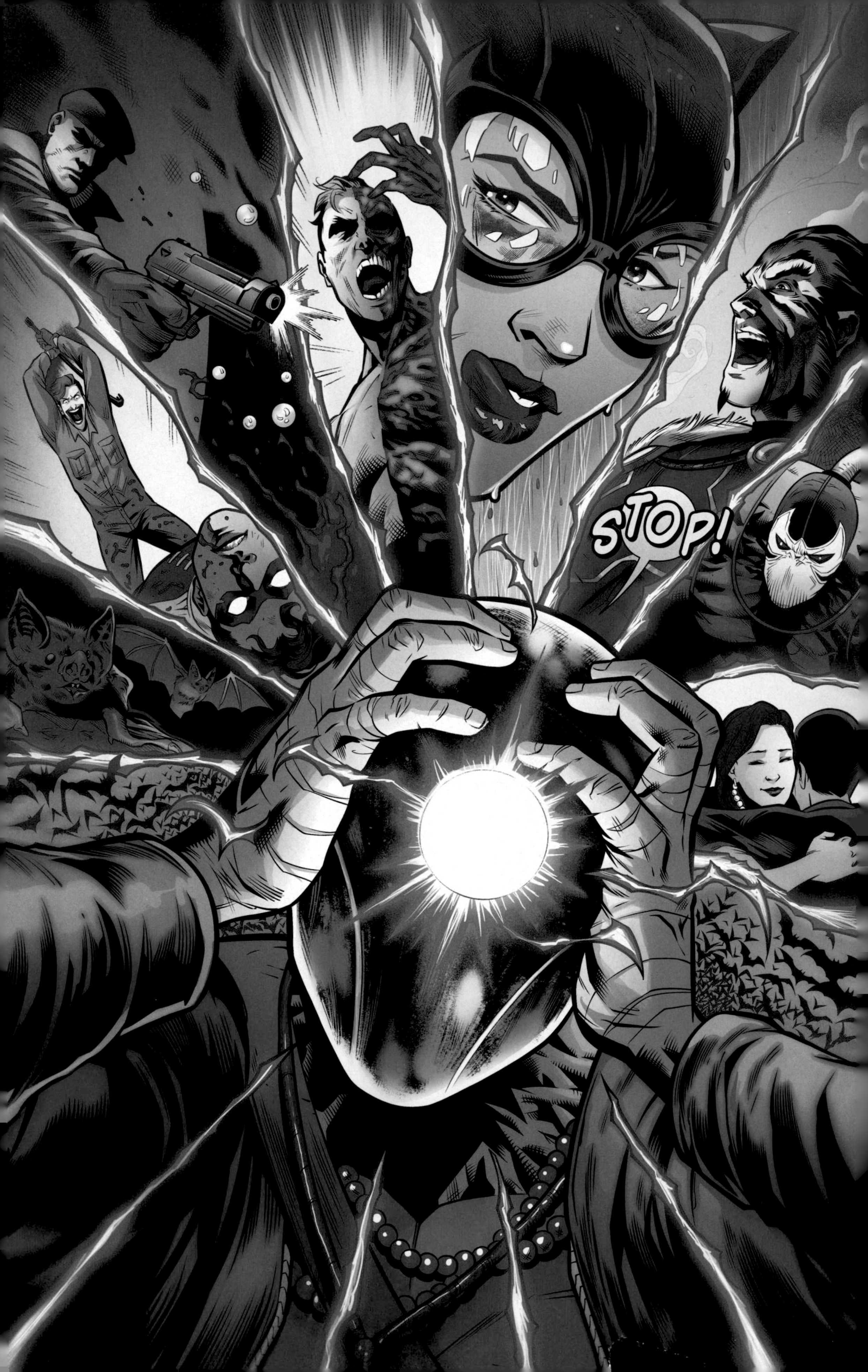
STOP!

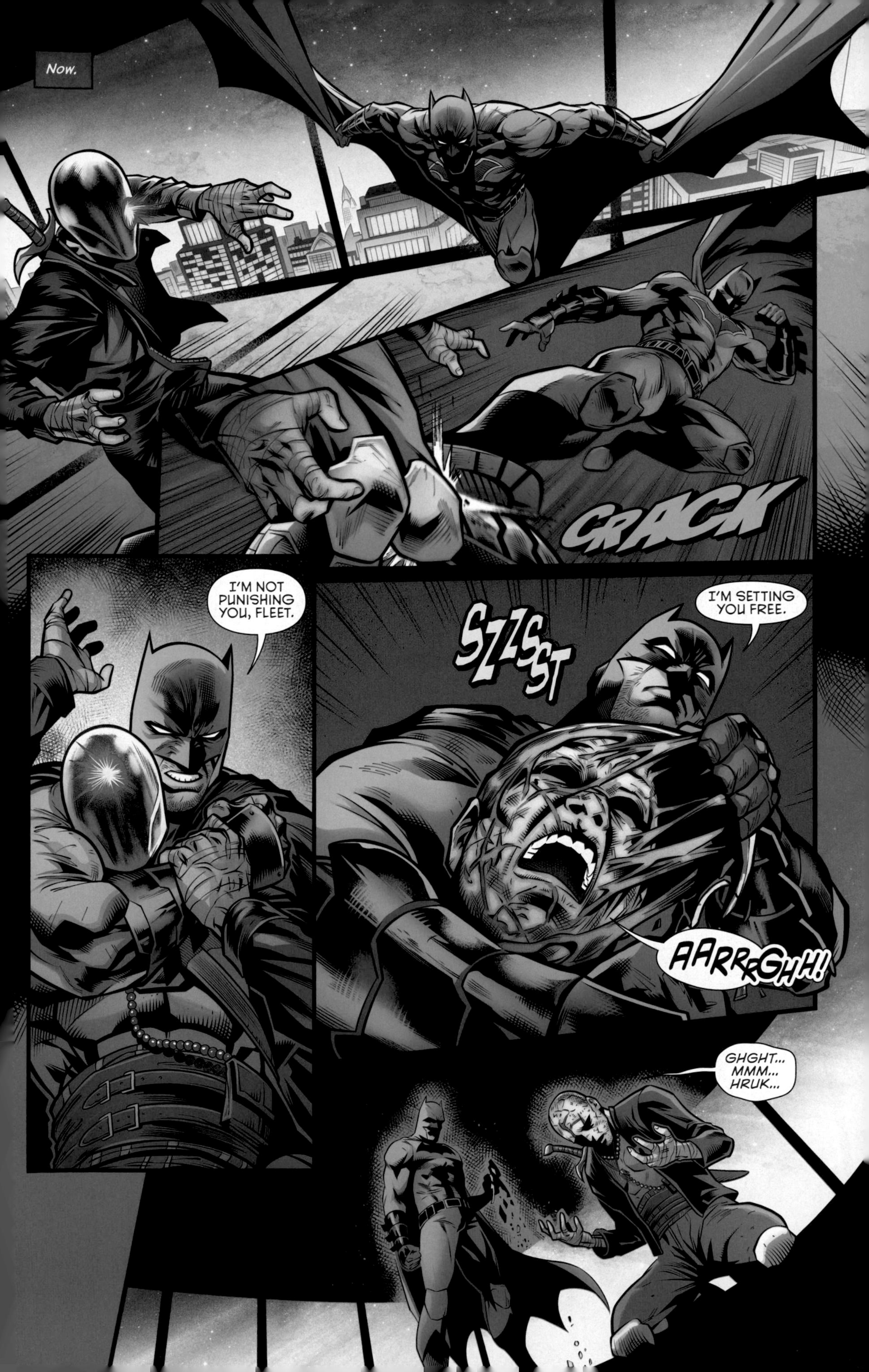
Now.
CRACK
I'M NOT PUNISHING YOU, FLEET.
SZZSST
I'M SETTING YOU FREE.
AARRRGHH!
GHGHT... MMM... HRUK...

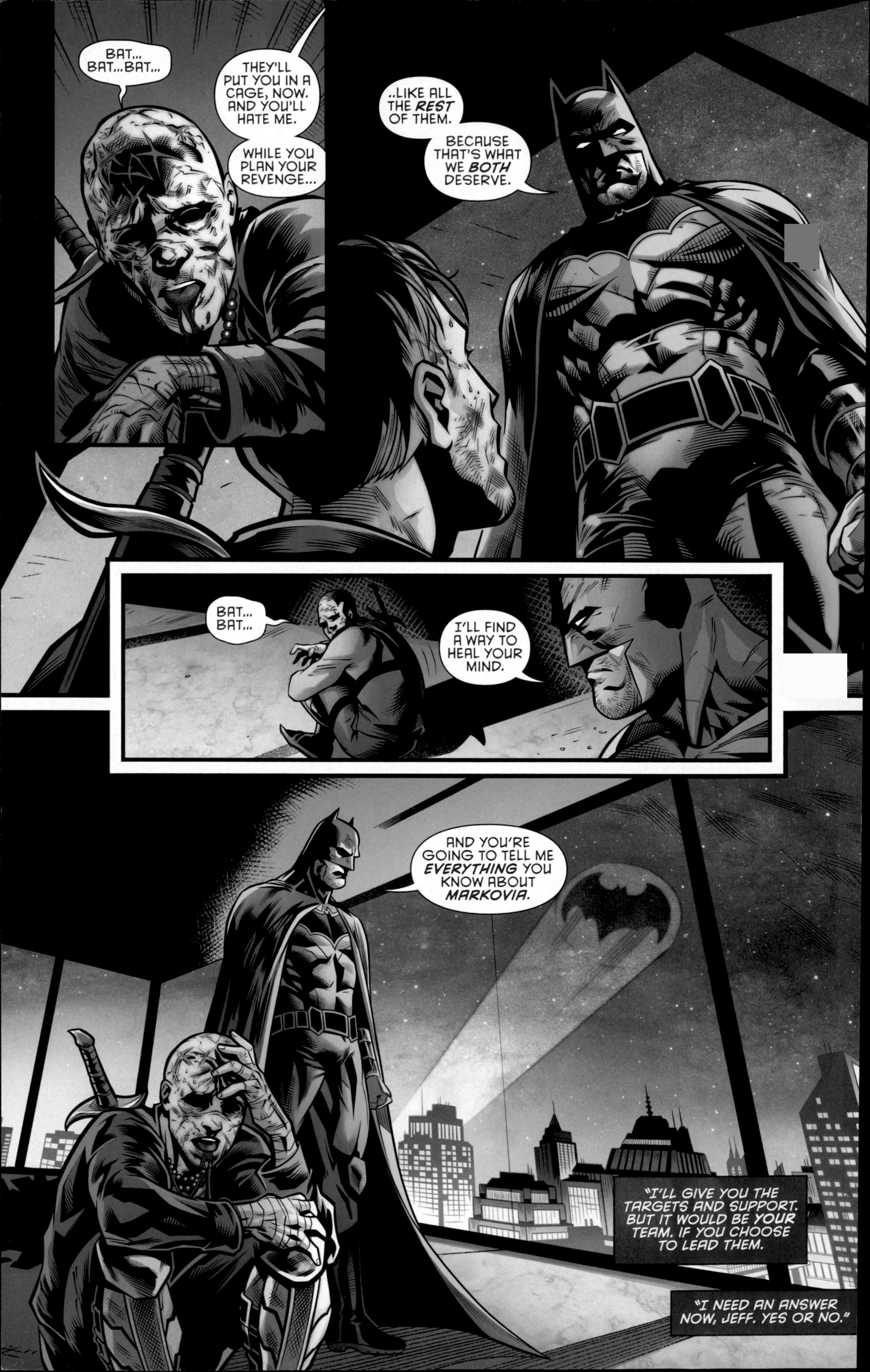
BAT... BAT...BAT...
THEY'LL PUT YOU IN A CAGE, NOW. AND YOU'LL HATE ME.
WHILE YOU PLAN YOUR REVENGE...
..LIKE ALL THE *REST* OF THEM.
BECAUSE THAT'S WHAT WE *BOTH* DESERVE.
BAT... BAT...
I'LL FIND A WAY TO HEAL YOUR MIND.
AND YOU'RE GOING TO TELL ME *EVERYTHING* YOU KNOW ABOUT *MARKOVIA*.
"I'LL GIVE YOU THE TARGETS AND SUPPORT. BUT IT WOULD BE *YOUR* TEAM, IF YOU CHOOSE TO LEAD THEM.
"I NEED AN ANSWER NOW, JEFF. YES OR NO."

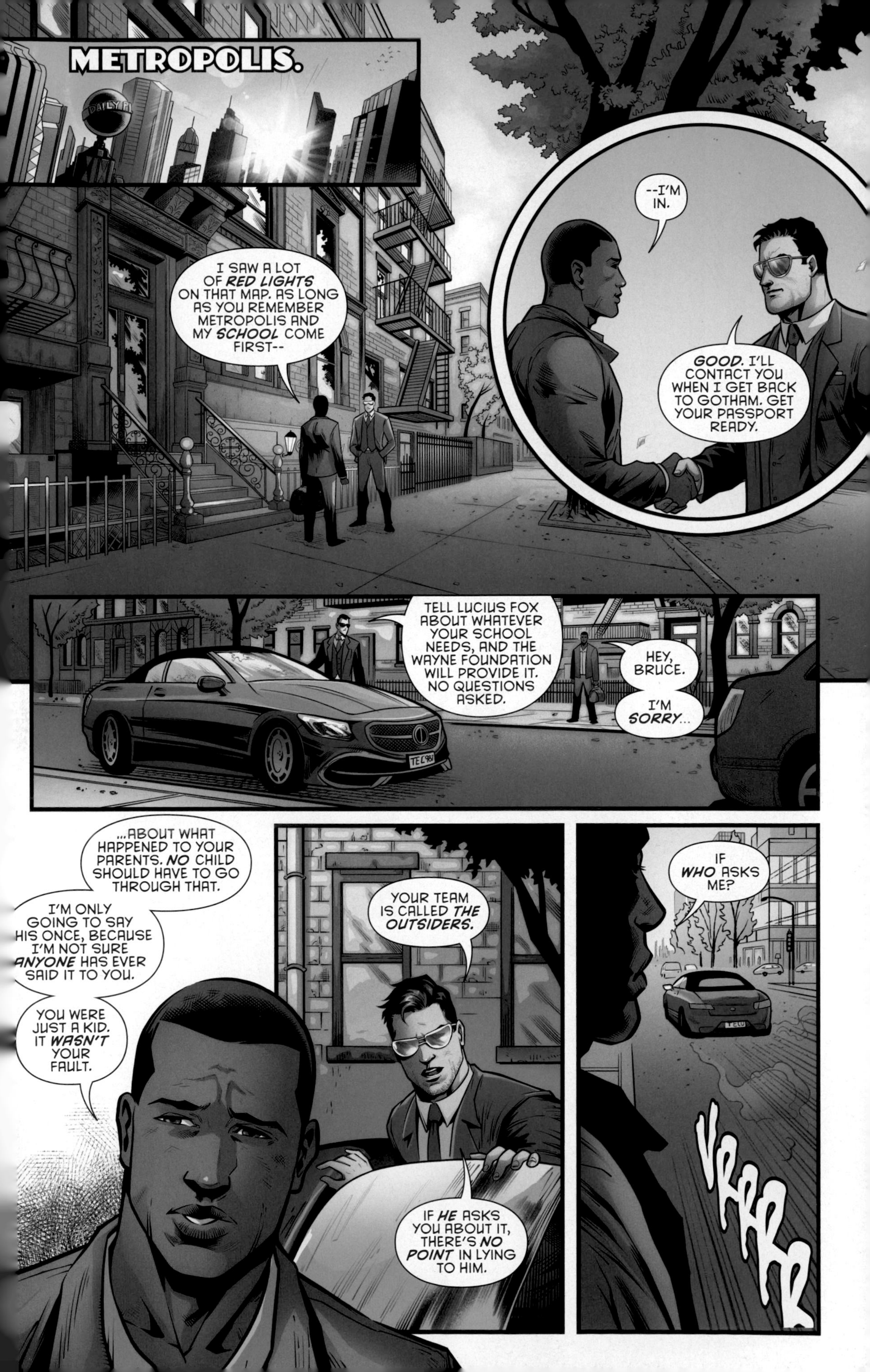
METROPOLIS.
I SAW A LOT OF RED LIGHTS ON THAT MAP. AS LONG AS YOU REMEMBER METROPOLIS AND MY SCHOOL COME FIRST--
--I'M IN.
GOOD. I'LL CONTACT YOU WHEN I GET BACK TO GOTHAM. GET YOUR PASSPORT READY.
TELL LUCIUS FOX ABOUT WHATEVER YOUR SCHOOL NEEDS, AND THE WAYNE FOUNDATION WILL PROVIDE IT. NO QUESTIONS ASKED.
HEY, BRUCE.
I'M SORRY...
...ABOUT WHAT HAPPENED TO YOUR PARENTS. NO CHILD SHOULD HAVE TO GO THROUGH THAT.
I'M ONLY GOING TO SAY HIS ONCE, BECAUSE I'M NOT SURE ANYONE HAS EVER SAID IT TO YOU.
YOU WERE JUST A KID. IT WASN'T YOUR FAULT.
YOUR TEAM IS CALLED THE OUTSIDERS.
IF HE ASKS YOU ABOUT IT, THERE'S NO POINT IN LYING TO HIM.
IF WHO ASKS ME?
VRRRR

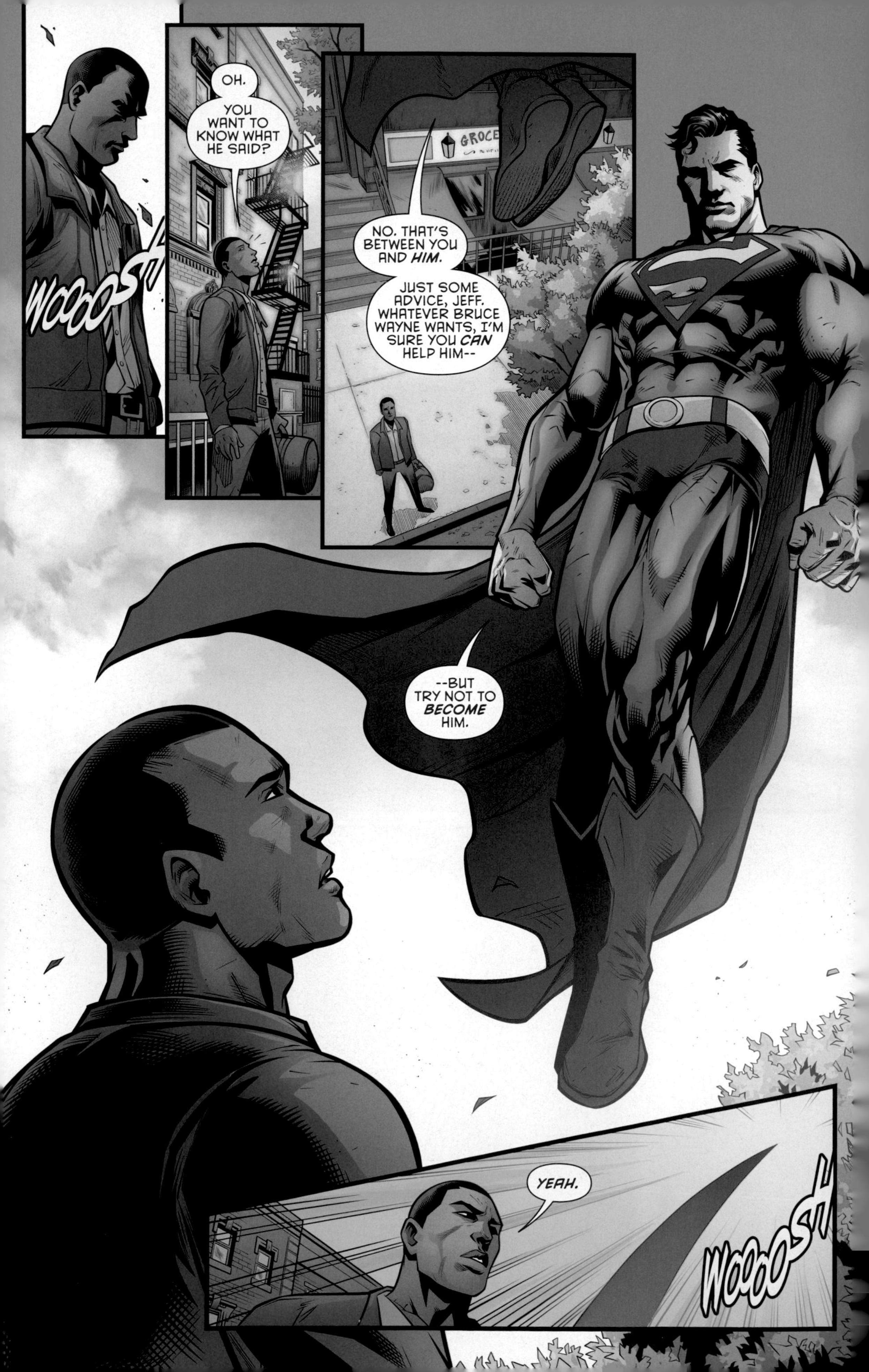
WOOOOSH
OH.
YOU WANT TO KNOW WHAT HE SAID?
NO. THAT'S BETWEEN YOU AND *HIM*.
JUST SOME ADVICE, JEFF. WHATEVER BRUCE WAYNE WANTS, I'M SURE YOU *CAN* HELP HIM--
--BUT TRY NOT TO *BECOME* HIM.
YEAH.
WOOOOSH

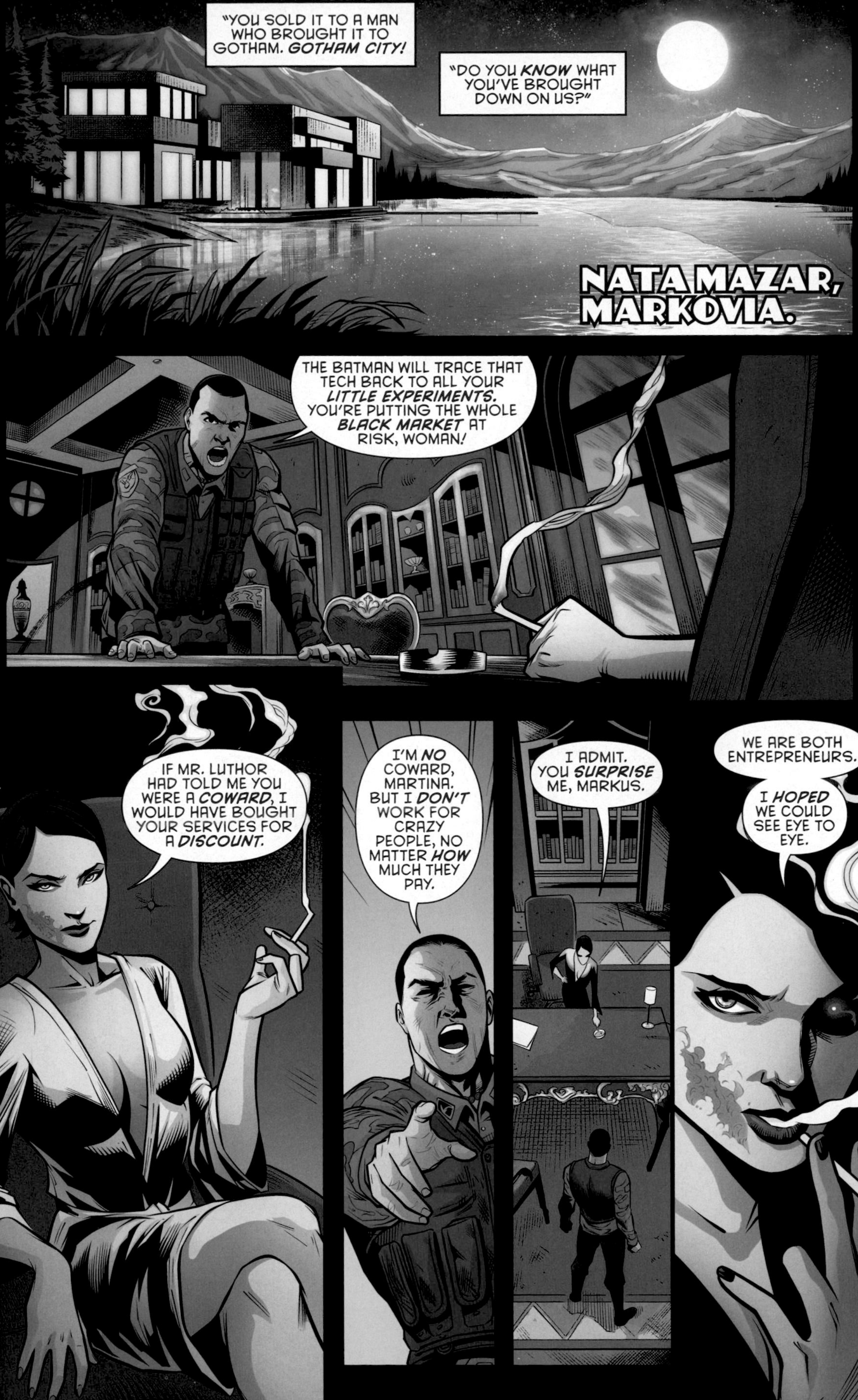
"YOU SOLD IT TO A MAN WHO BROUGHT IT TO GOTHAM. *GOTHAM CITY!*
"DO YOU *KNOW* WHAT YOU'VE BROUGHT DOWN ON US?"
NATA MAZAR, MARKOVIA.
THE BATMAN WILL TRACE THAT TECH BACK TO ALL YOUR *LITTLE EXPERIMENTS.* YOU'RE PUTTING THE WHOLE *BLACK MARKET* AT RISK, WOMAN!
IF MR. LUTHOR HAD TOLD ME YOU WERE A *COWARD*, I WOULD HAVE BOUGHT YOUR SERVICES FOR A *DISCOUNT.*
I'M *NO* COWARD, MARTINA. BUT I *DON'T* WORK FOR CRAZY PEOPLE, NO MATTER *HOW* MUCH THEY PAY.
I ADMIT. YOU *SURPRISE* ME, MARKUS.
WE ARE BOTH ENTREPRENEURS.
I *HOPED* WE COULD SEE EYE TO EYE.

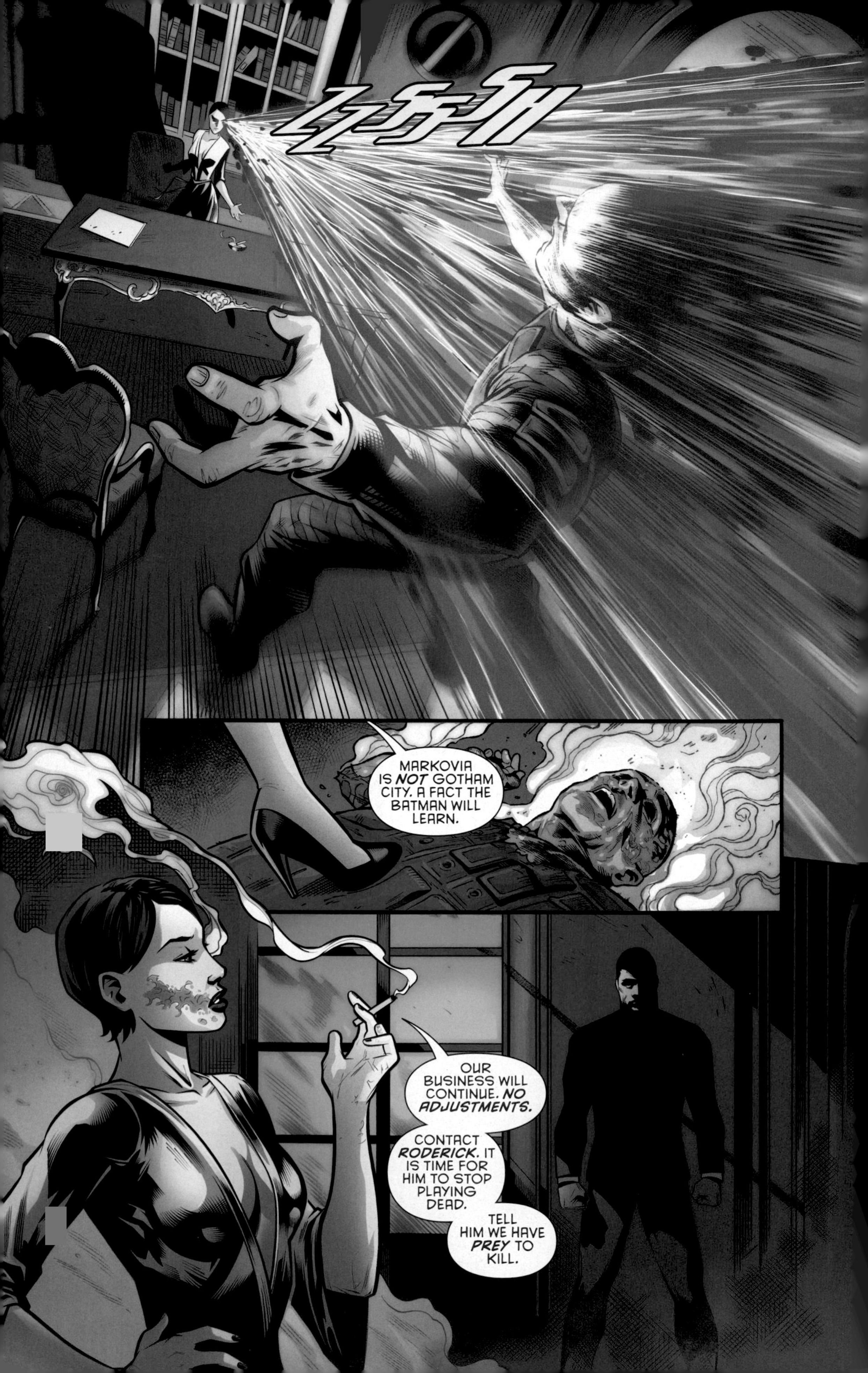
ZZSSSH
MARKOVIA IS *NOT* GOTHAM CITY. A FACT THE BATMAN WILL LEARN.
OUR BUSINESS WILL CONTINUE. *NO ADJUSTMENTS.*
CONTACT *RODERICK.* IT IS TIME FOR HIM TO STOP PLAYING DEAD.
TELL HIM WE HAVE *PREY* TO KILL.

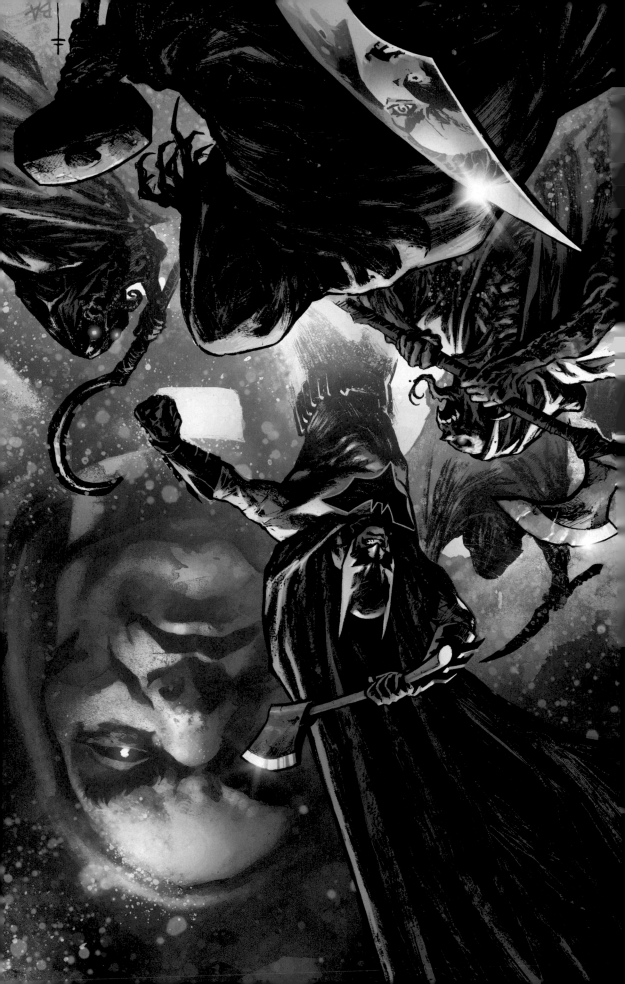

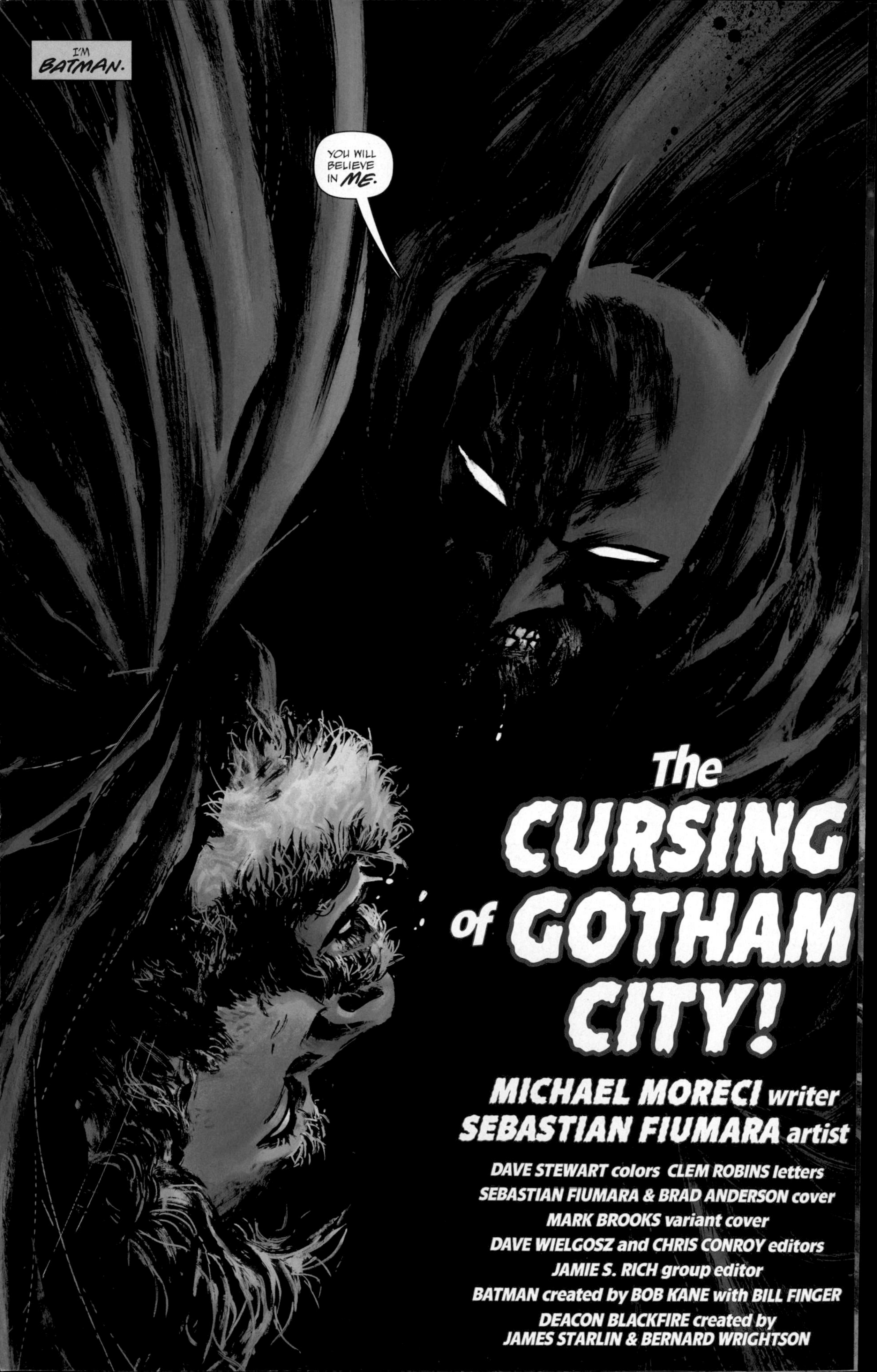
I'M BATMAN.
YOU WILL BELIEVE IN ME.

The CURSING of GOTHAM CITY!

MICHAEL MORECI writer
SEBASTIAN FIUMARA artist

DAVE STEWART colors **CLEM ROBINS** letters
SEBASTIAN FIUMARA & BRAD ANDERSON cover
MARK BROOKS variant cover
DAVE WIELGOSZ and **CHRIS CONROY** editors
JAMIE S. RICH group editor
BATMAN created by **BOB KANE** with **BILL FINGER**
DEACON BLACKFIRE created by
JAMES STARLIN & BERNARD WRIGHTSON

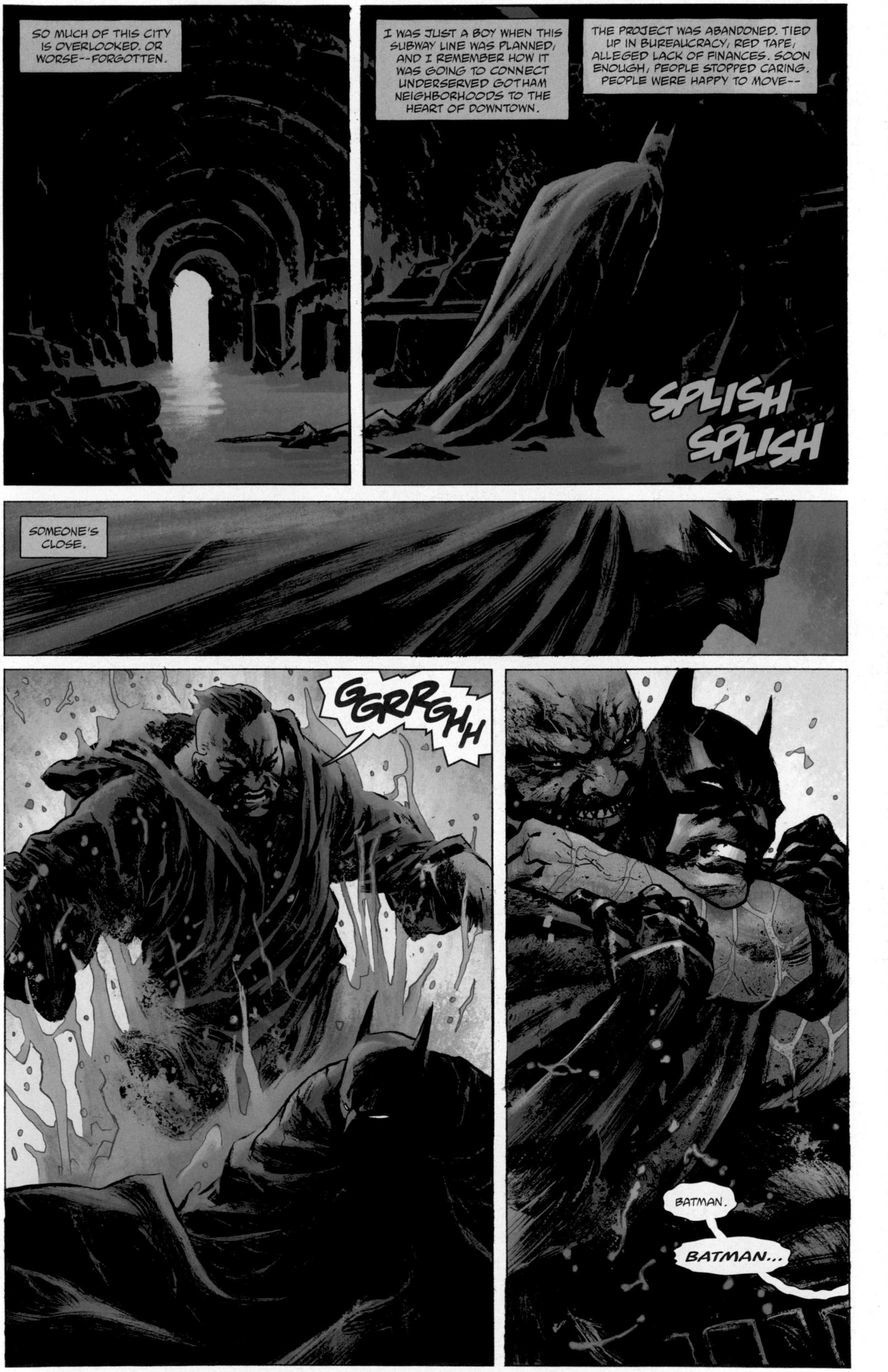

SO MUCH OF THIS CITY IS OVERLOOKED. OR WORSE--FORGOTTEN.
I WAS JUST A BOY WHEN THIS SUBWAY LINE WAS PLANNED, AND I REMEMBER HOW IT WAS GOING TO CONNECT UNDERSERVED GOTHAM NEIGHBORHOODS TO THE HEART OF DOWNTOWN.
THE PROJECT WAS ABANDONED. TIED UP IN BUREAUCRACY, RED TAPE, ALLEGED LACK OF FINANCES. SOON ENOUGH, PEOPLE STOPPED CARING. PEOPLE WERE HAPPY TO MOVE--
SPLISH
SPLISH
SOMEONE'S CLOSE.
GGRRRGHH
BATMAN.
BATMAN...

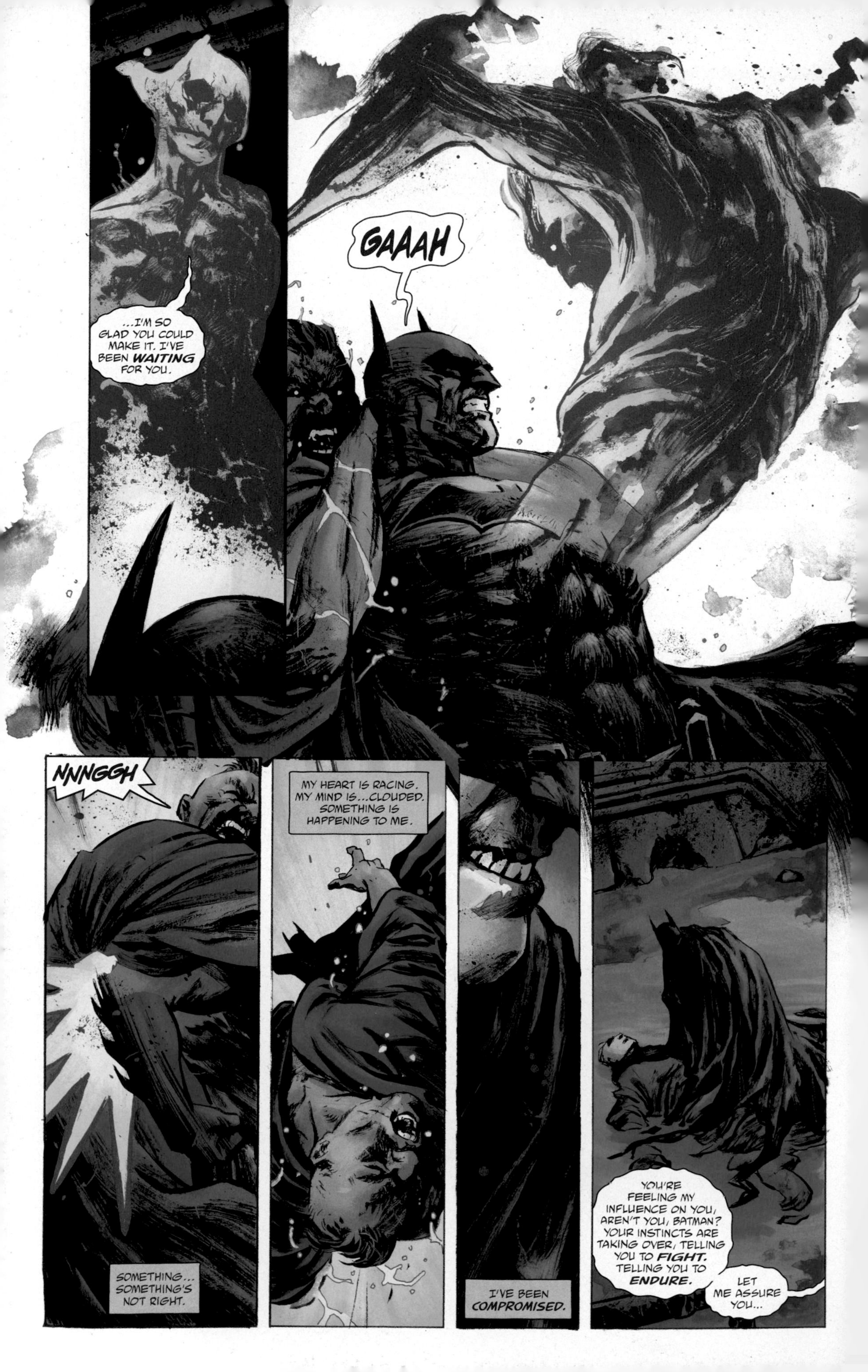
...I'M SO GLAD YOU COULD MAKE IT. I'VE BEEN **WAITING** FOR YOU.
GAAAH
NNNGGH
SOMETHING... SOMETHING'S NOT RIGHT.
MY HEART IS RACING. MY MIND IS...CLOUDED. SOMETHING IS HAPPENING TO ME.
I'VE BEEN **COMPROMISED.**
YOU'RE FEELING MY INFLUENCE ON YOU, AREN'T YOU, BATMAN? YOUR INSTINCTS ARE TAKING OVER, TELLING YOU TO **FIGHT.** TELLING YOU TO **ENDURE.**
LET ME ASSURE YOU...

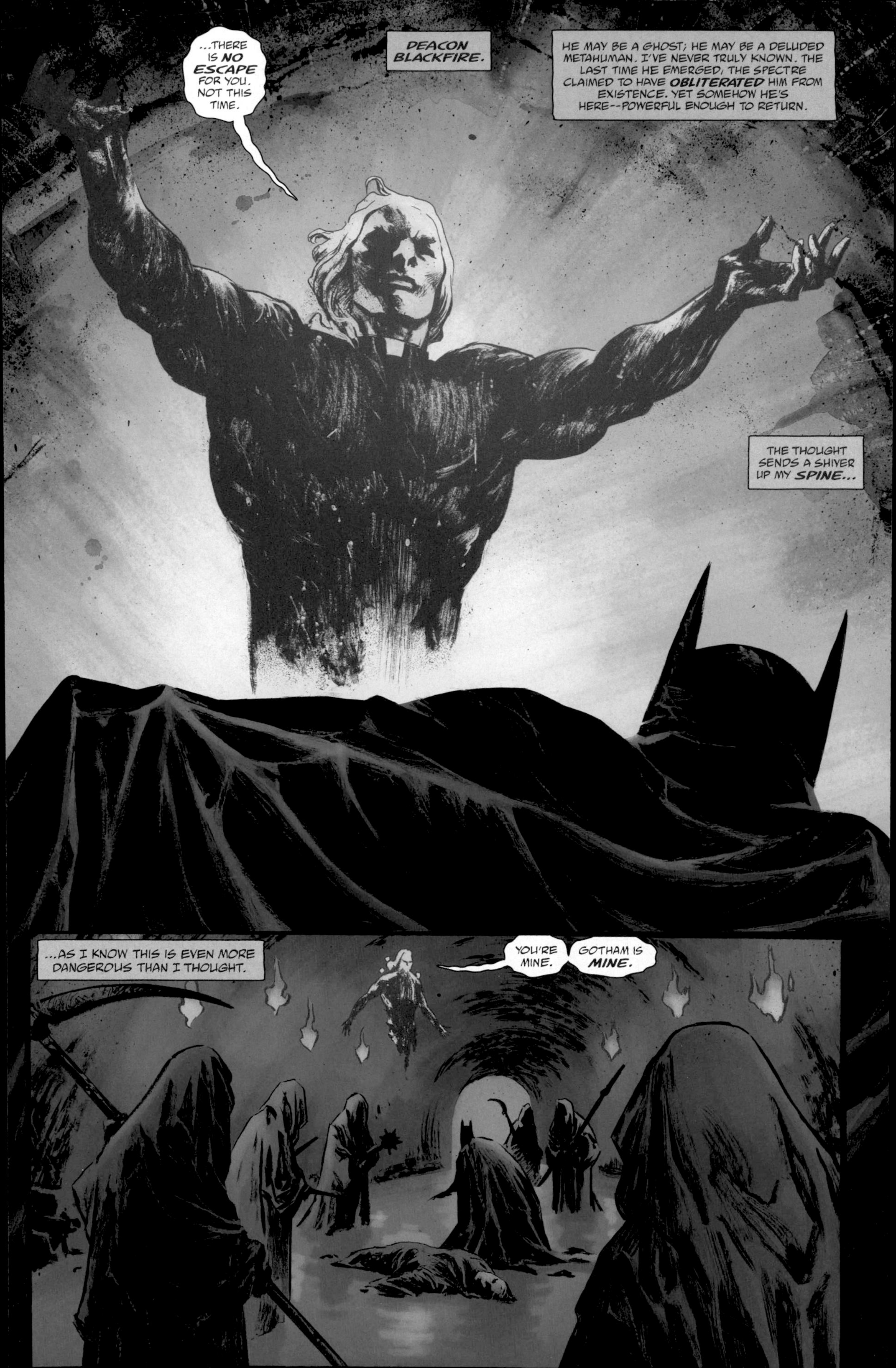
...THERE IS **NO ESCAPE** FOR YOU. NOT THIS TIME.
DEACON BLACKFIRE.
HE MAY BE A GHOST; HE MAY BE A DELUDED METAHUMAN. I'VE NEVER TRULY KNOWN. THE LAST TIME HE EMERGED, THE SPECTRE CLAIMED TO HAVE **OBLITERATED** HIM FROM EXISTENCE. YET SOMEHOW HE'S HERE--POWERFUL ENOUGH TO RETURN.
THE THOUGHT SENDS A SHIVER UP MY **SPINE**...
...AS I KNOW THIS IS EVEN MORE DANGEROUS THAN I THOUGHT.
YOU'RE MINE.
GOTHAM IS **MINE.**

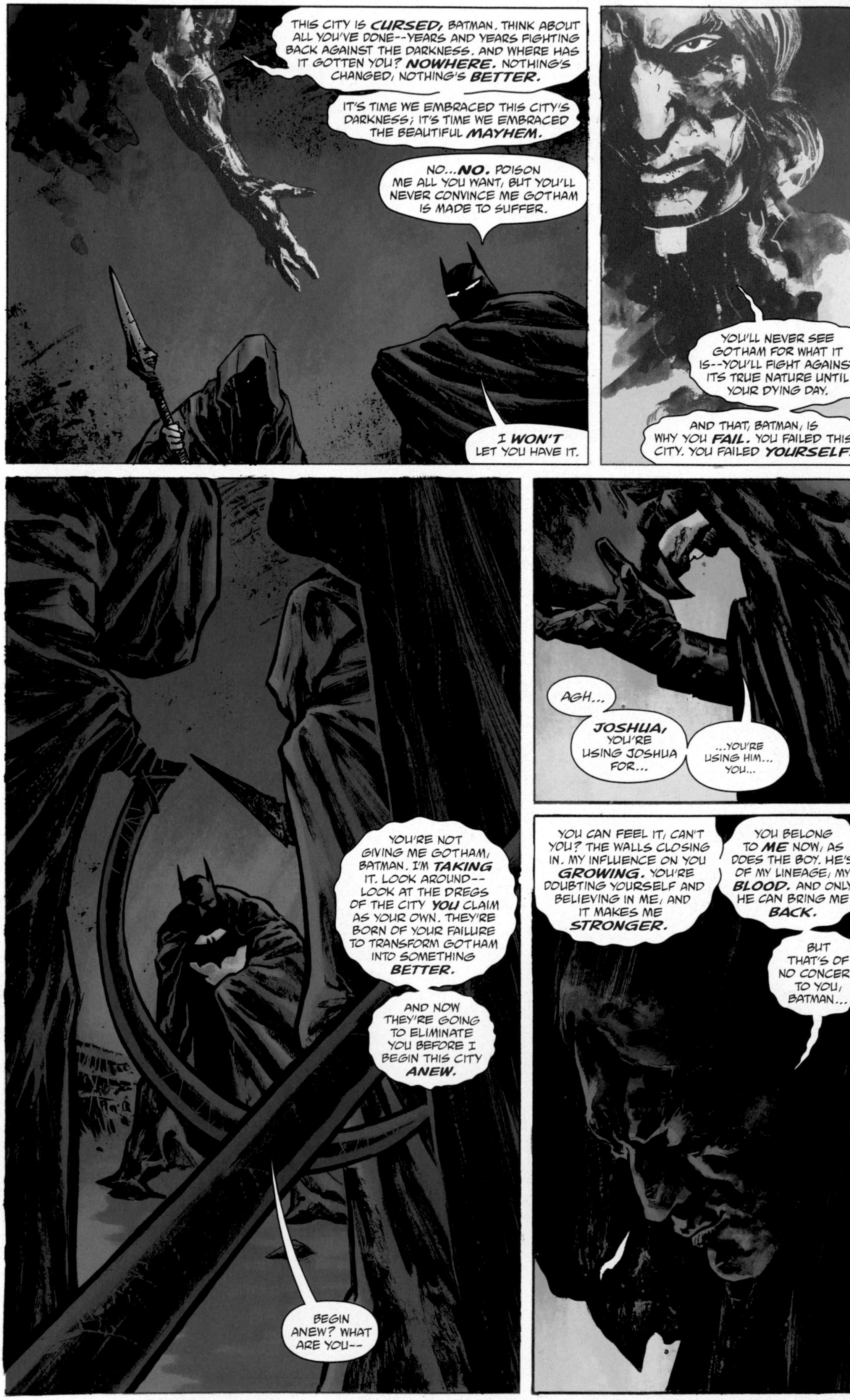

THIS CITY IS **CURSED,** BATMAN. THINK ABOUT ALL YOU'VE DONE--YEARS AND YEARS FIGHTING BACK AGAINST THE DARKNESS. AND WHERE HAS IT GOTTEN YOU? **NOWHERE.** NOTHING'S CHANGED, NOTHING'S **BETTER.**
IT'S TIME WE EMBRACED THIS CITY'S DARKNESS; IT'S TIME WE EMBRACED THE BEAUTIFUL **MAYHEM.**
NO...**NO.** POISON ME ALL YOU WANT, BUT YOU'LL NEVER CONVINCE ME GOTHAM IS MADE TO SUFFER.
I **WON'T** LET YOU HAVE IT.
YOU'LL NEVER SEE GOTHAM FOR WHAT IT IS--YOU'LL FIGHT AGAINST ITS TRUE NATURE UNTIL YOUR DYING DAY.
AND THAT, BATMAN, IS WHY YOU **FAIL.** YOU FAILED THIS CITY. YOU FAILED **YOURSELF.**
YOU'RE NOT GIVING ME GOTHAM, BATMAN. I'M **TAKING** IT. LOOK AROUND-- LOOK AT THE DREGS OF THE CITY **YOU** CLAIM AS YOUR OWN. THEY'RE BORN OF YOUR FAILURE TO TRANSFORM GOTHAM INTO SOMETHING **BETTER.**
AND NOW THEY'RE GOING TO ELIMINATE YOU BEFORE I BEGIN THIS CITY **ANEW.**
BEGIN ANEW? WHAT ARE YOU--
AGH...
JOSHUA, YOU'RE USING JOSHUA FOR...
...YOU'RE USING HIM... YOU...
YOU CAN FEEL IT, CAN'T YOU? THE WALLS CLOSING IN. MY INFLUENCE ON YOU **GROWING.** YOU'RE DOUBTING YOURSELF AND BELIEVING IN ME, AND IT MAKES ME **STRONGER.**
YOU BELONG TO **ME** NOW, AS DOES THE BOY. HE'S OF MY LINEAGE, MY **BLOOD.** AND ONLY HE CAN BRING ME **BACK.**
BUT THAT'S OF NO CONCERN TO YOU, BATMAN...

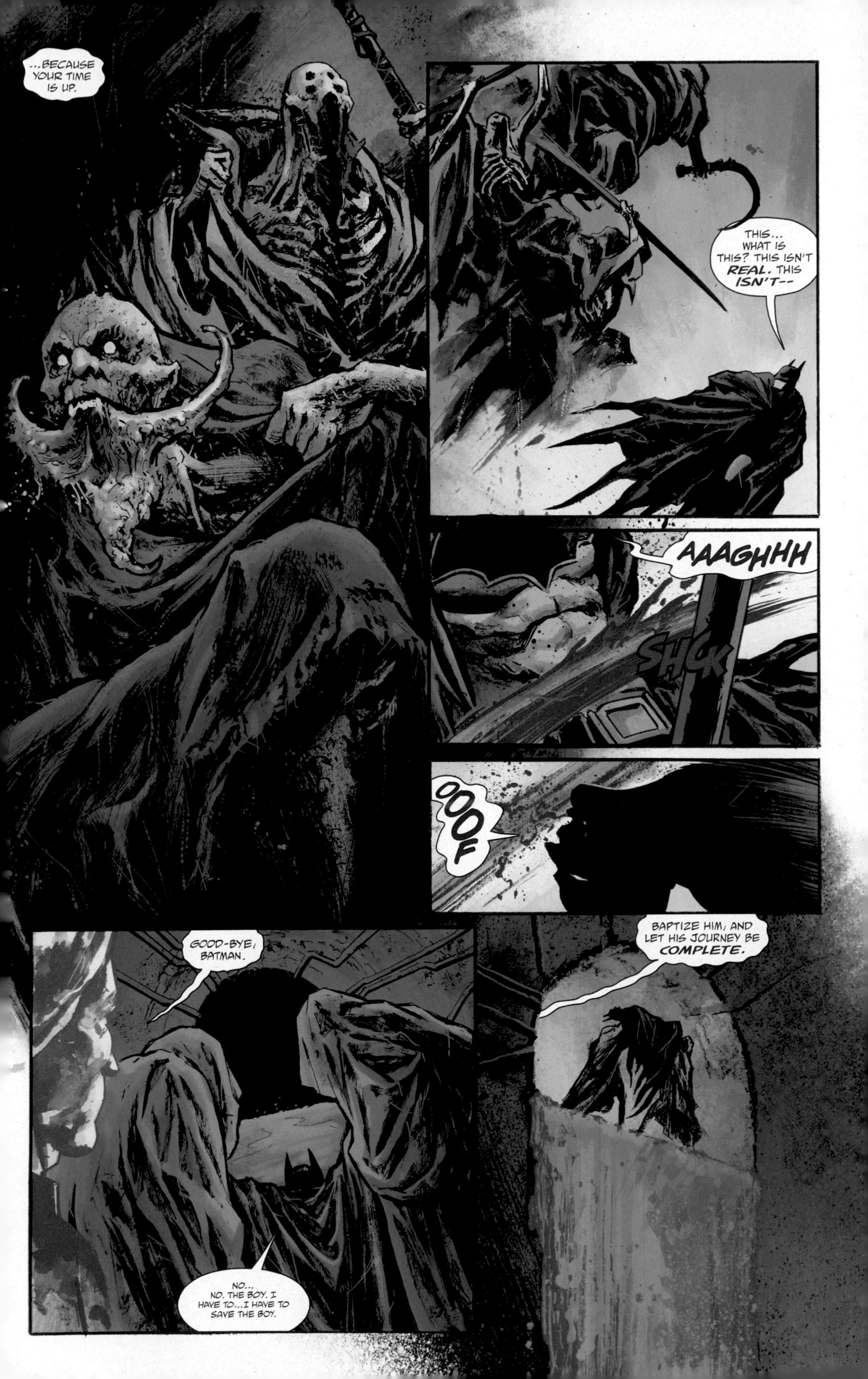
...BECAUSE YOUR TIME IS UP.
THIS... WHAT IS THIS? THIS ISN'T REAL. THIS ISN'T--
AAAGHHH
SHCK
OOOF
GOOD-BYE, BATMAN.
NO... NO. THE BOY. I HAVE TO...I HAVE TO SAVE THE BOY.
BAPTIZE HIM, AND LET HIS JOURNEY BE COMPLETE.

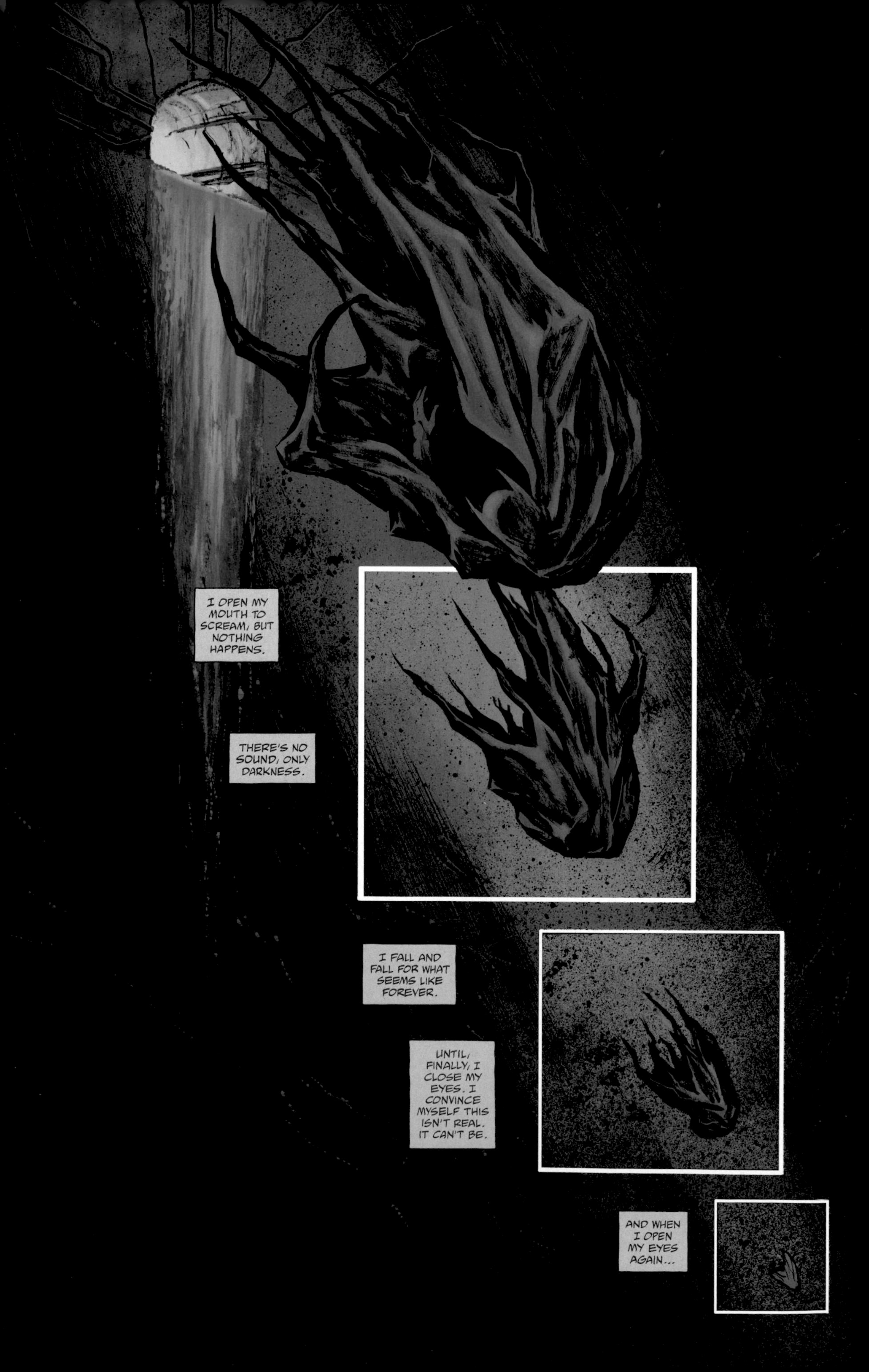
I OPEN MY MOUTH TO SCREAM, BUT NOTHING HAPPENS.
THERE'S NO SOUND, ONLY DARKNESS.
I FALL AND FALL FOR WHAT SEEMS LIKE FOREVER.
UNTIL, FINALLY, I CLOSE MY EYES. I CONVINCE MYSELF THIS ISN'T REAL. IT CAN'T BE.
AND WHEN I OPEN MY EYES AGAIN...

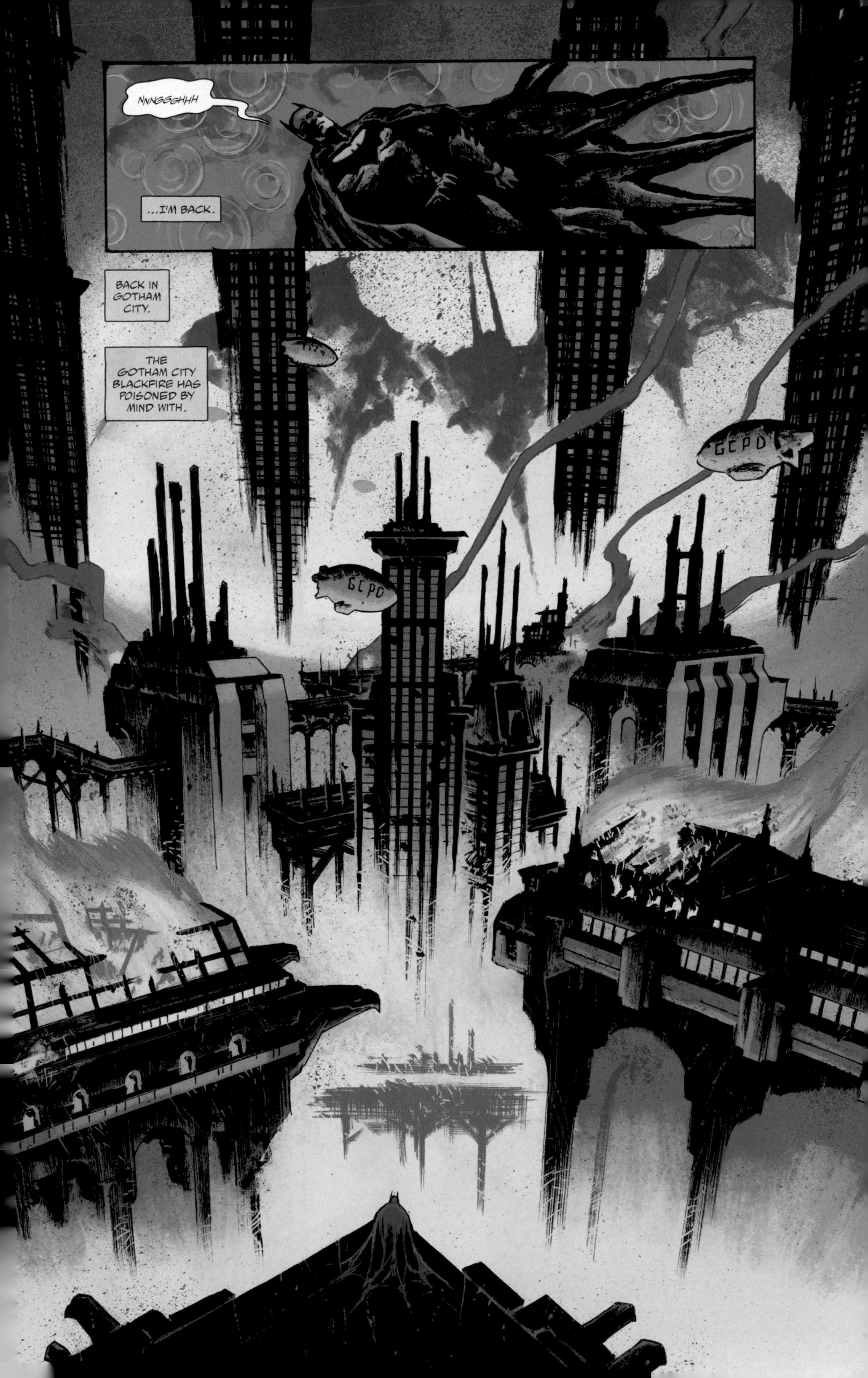
NNNGGGHHH
...I'M BACK.
BACK IN GOTHAM CITY.
THE GOTHAM CITY BLACKFIRE HAS POISONED BY MIND WITH.
GCPD
GCPD

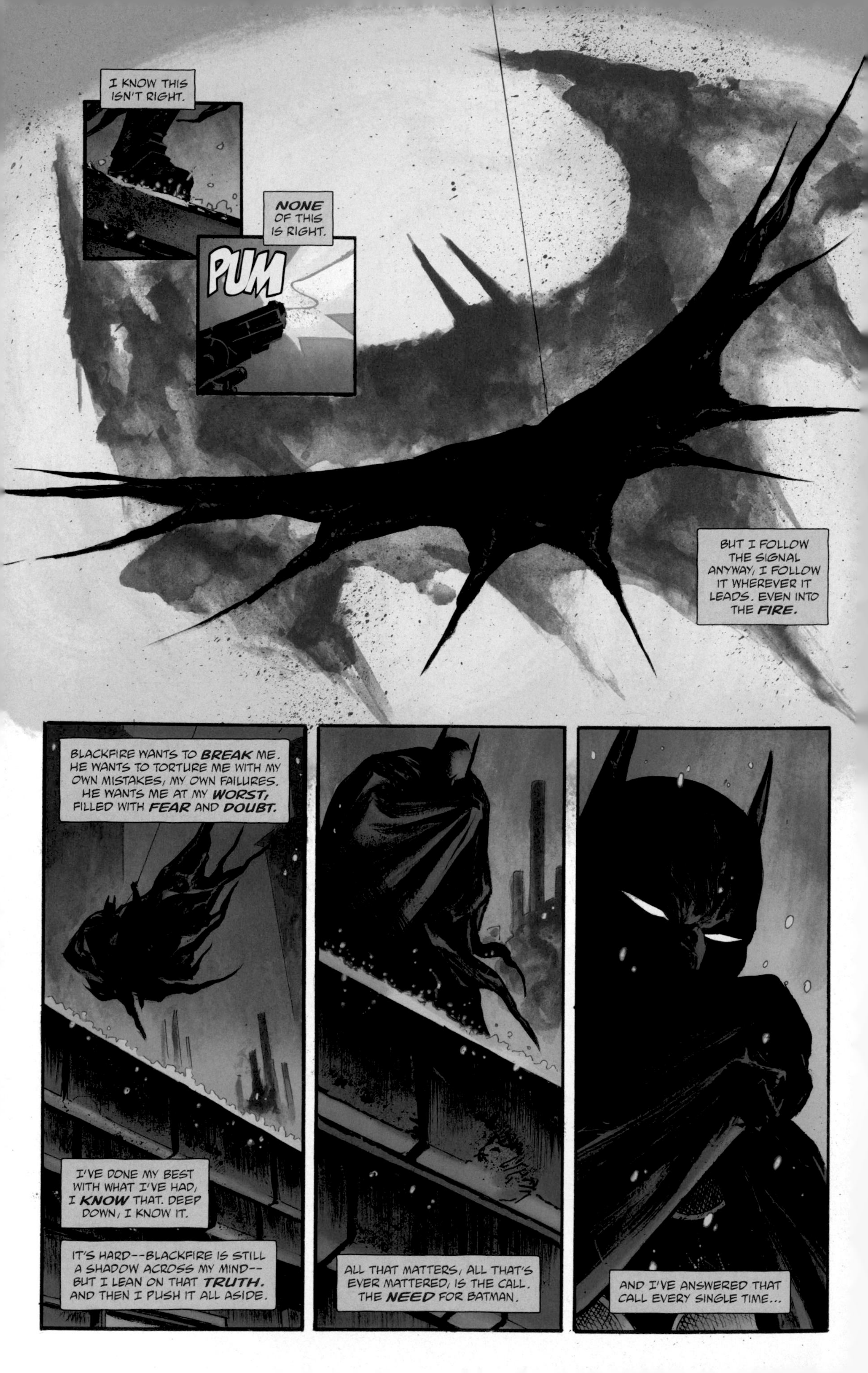
I KNOW THIS ISN'T RIGHT.
NONE OF THIS IS RIGHT.
PUM
BUT I FOLLOW THE SIGNAL ANYWAY, I FOLLOW IT WHEREVER IT LEADS. EVEN INTO THE FIRE.
BLACKFIRE WANTS TO BREAK ME. HE WANTS TO TORTURE ME WITH MY OWN MISTAKES, MY OWN FAILURES. HE WANTS ME AT MY WORST, FILLED WITH FEAR AND DOUBT.
I'VE DONE MY BEST WITH WHAT I'VE HAD, I KNOW THAT. DEEP DOWN, I KNOW IT.
IT'S HARD--BLACKFIRE IS STILL A SHADOW ACROSS MY MIND--BUT I LEAN ON THAT TRUTH. AND THEN I PUSH IT ALL ASIDE.
ALL THAT MATTERS, ALL THAT'S EVER MATTERED, IS THE CALL. THE NEED FOR BATMAN.
AND I'VE ANSWERED THAT CALL EVERY SINGLE TIME...

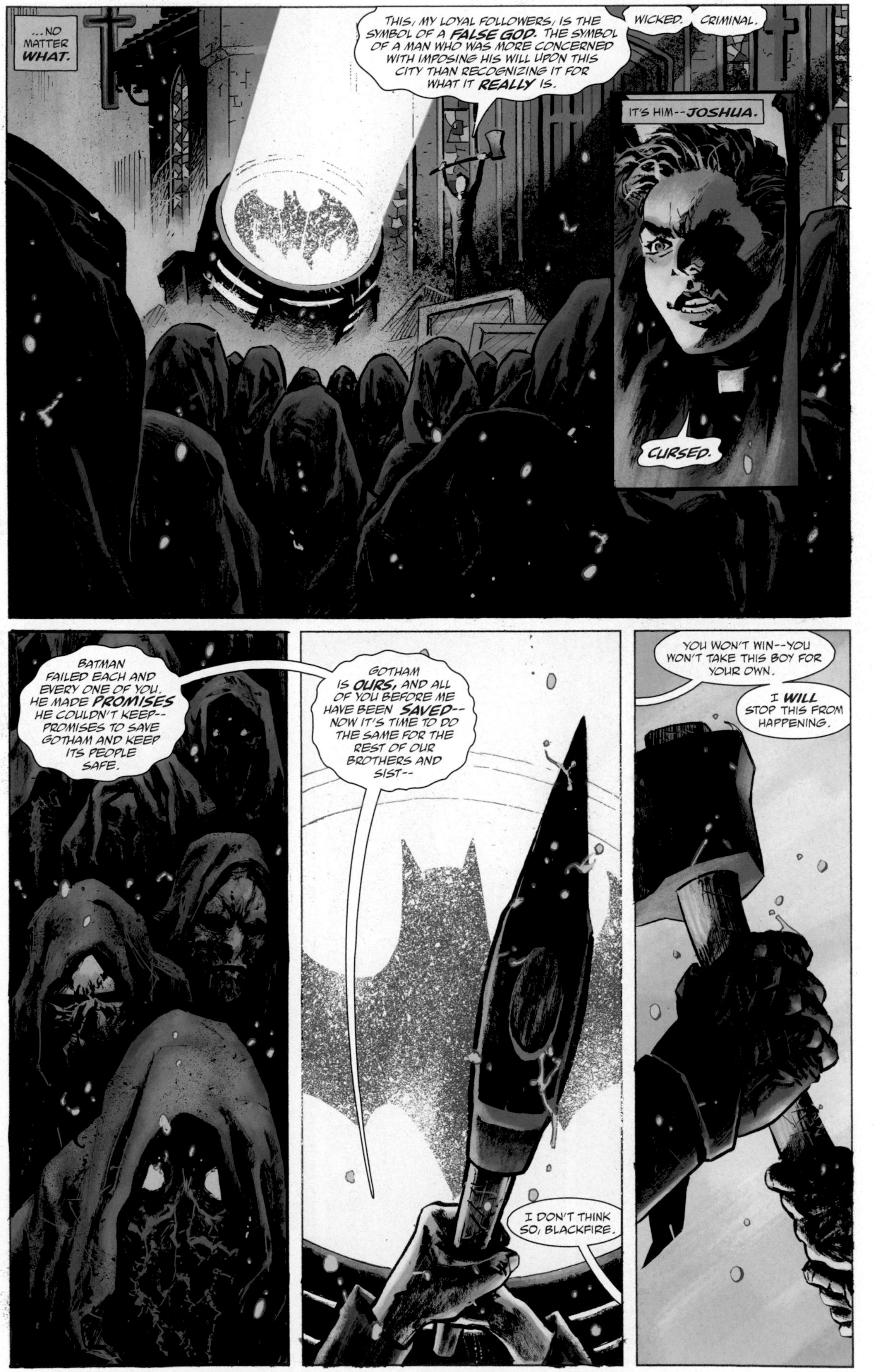
...NO MATTER **WHAT**.
THIS, MY LOYAL FOLLOWERS, IS THE SYMBOL OF A **FALSE GOD**. THE SYMBOL OF A MAN WHO WAS MORE CONCERNED WITH IMPOSING HIS WILL UPON THIS CITY THAN RECOGNIZING IT FOR WHAT IT **REALLY** IS.
WICKED.
CRIMINAL.
IT'S HIM--**JOSHUA**.
CURSED.
BATMAN FAILED EACH AND EVERY ONE OF YOU. HE MADE **PROMISES** HE COULDN'T KEEP--PROMISES TO SAVE GOTHAM AND KEEP ITS PEOPLE SAFE.
GOTHAM IS **OURS**, AND ALL OF YOU BEFORE ME HAVE BEEN **SAVED**--NOW IT'S TIME TO DO THE SAME FOR THE REST OF OUR BROTHERS AND SIST--
I DON'T THINK SO, BLACKFIRE.
YOU WON'T WIN--YOU WON'T TAKE THIS BOY FOR YOUR OWN.
I **WILL** STOP THIS FROM HAPPENING.

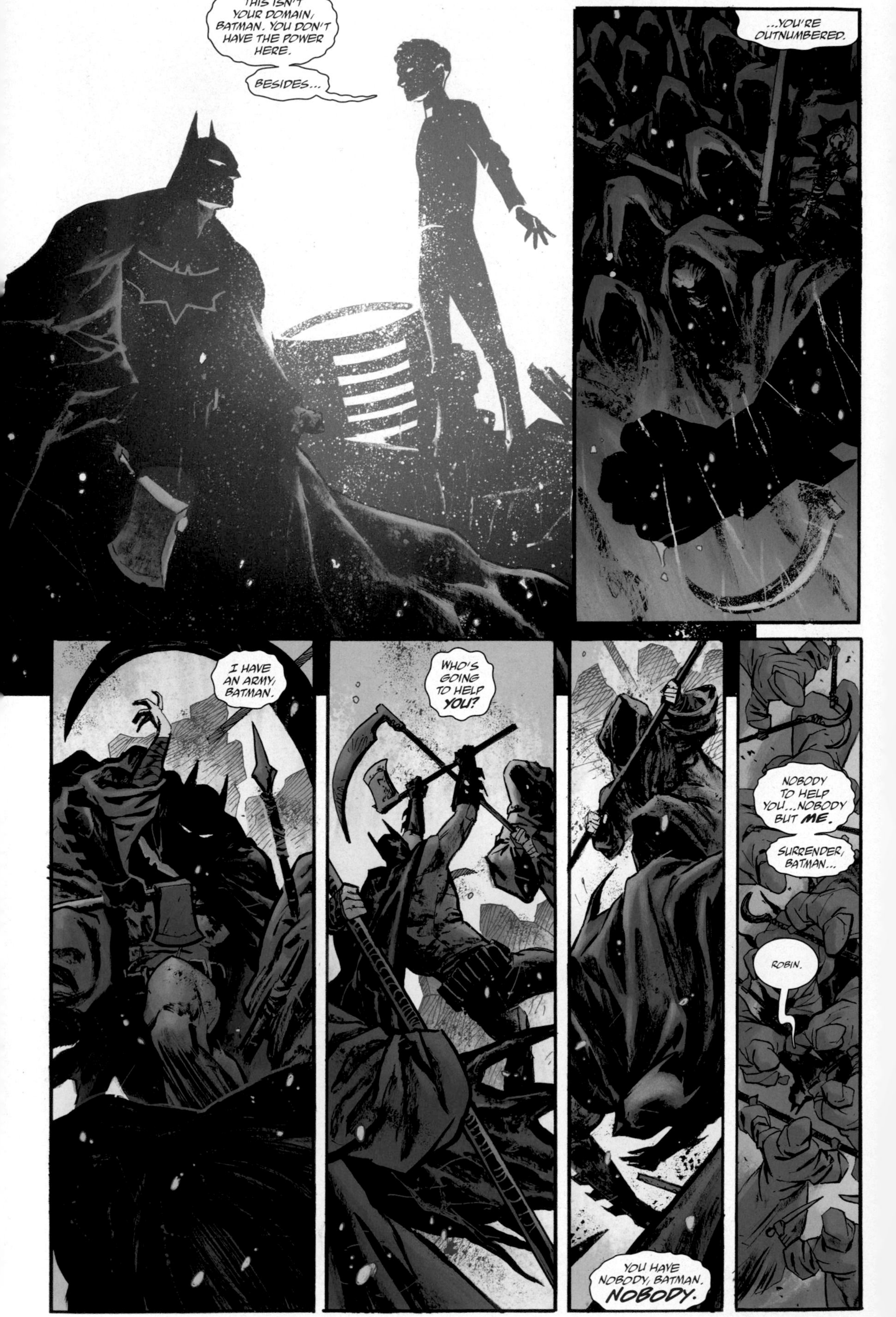
THIS ISN'T YOUR DOMAIN, BATMAN. YOU DON'T HAVE THE POWER HERE.
BESIDES...
...YOU'RE OUTNUMBERED.
I HAVE AN ARMY, BATMAN.
WHO'S GOING TO HELP **YOU?**
YOU HAVE NOBODY, BATMAN. **NOBODY.**
NOBODY TO HELP YOU...NOBODY BUT **ME.**
SURRENDER, BATMAN...
ROBIN.

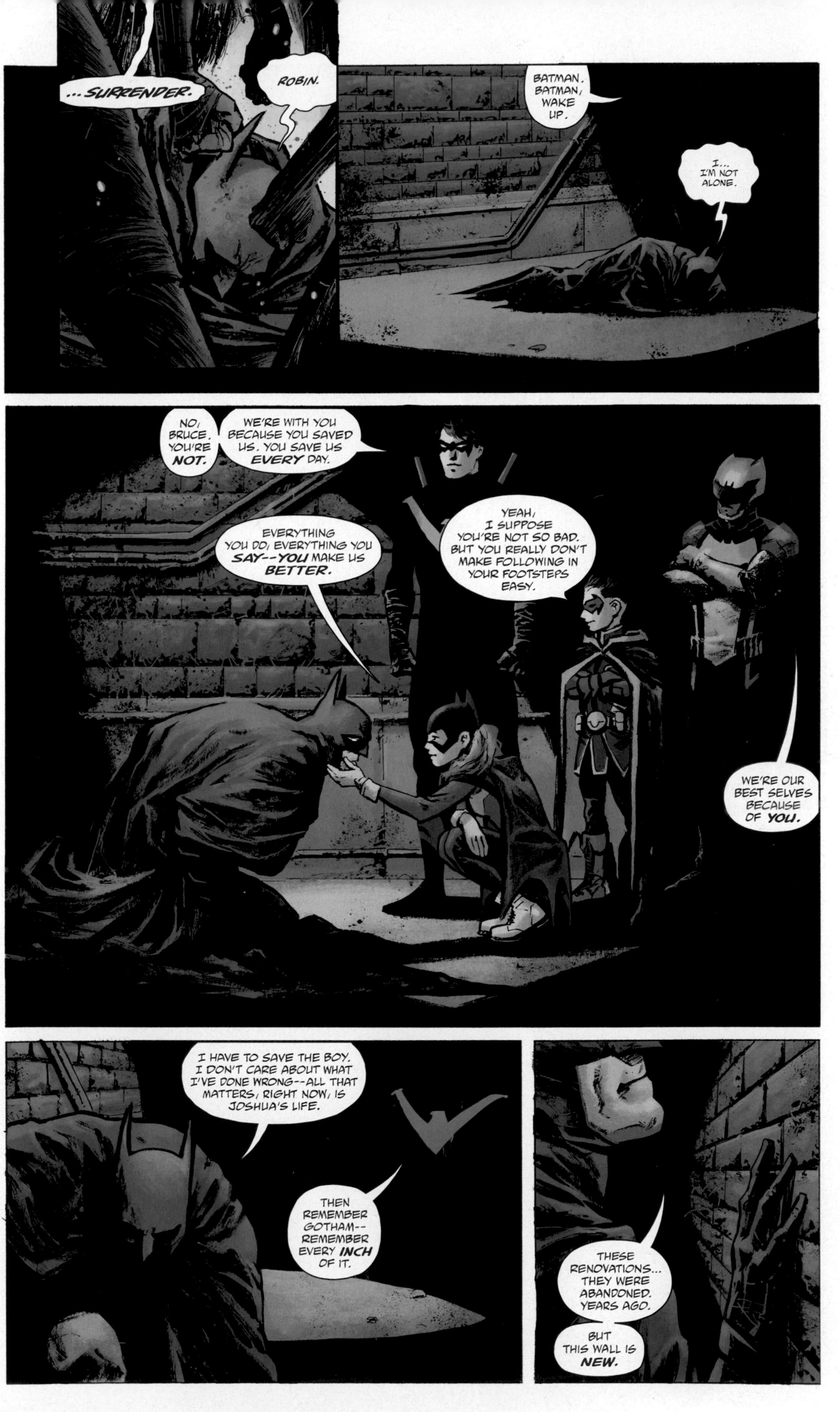
...SURRENDER.
ROBIN.
BATMAN. BATMAN, WAKE UP.
I... I'M NOT ALONE.
NO, BRUCE. YOU'RE NOT.
WE'RE WITH YOU BECAUSE YOU SAVED US. YOU SAVE US EVERY DAY.
EVERYTHING YOU DO, EVERYTHING YOU SAY--YOU MAKE US BETTER.
YEAH, I SUPPOSE YOU'RE NOT SO BAD. BUT YOU REALLY DON'T MAKE FOLLOWING IN YOUR FOOTSTEPS EASY.
WE'RE OUR BEST SELVES BECAUSE OF YOU.
I HAVE TO SAVE THE BOY. I DON'T CARE ABOUT WHAT I'VE DONE WRONG--ALL THAT MATTERS, RIGHT NOW, IS JOSHUA'S LIFE.
THEN REMEMBER GOTHAM--REMEMBER EVERY INCH OF IT.
THESE RENOVATIONS... THEY WERE ABANDONED. YEARS AGO.
BUT THIS WALL IS NEW.

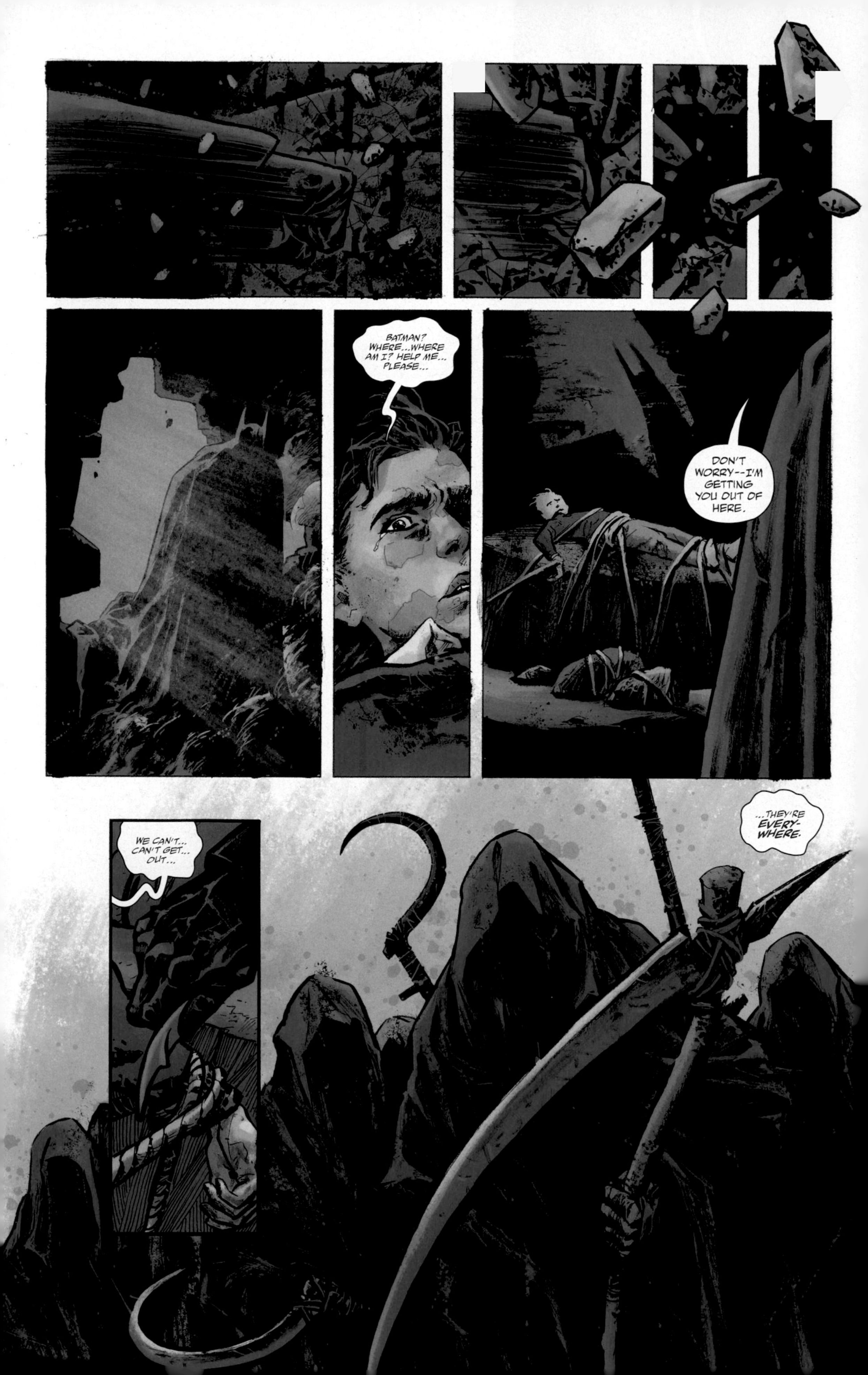
BATMAN? WHERE...WHERE AM I? HELP ME... PLEASE...
DON'T WORRY--I'M GETTING YOU OUT OF HERE.
WE CAN'T... CAN'T GET... OUT...
...THEY'RE EVERY-WHERE.

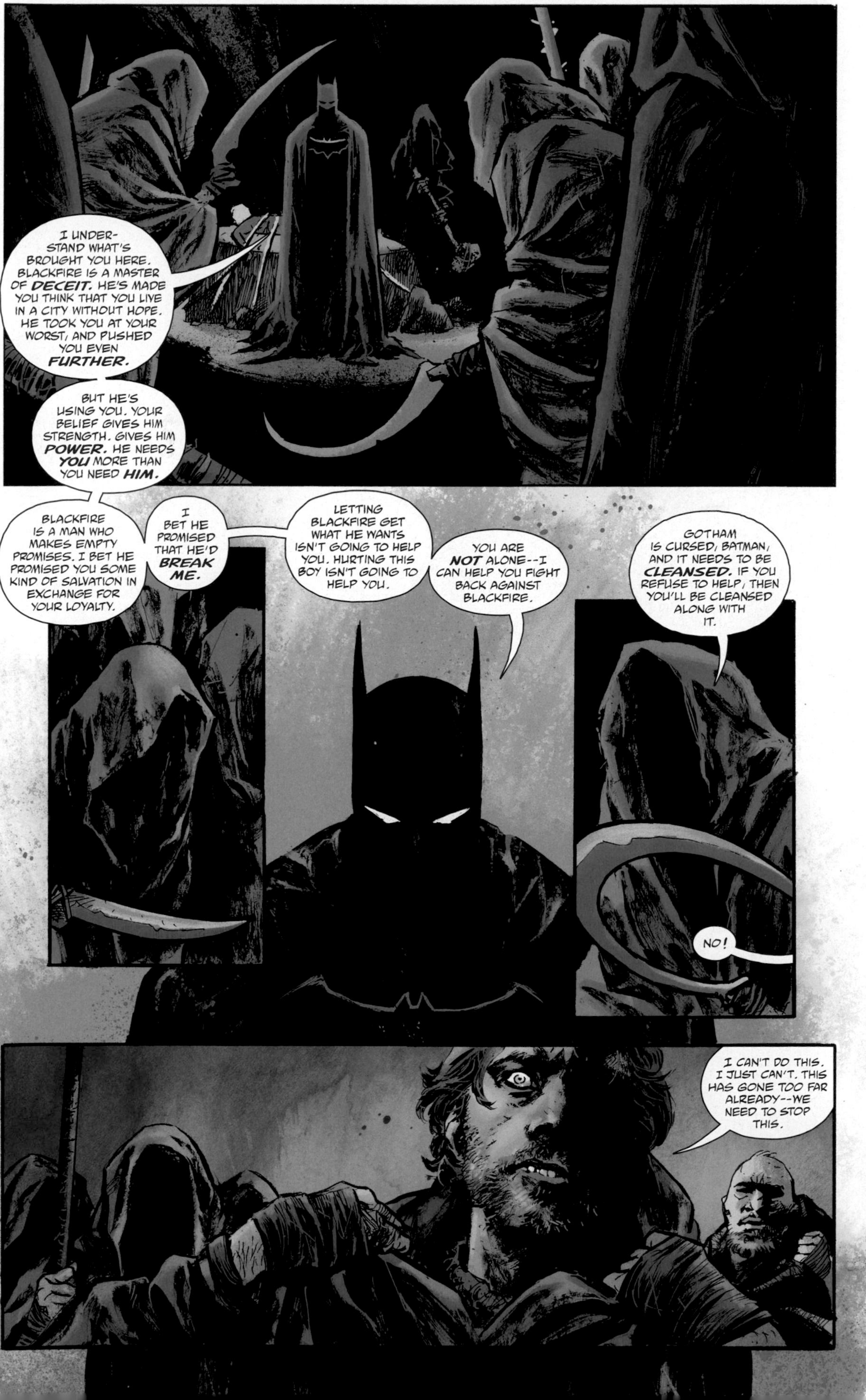
I UNDERSTAND WHAT'S BROUGHT YOU HERE. BLACKFIRE IS A MASTER OF **DECEIT.** HE'S MADE YOU THINK THAT YOU LIVE IN A CITY WITHOUT HOPE. HE TOOK YOU AT YOUR WORST, AND PUSHED YOU EVEN **FURTHER.**
BUT HE'S USING YOU. YOUR BELIEF GIVES HIM STRENGTH. GIVES HIM **POWER.** HE NEEDS **YOU** MORE THAN YOU NEED **HIM.**
BLACKFIRE IS A MAN WHO MAKES EMPTY PROMISES. I BET HE PROMISED YOU SOME KIND OF SALVATION IN EXCHANGE FOR YOUR LOYALTY.
I BET HE PROMISED THAT HE'D **BREAK ME.**
LETTING BLACKFIRE GET WHAT HE WANTS ISN'T GOING TO HELP YOU. HURTING THIS BOY ISN'T GOING TO HELP YOU.
YOU ARE **NOT** ALONE--I CAN HELP YOU FIGHT BACK AGAINST BLACKFIRE.
GOTHAM IS CURSED, BATMAN, AND IT NEEDS TO BE **CLEANSED.** IF YOU REFUSE TO HELP, THEN YOU'LL BE CLEANSED ALONG WITH IT.
NO!
I CAN'T DO THIS. I JUST CAN'T. THIS HAS GONE TOO FAR ALREADY--WE NEED TO STOP THIS.

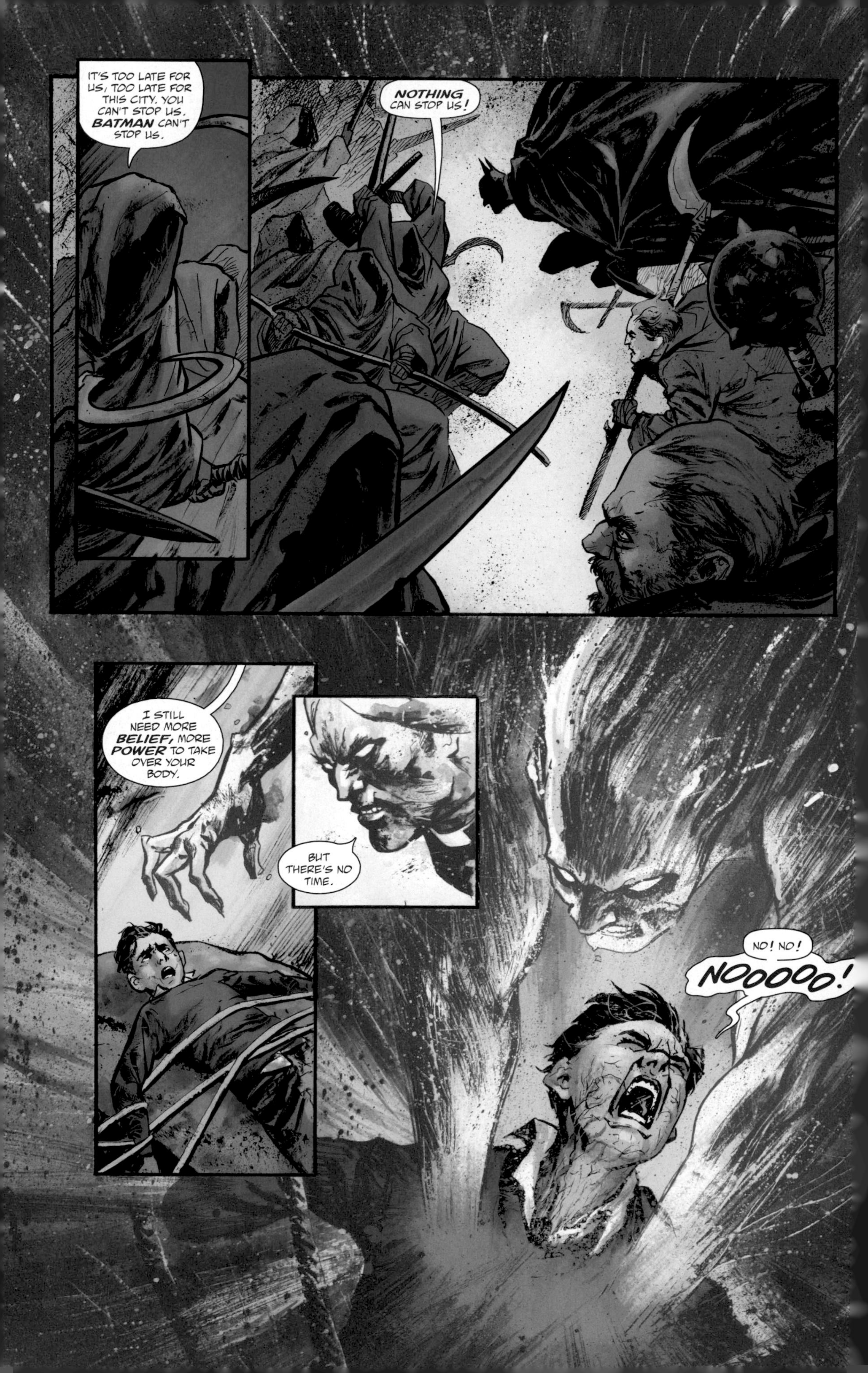
IT'S TOO LATE FOR US, TOO LATE FOR THIS CITY. YOU CAN'T STOP US. **BATMAN** CAN'T STOP US.
NOTHING CAN STOP US!
I STILL NEED MORE **BELIEF,** MORE **POWER** TO TAKE OVER YOUR BODY.
BUT THERE'S NO TIME.
NO! NO!
NOOOOO!

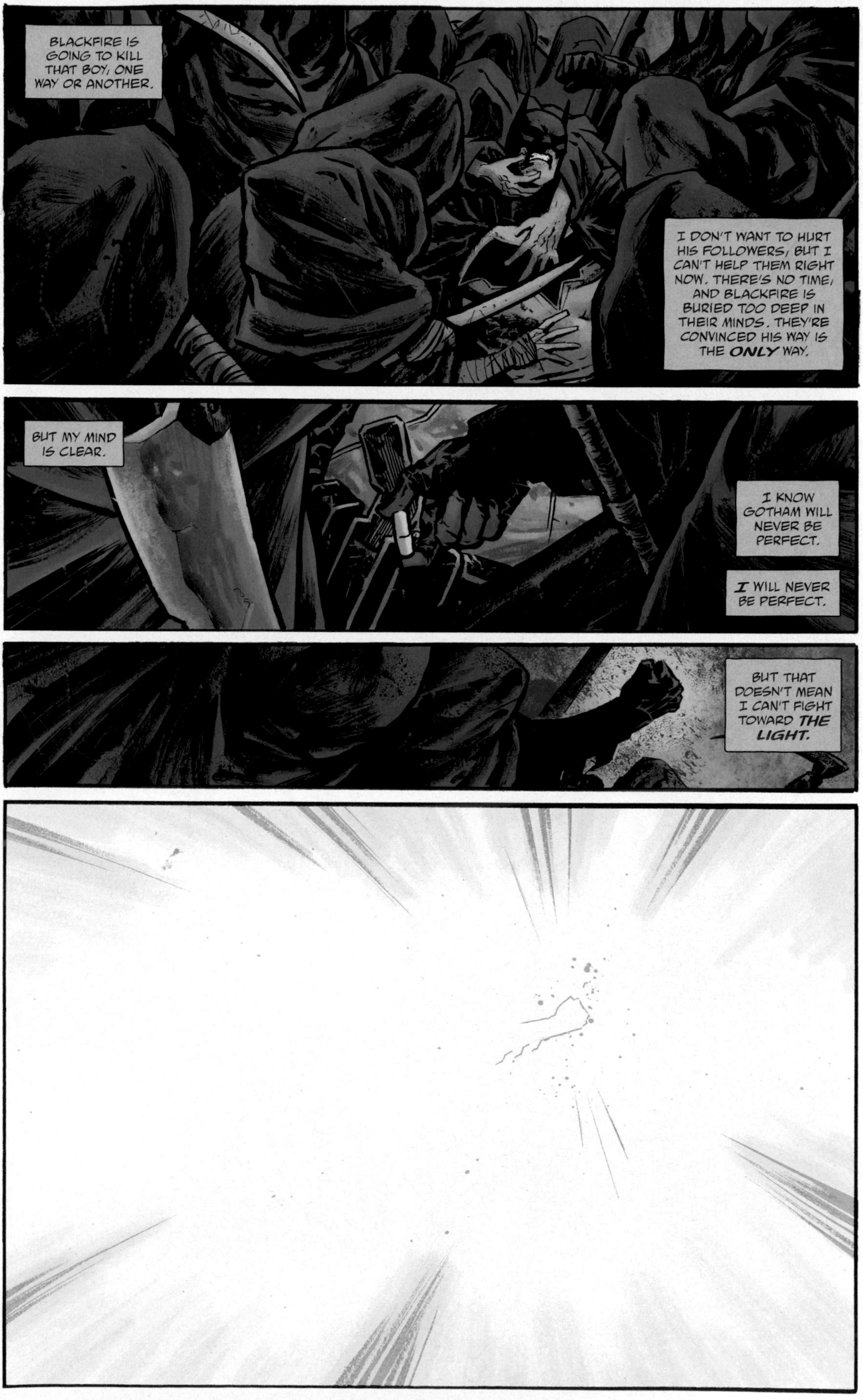
BLACKFIRE IS GOING TO KILL THAT BOY, ONE WAY OR ANOTHER.
I DON'T WANT TO HURT HIS FOLLOWERS, BUT I CAN'T HELP THEM RIGHT NOW. THERE'S NO TIME, AND BLACKFIRE IS BURIED TOO DEEP IN THEIR MINDS. THEY'RE CONVINCED HIS WAY IS THE **ONLY** WAY.
BUT MY MIND IS CLEAR.
I KNOW GOTHAM WILL NEVER BE PERFECT.
I WILL NEVER BE PERFECT.
BUT THAT DOESN'T MEAN I CAN'T FIGHT TOWARD ***THE LIGHT.***

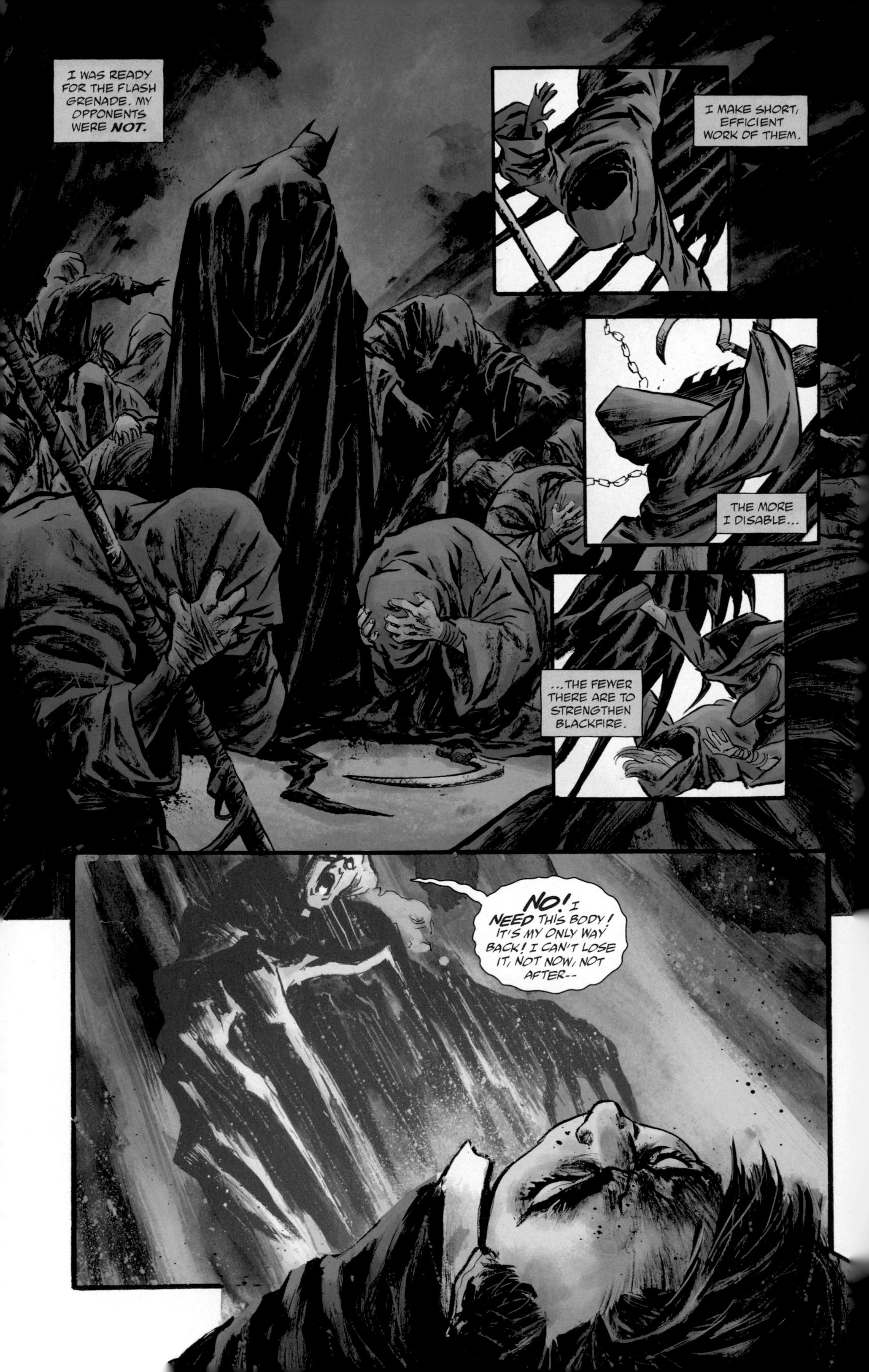
I WAS READY FOR THE FLASH GRENADE. MY OPPONENTS WERE **NOT.**
I MAKE SHORT, EFFICIENT WORK OF THEM.
THE MORE I DISABLE...
...THE FEWER THERE ARE TO STRENGTHEN BLACKFIRE.
NO! I **NEED** THIS BODY! IT'S MY ONLY WAY BACK! I CAN'T LOSE IT, NOT NOW, NOT AFTER--

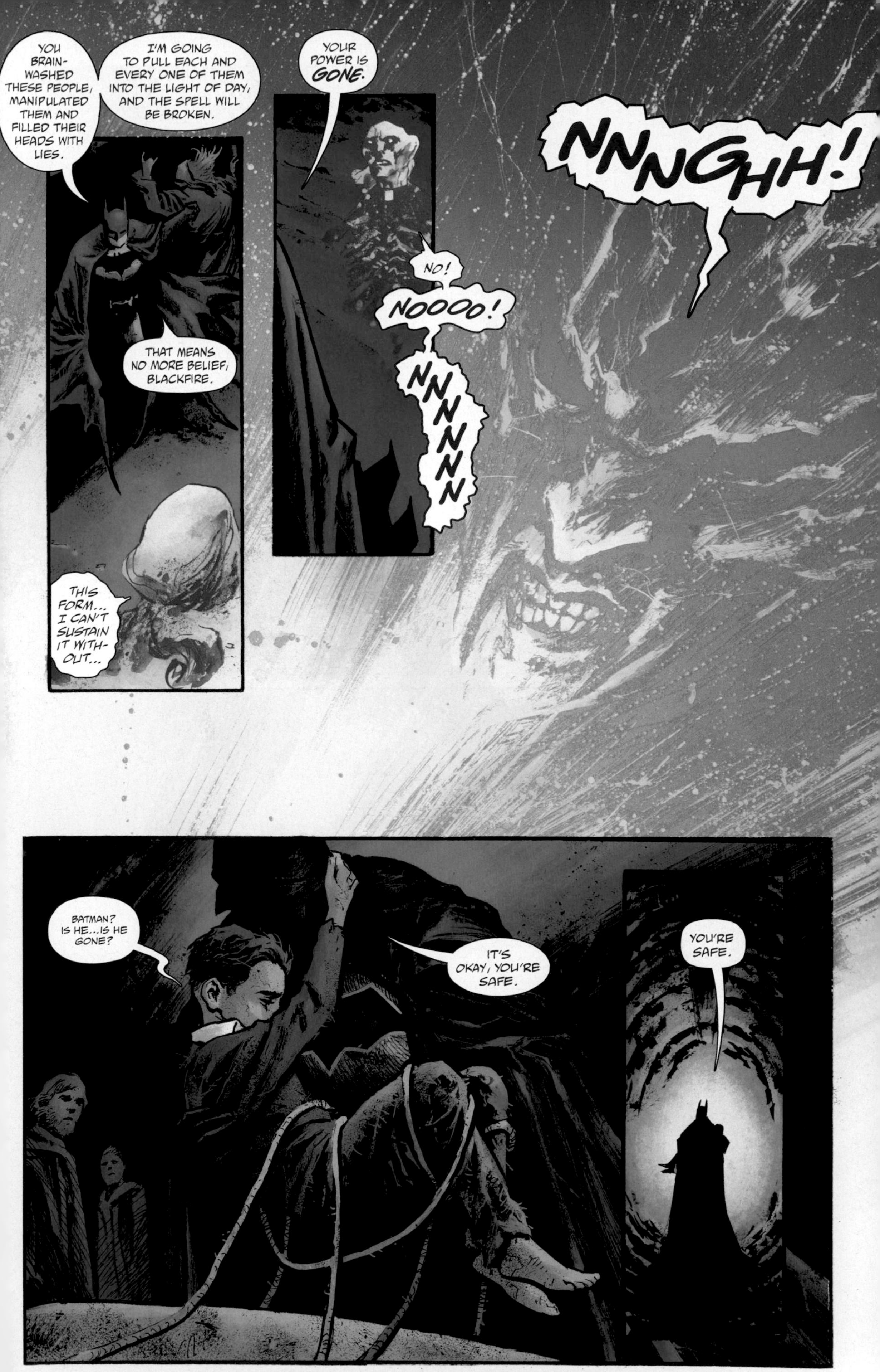
YOU BRAIN-WASHED THESE PEOPLE, MANIPULATED THEM AND FILLED THEIR HEADS WITH LIES.
I'M GOING TO PULL EACH AND EVERY ONE OF THEM INTO THE LIGHT OF DAY, AND THE SPELL WILL BE BROKEN.
THAT MEANS NO MORE BELIEF, BLACKFIRE.
THIS FORM... I CAN'T SUSTAIN IT WITH-OUT...
YOUR POWER IS GONE.
NO!
NOOOO!
NNNNNNN
NNNGHH!
BATMAN? IS HE...IS HE GONE?
IT'S OKAY, YOU'RE SAFE.
YOU'RE SAFE.

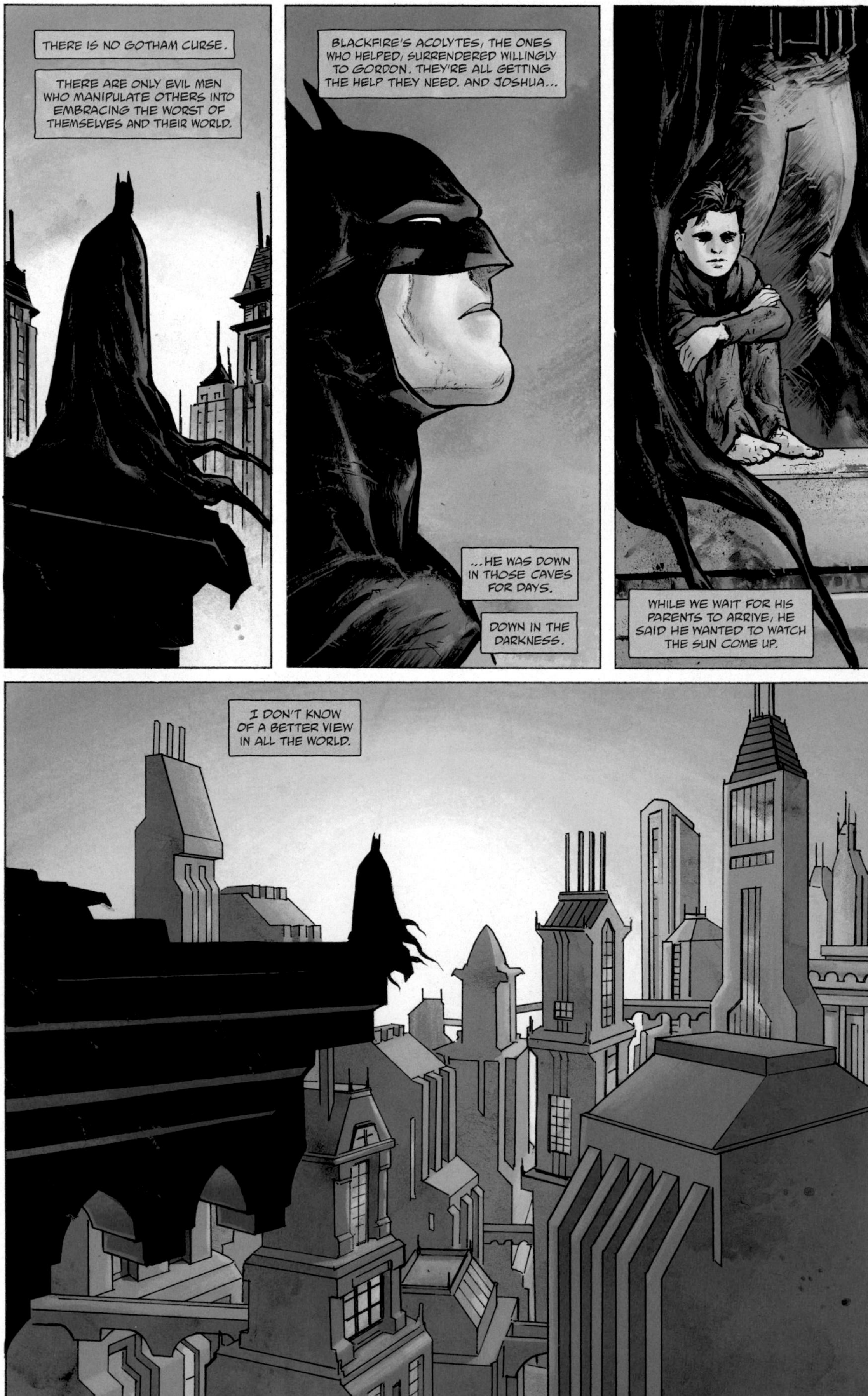
THERE IS NO GOTHAM CURSE.
THERE ARE ONLY EVIL MEN WHO MANIPULATE OTHERS INTO EMBRACING THE WORST OF THEMSELVES AND THEIR WORLD.
BLACKFIRE'S ACOLYTES, THE ONES WHO HELPED, SURRENDERED WILLINGLY TO GORDON. THEY'RE ALL GETTING THE HELP THEY NEED. AND JOSHUA...
...HE WAS DOWN IN THOSE CAVES FOR DAYS.
DOWN IN THE DARKNESS.
WHILE WE WAIT FOR HIS PARENTS TO ARRIVE, HE SAID HE WANTED TO WATCH THE SUN COME UP.
I DON'T KNOW OF A BETTER VIEW IN ALL THE WORLD.

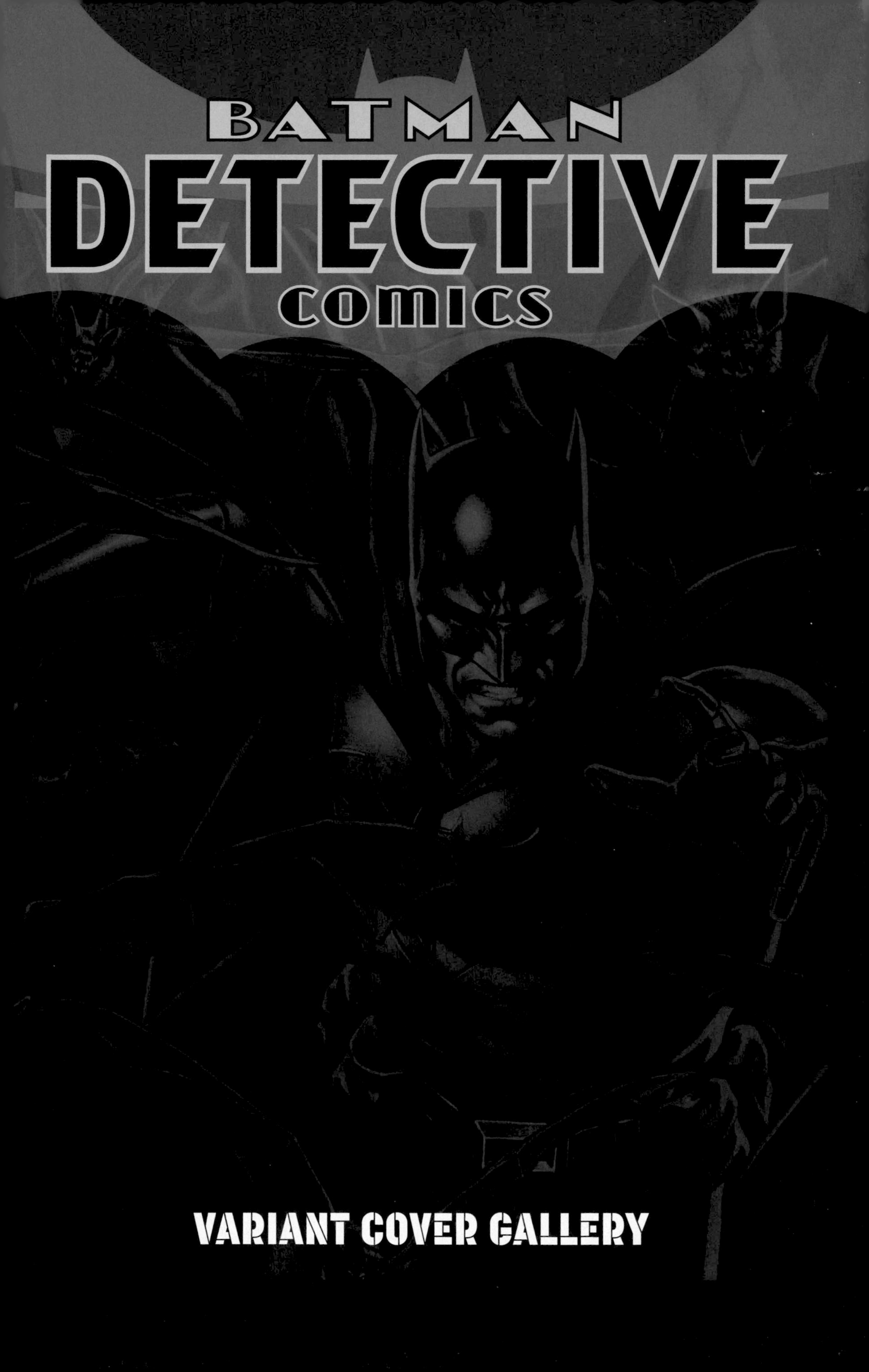
BATMAN
DETECTIVE
COMICS
VARIANT COVER GALLERY

DETECTIVE COMICS #982 variant cover by MARK BROOKS

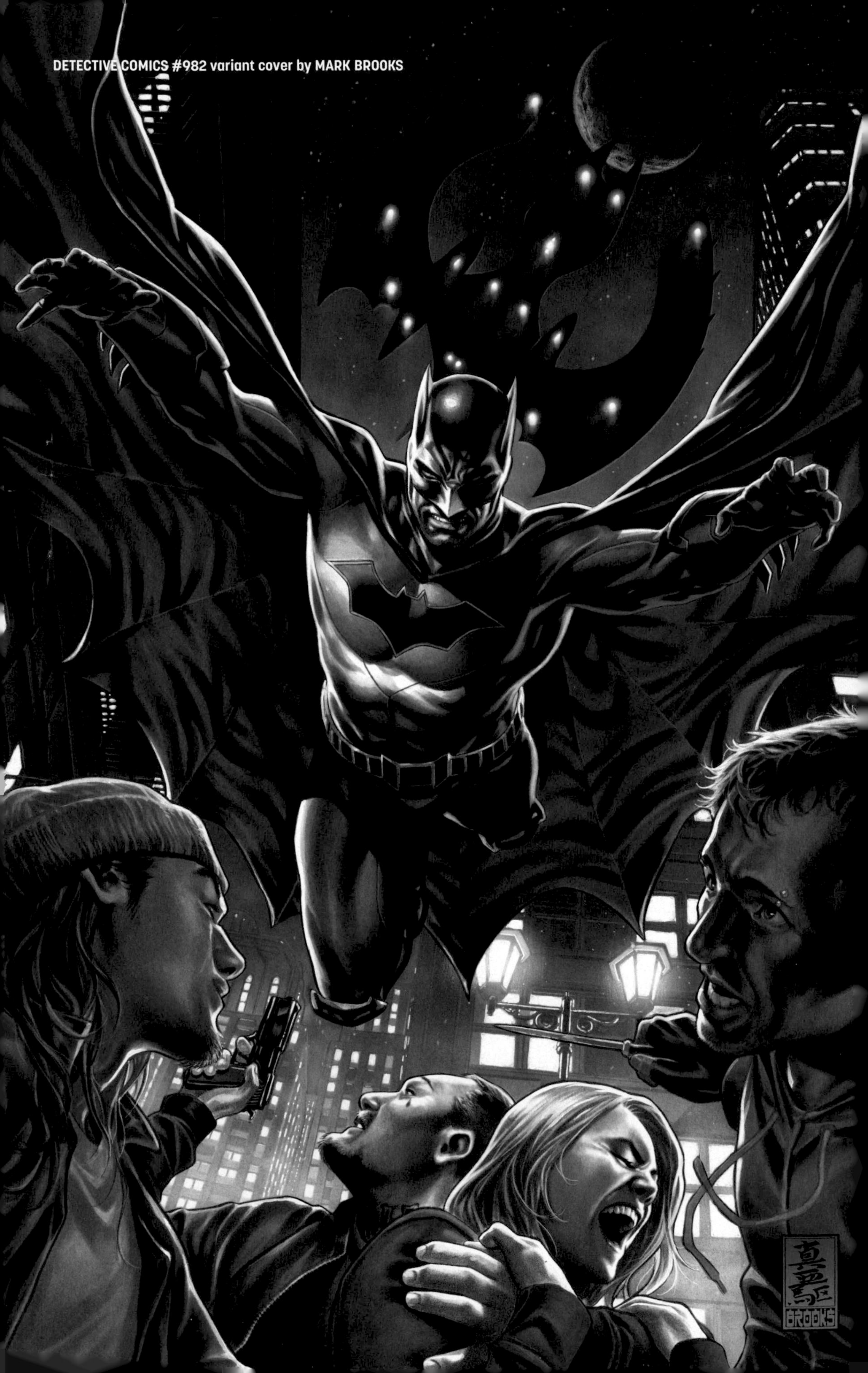
BROOKS

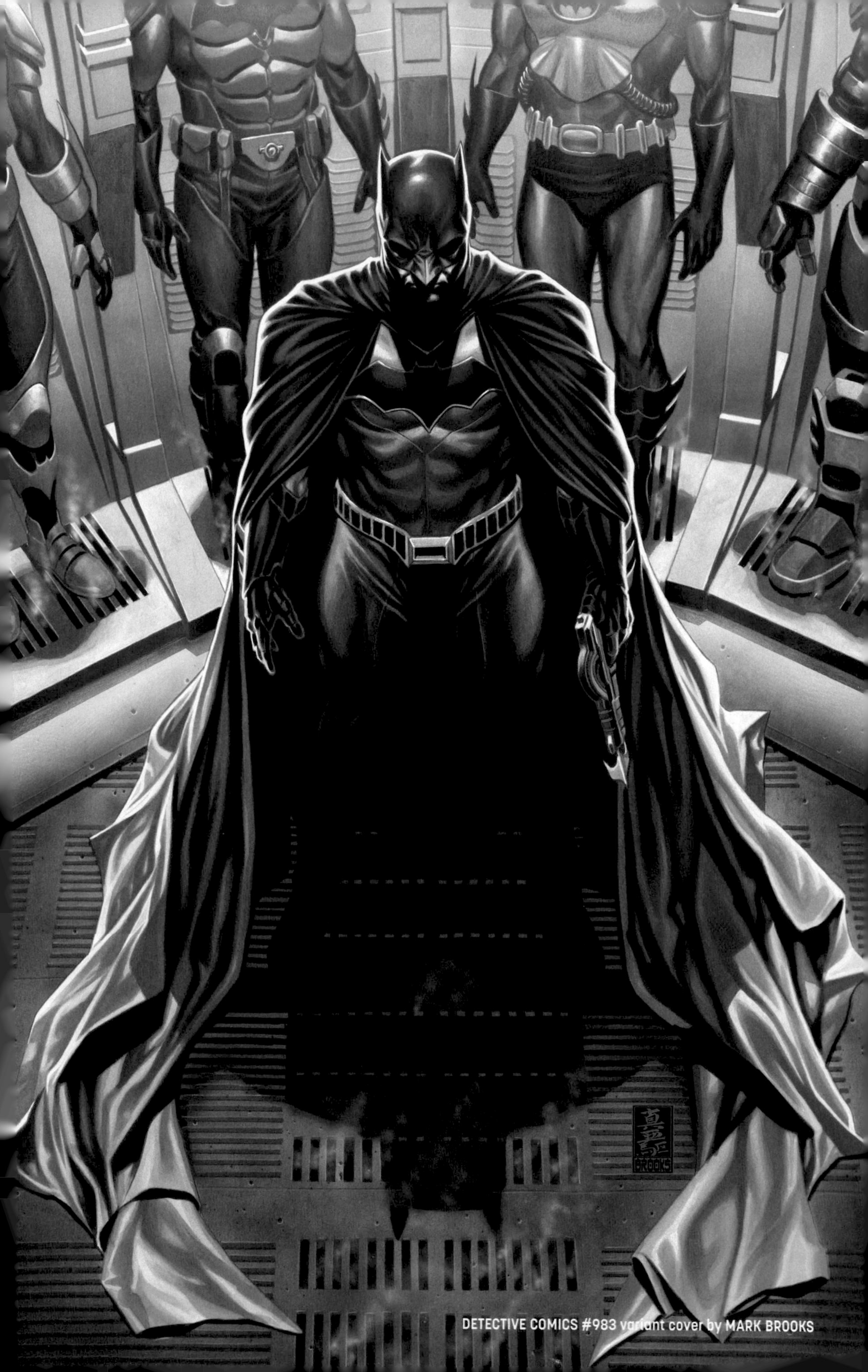
BROOKS
DETECTIVE COMICS #983 variant cover by MARK BROOKS

DETECTIVE COMICS #984 variant cover by MARK BROOKS

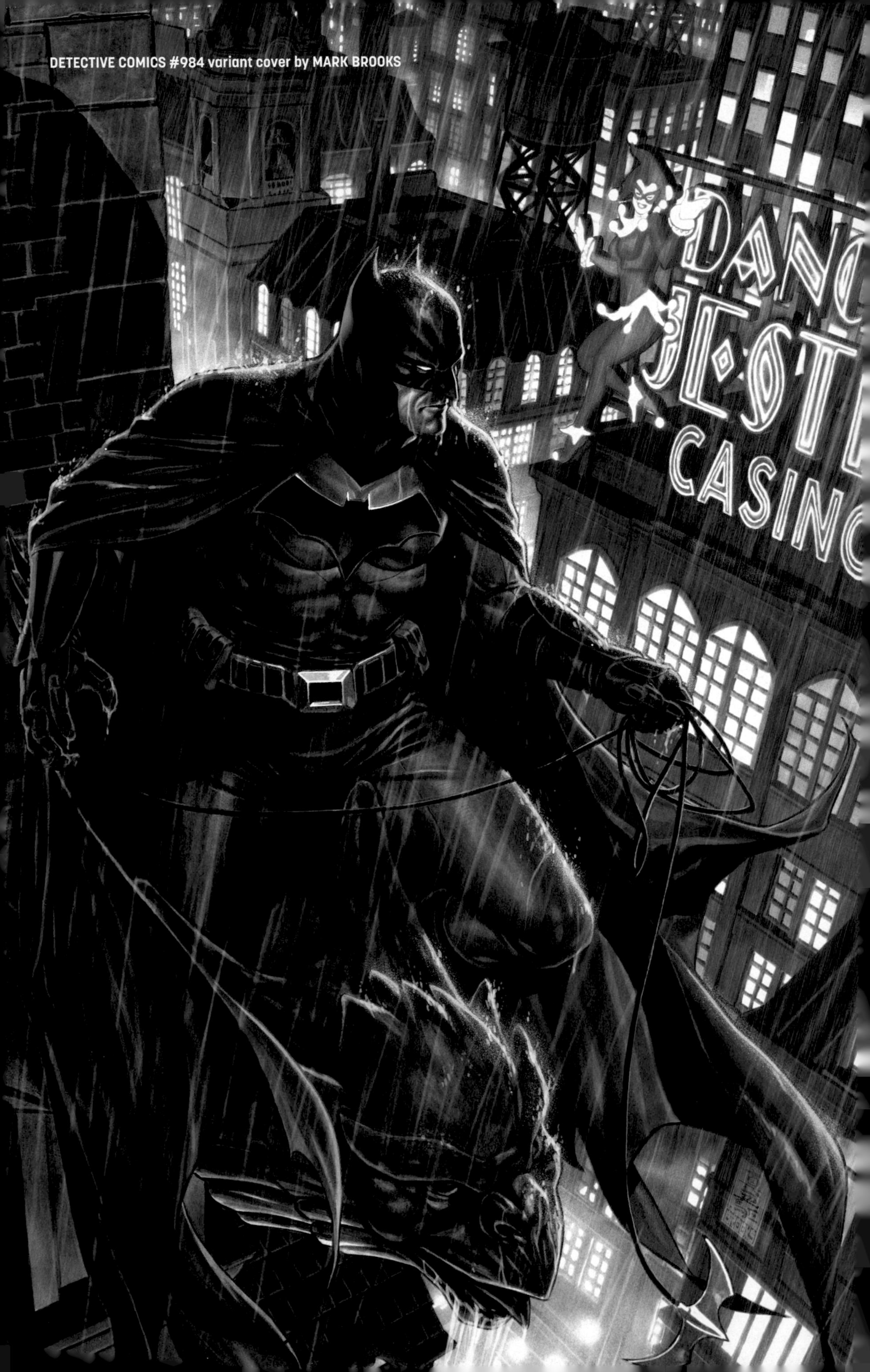
CASINO

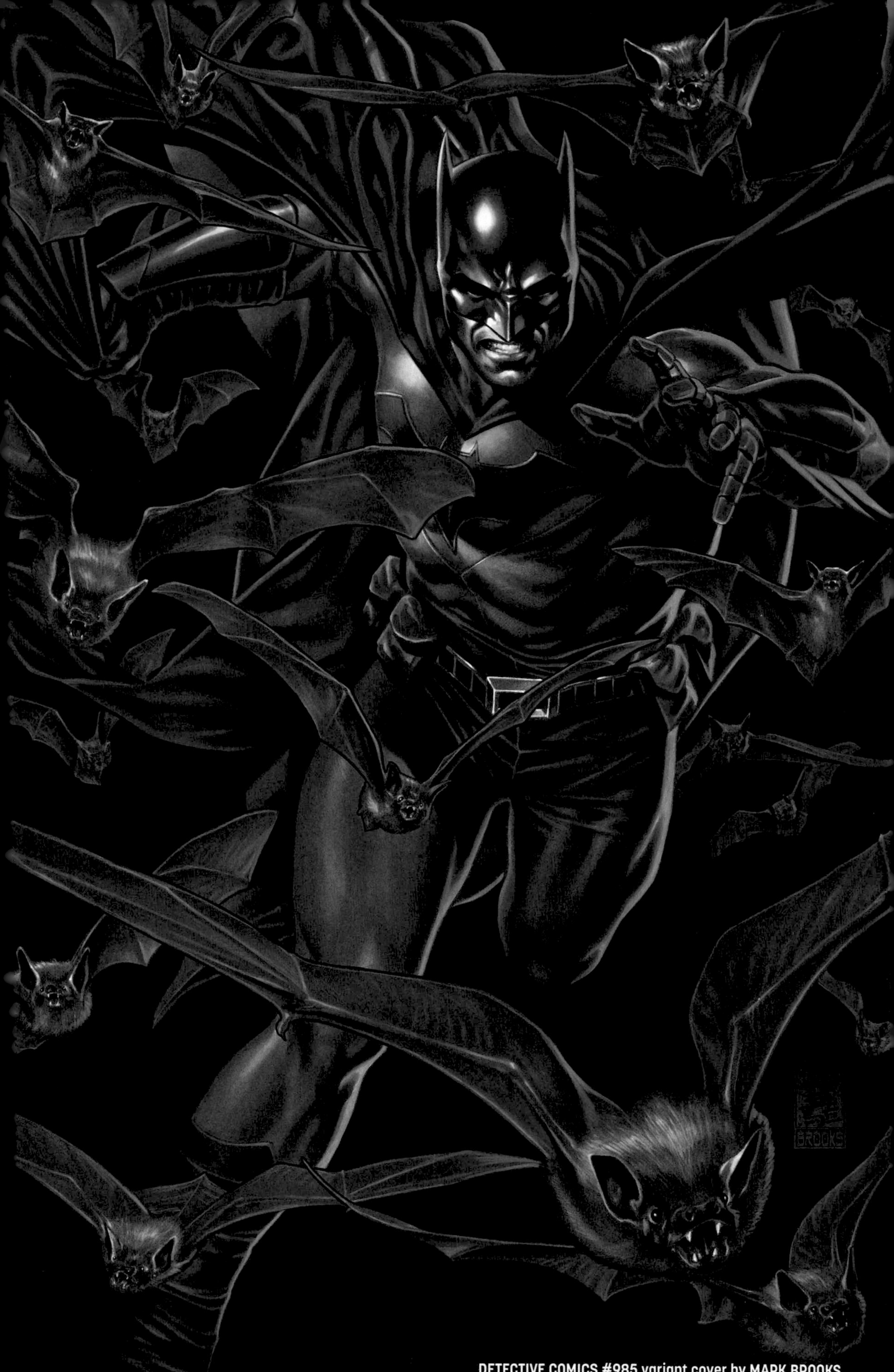
BROOKS
DETECTIVE COMICS #985 variant cover by MARK BROOKS

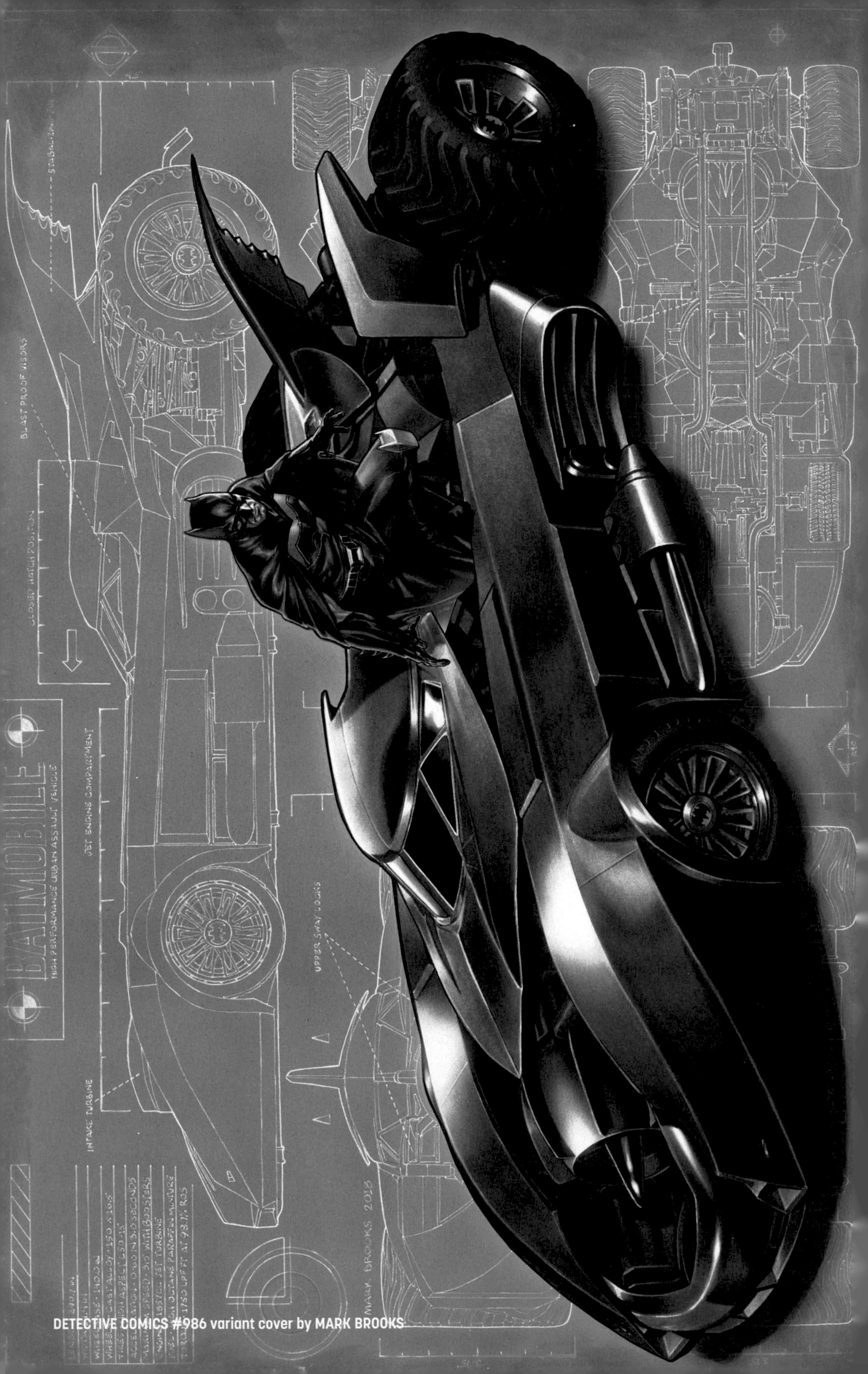
BATMOBILE
HIGH PERFORMANCE URBAN ASSAULT VEHICLE
JET ENGINE COMPARTMENT
INTAKE TURBINE
UPPER SWAY LOCKS
CLOSED HATCH POSITION
BLAST PROOF VISORS
MARK BROOKS 2018

DETECTIVE COMICS #986 variant cover by MARK BROOKS

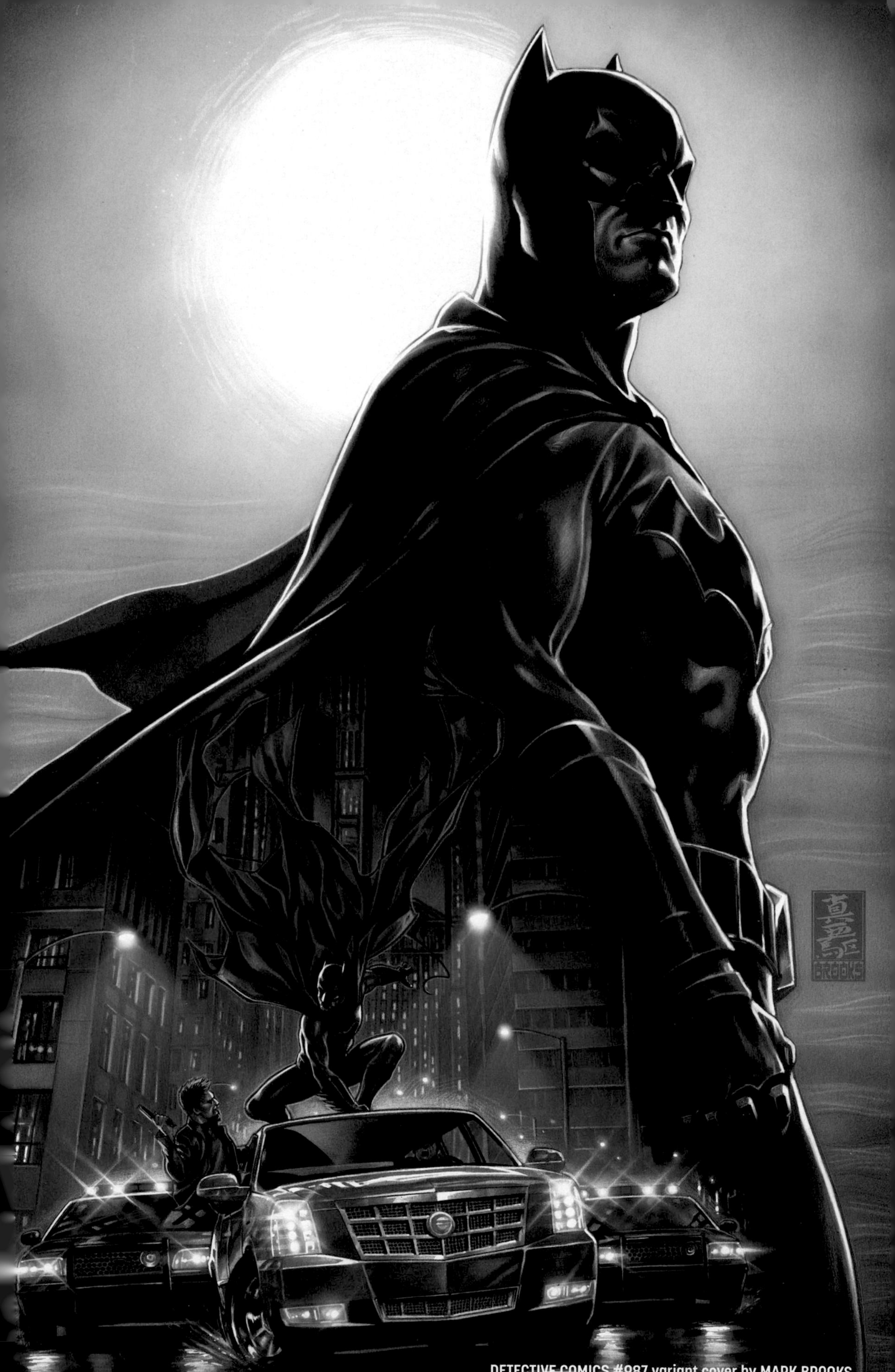
BROOKS

DETECTIVE COMICS #987 variant cover by MARK BROOKS

BATMAN & ROBIN VOL. 2:
PEARL

PETER J. TOMASI PATRICK GLEASON MICK GRAY

BATMAN & ROBIN VOL. 3:
DEATH OF THE FAMILY

PETER J. TOMASI PATRICK GLEASON MICK GRAY

READ THE ENTIRE EPIC!

BATMAN & ROBIN VOL. 4:
REQUIEM FOR DAMIAN

BATMAN & ROBIN VOL. 5:
THE BIG BURN

BATMAN & ROBIN VOL. 6:
THE HUNT FOR ROBIN

BATMAN & ROBIN VOL. 7:
ROBIN RISES

BATMAN & ROBIN
VOL. 1: BORN TO KILL
PETER J. TOMASI
with PATRICK GLEASON

– THE ONION / AV CLUB

"This is the kind of Batman story I like to read: an actual mystery with an emotional hook."

– IGN

"Rock solid."

"PETER J. TOMASI AND
PATRICK GLEASON ARE
KNOCKING IT OUT ISSUE
AFTER ISSUE."

– WIRED.COM